BLACK LEGACY

BLACK LEGACY

AMERICA'S
HIDDEN
HERITAGE

William D. Piersen

THE UNIVERSITY OF MASSACHUSETTS PRESS   AMHERST

HOUSTON PUBLIC LIBRARY

Copyright © 1993 by
The University of Massachusetts Press
All rights reserved
Printed in the United States of America
LC 92-41003
ISBN 0-87023-854-X (cloth); 859-0 (pbk.)

Designed by Rebecca S. Neimark
Set in Ehrhardt and Gill Sans by Keystone Typesetting, Inc.
Printed and bound by Thomson-Shore, Inc.

Library of Congress Cataloging-in-Publication Data
Piersen, William Dillon, 1942–
      Black legacy : America's hidden heritage / William D. Piersen.
          p.   cm.
      Includes bibliographical references and index.
      ISBN 0–87023–854–X (alk. paper). — ISBN 0–87023–859–0 (pbk. :
alk. paper)
        1. United States—Civilization—Afro-American influences.   2. Afro-
Americans.   I. Title.
      E169.1.P553   1993
      973′.0496073—dc20   92–41003
                                                                CIP

British Library Cataloguing in Publication data are available.

For Charlotte and Katie

CONTENTS

PREFACE

An interesting artistic effect most of us have experienced is the way certain black and white designs can be made to contain two vastly different pictures, the observed pattern depending upon which color our mind perceives at a particular moment to be dominant. So it is with history; what the historian sees is influenced by what the historian believes is important. What would happen if we shifted our normal perspective so as to make our nation's black legacy a primary point of reference? Just as in the visual image, the patterns of American history would instantly seem to reverse themselves. Such a process would not change the history, but it would offer a flash of Afrocentric insight— how changed the world could be if only we thought differently about things, at least for a moment.

Taking the African heritage seriously can be disorienting, for it is not often (or at least not often enough) that Africans and African Americans are presented as cultural founding fathers and mothers with life-building agendas of their own. We have no trouble assuming the influence of Europe and Europeans on our history and culture, but until recently we have tended to reject the idea that the cultures of Africa could also have had significant effect.

Indeed, how could influence from Africa have survived the brutal filter of the Atlantic slave trade and the oppressions of American bondage? Moreover, given the great numbers of African cultures involved, would not African perceptions simply have canceled each other out when crushed down by the ethnocentric values of dominant Europeans? Let us assume for a moment that despite such difficulties the African cultural heritage was not destroyed, that aspects of Africa did survive in the Americas, at least in generalized form, and that African-American culture not only stood up to the challenge of the white world but sometimes changed the ways that whites themselves lived. Let us look at our past with eyes focused on new patterns.

We can learn a great deal from shifting our horizons so as to take Africa seriously. Take the long-held view that African Americans were America's true peasantry. No one seemed to think it unfitting when the African-American scholar W. E. B. Du Bois entitled his classic study of black life *The Souls of Black Folk;* yet given Du Bois's personal demeanor—he was about as aristocratic as an American could be—might not the black world be envisioned from a different perspective? Yes, it could be, for in a nation of immigrants from the middling and lower orders, only African Americans had among them men and women of noble and royal lineage. It is these people of quality this book recalls, an African and African-American elite who imparted gentility, manners, and honor into the American South—not the other way around. If we come to appreciate that America's underclass has aristocratic and royal blood, we might stop confusing the results of the American social system with biological destiny.

Once we start shifting perspectives, very little about our interracial past remains secure. Consider those bizarrely costumed southern defenders of the Anglo-Saxon way of life, the Ku Klux Klan. We all know how they despised any possible Africanization of America. And yet, if we change our viewpoint so as to look at how they began rather than at what they became, we find something most unexpected. In their earliest years, the white founders of the Klan were not paralleling typical European masking forms or social behaviors, but their masks and actions would have been familiar enough to West African secret societies. Indeed, it looks as if the first Klansmen were furtively adopting masking traditions modeled after the secret societies of the West African coast and the African-American New World. In doing so, the Klan was not race mixing. But Klansmen were surely culture mixing; and if that is the case, the Ku Klux Klan should never look the same to us again.

By going back in time and looking from the other side of the racial mirror, from the folk customs and perspectives of Africa and Afro-America, we see the norms of history alter; it is the whites who appear to be the cannibals, and the blacks who are revealed as God's favorites. From the side of the traditional other, it is Africans and African Americans who have the deepest understanding of what lay behind the slave trade and who accept their own share of the blame for what happened.

The first major section of this book, Part I, "The Comforts of Job," discusses a series of African and African-American tales and legends that explain enslavement and the disparity of power between blacks and whites from the black point of view. Chapter 1, "Why God's Black Children Suffer," first examines a pervasive African folk belief that the slave trade was the result of white cannibalism, and then looks at a series of tales about God's gifts to the races which spread across the African continent from the sixteenth to twentieth centuries and also immigrated to the Americas where African-American variants developed. This tale series is especially important because it encompasses the only authentic folk tradition with wide circulation among black populations that explains why God could have allowed the slave trade, colonialism, and white supremacy. Moreover, since the explanations evolved across time and space, the tales capture important historical and cultural changes in attitude as well as larger, more constant, truths.

In Chapter 2, "Das How Dey Ketch Um," African folk narratives give way before African-American tales and legends that explain how and why Africans came to be enslaved. These stories, like the others in Part I, were not intended by their narrators as historical truths in the way modern scholars understand historical truth; rather, they were about a deeper reality, the realm of moral truth. As such, they are the missing last testament of the slave trade generations on the meaning of their experience.

The second major section of the book, Part II, "No Simple Black Folk Here," looks at specific ways that certain highly sophisticated African traditions shaped both black and white life in the Americas. Chapter 3, "A Resistance Too Civilized to Notice," traces the use of satiric social control mechanisms that were brought from Africa to the Americas, paying special attention to the public ridicule of white authority figures, a lampooning much relished by blacks in both Africa and the New World. To understand that slave music was more than sorrow songs gives us a new perspective on bondage. Slaves who intellectually and artistically mocked their masters before their faces surely were not the sulking, emasculated bondsmen of historical imagination. We have too often missed intellectual resistance because we were blinded by a national predilection for physical violence. Valuing the brute force of isolated rebellions, we overlooked more civilized and more common forms of social pressure based on the African predisposition for wry humor and verbal cleverness.

Chapter 4, "The Aristocratic Heritage of Black America," carries the inversion of perspective and values farther by recapturing the lost stereotype of Guinea's captive kings and in the process reminds us where true nobility in America was to be found. Ironically, given our traditional historical imagination, black folk—along with Native Americans and their Mexican-American kin—own almost all of the nation's bluest blood.

Chapter 5, "Duh Root Doctuh Wuz All We Needed," the last chapter of Part II, looks comparatively at the transfer of traditional African medical knowledge to the Americas and argues for the superiority of "folk-trained" African-American antebellum medicine over the era's "professionalized" European-American health care. Three larger traditions were creating the medicine of the Americas—African, European, and Native American—and all three mixed into what would become African-American medicine. Although this chapter stresses the African inheritance, that does not imply that black medical specialists were any more impervious to new ideas than were European or Native American ones. Nonetheless, African medicine predominated in the early health care of African Americans because it worked best.

The final section of the book, Part III, "Nigger in the Woodpile," takes its title from an old American proverb suggesting something hidden, such as a suspect ancestry. This section argues that there are hidden African and African-American bloodlines in certain well-known and nominally "white" institutions. Thus Chapter 6, "The Hidden Heritage of Mardi Gras," reexamines the shaky assumption that the American Mardi Gras is simply a transferred European holiday and postulates a revised argument that what we are seeing is something new, featuring at its core a white adaptation of African-American festive style. And Chapter 7, "The Mixed Bloodlines of the Early Ku Klux Klan," develops the case that the early KKK surreptitiously mimicked masking traditions of West African and African-American secret societies.

In the final chapter entitled "Mammy, Indeed!" we move to a more general examination of the African legacy that suckled the South. The evidence is compelling that white southerners adopted much from the culture of the blacks who raised their children and who lived alongside them. In speech patterns, in traditions of manners and honor, in the region's ways of cooking, work habits, religious styles, in southern "superstitious beliefs," holiday celebrations, and music, the white American South developed a distinctive and African-American way of life. And if southern culture had such strong African bloodlines, then clearly the effects of the master class's physical and political control have been overstated to the detriment of our understanding of the countervailing power of African-American culture.

I expect that in the course of this book some readers will be made uneasy by my tendency to wander across so many national boundaries, eras, and disciplines, but that is the nature of African-American studies, a research area that is international by the heritage of the slave trade and interdisciplinary by the mandates of its evidence. Early African Americans were not able to leave behind the wealth of written records we typically have from European Americans. Yet in fragments of black songs and tales a sophisticated intellectual heritage remains to be rediscovered. Because of the folkloristic nature of the evidence and because the processes of cultural change are not defined by political eras, I have loosened the chronology of individual chapters. The first sections of the book, especially, range widely in both geography and time; later chapters, however, begin to narrow down toward a concluding discussion of the origins of southern culture.

In African-American studies, we often need a wider comparative context because so much of our evidence remains fragmentary. To understand the function of the satiric songs of Afro-America, for example, requires knowledge about how similar tunes worked in both Africa and other cultures of the diaspora. In that sense, writing early African-American cultural history is something like doing archaeology. We can often discover intriguing fragments of tradition but rarely whole beliefs or customs clearly defined within their historical contexts. Thus we might say metaphorically that in African-American studies there are often potsherds to be found but seldom pots. Shall we refuse tentatively to reconstruct the past because so much of our evidence is broken or remains covered by layers of more recent history? Must we wait for the day when a figurative royal tomb is found to reveal finally the full truth of what all the fragments we have been collecting really imply?

While waiting for that great day of discovery—a day that might never come—it would be best to continue looking elsewhere for similar fragments, parallel motifs, and related pot types so as to make a tentative reconstruction of the precious remains we have in our possession now. In such reconstruction comparative evidence is crucial because we can develop a pretty good idea about what early African-American culture was like by building our models from clearly related cultural traditions taken from a variety of nearby historical sites. Admittedly, this method of analogy can lead to overgeneralization and outright mistakes, but there is nothing so unusual in history about the process of inference or the possibility of error. Historians, like archaeologists, must come to terms with the reality that there is always evidence now buried that will eventually alter, improve, and even completely revise the models we are now creating to understand history.

There is one other reason for using comparative evidence. Too often, citizens of the United States think African-American culture is encompassed within a minority subsection of our national history. It would be wiser to recognize that African-American culture spans the Americas. Whereas European cultures split the Americas into Portuguese, Spanish, English, French, and Dutch influenced regions, the heritage of African cultures reunites them all into the wider realm of the African diaspora. Let us be truthful; recognition of this wider heritage reverses the concept of minority cultures, minority history. The cultures of the Americas can no more be understood without recognition of their wider African component than they can be understood without attention to their particular European and Native American variations.

Certainly, some readers will suspect that in my chapters on African cultural influences I go overboard, overlooking possible European precedents while overemphasizing potential African ones. From my point of view, scholarship has too often, and more often, taken precisely the opposite approach. But reading the work of fellow authors—more Eurocentric authors—and talking to friendly critics, I realize that because I have a thesis I am as vulnerable to such criticism as they are. In the end, we all have a perspective. I have tried to argue mine objectively, but it is still an argument, an argument that the legacy of African culture is important to the understanding of America.

History works best when the past has something to say to the present. By looking backward, we should indirectly come to a better understanding of our own lives in the here and now. In the debate over the meaning of cultural diversity and national history, putting the "Afro" back into America does make a difference. The technique is not precisely Afrocentric because the conclusions are not particularly ethnocentric. The approach is more like stirring a can of cultural paint— as the separate colors swirl toward the vortex, an entirely new shade emerges.

If such an approach ends by supporting the old, discarded, but commonsensical stereotype of America as melting pot or mixing pot, so be it. The creation of American culture cannot be understood by adopting a single ethnic perspective. Whatever American culture is, it is a blending, a blending in which the Afro is an essential part.

PART I

THE

COMFORTS

OF JOB

CHAPTER I

Why God's Black Children Suffer

Looking back, modern scholars have seen that the Atlantic slave trade was shaped by the emergence of an international economy that created a nearly insatiable demand for cheap labor in the Americas and a technological revolution that provided the means to transport forcibly millions of African workers across the seas to help meet that demand. Does that mean, then, that we finally understand what happened? Not really. Such cold, after-the-fact rationalizing is a product of our own secular, scientific, and business-oriented era; it does not at all suggest how the Africans and African Americans who experienced enslavement interpreted this same brutal commerce.

In the years of the slave trade, people used value systems and frames of reference far different from our own to understand both the world and their own place in it. So to appreciate fully the meaning and nature of enslavement, we must try to grasp the victims' understanding of a process that has lain at the core of American race relations for almost three centuries. We must ask the type of question that enslaved Africans and generations of their progeny asked in their darkest hours of despair: Why? Why me? What have I done to deserve this?

Unfortunately, the victims of the slave trade rarely left written records documenting their understanding of their victimization. Few African slaves had the autonomy to produce such artifacts, and almost all lacked the literacy to do so. In fact, the idea would have come to very few of them, since among the African peoples involved in the Atlantic trade traditional wisdom and experience were passed on by word of mouth from narrator to narrator, not by the written word.

The oral histories of African peoples were communal products, the results of a series of interchanges between narrators and their audiences; they were not the personal opinion or experience of any single individual. They were a property of group creation over time. The end result was not individual history as we know it. Folk memory is simply not as exact in detail or moment as written history, but, on the other hand, neither is it as subjective or idiosyncratic. Folk narrative, because of its shared authorship and its oral transmission over a series of years, aims for, and tells, a larger truth than is recorded in individual written records. Folk history reflects the shared experiences and attitudes of a people.

In folk narratives about enslavement, Africans and their American children left behind their own insights into what they communally understood to be the causes of the human misery we call slavery. We know roughly what they thought because the ephemeral oral narratives they passed down were occasionally frozen into the written records of contemporary white and black writers. Our understanding of black attitudes about the enslavement process depends as much upon these folk sources as our reconstruction of the process itself relies upon more traditional kinds of historical evidence.

Ironically, given Western culture's tradition of joking about supposed African cannibalism, visitors to Africa in the slave trade era and later discovered that Africans reversed the stereotype—believing that it was whites who were the cannibals, buying slaves in order to eat them. The tradition of insatiable white man-eaters explained why no one ever returned after being purchased on the coast. A second cycle of narrative tales found in both Africa and the Americas centered around the significance of the different gifts God had originally given his black and white children, gifts that symbolized growing inequalities of racial power. And a third American sequence of anecdotal legends developed in the same era to explain how Africans came to be stolen away from their native shores. These three narrative series show black insights into the slave trade changing as the observers moved from Africa to America, just as they show the passage of time altering African and African-American understanding of racial power.

The people that first told these explanatory tales lived in cultures far more magical and mythopoeic than our own. As Africans and early

African Americans, they believed that truth had both a narrow literal meaning and a broader, more dynamic, symbolic dimension. And it is the mythopoeic or wider definition of reality contained in these tales that makes these old oral traditions so remarkably perceptive, despite all the narrow "factual" details that we have piled up in study after study of the Atlantic slave trade. Truth is not always in the facts; sometimes it is in the meaning.

White Cannibals and the Hunger for Human Labor

For most Africans the forced migration into American slavery was made all the more terrifying by their fears about the ultimate destiny of slave emigrants. Few of the new captives imagined themselves going west to become agricultural laborers; instead, they suspected they were to be cooked and eaten. From the seventeenth century onward, people in West and Central Africa from the Senegambia to Angola commonly explained the prodigious appetite of the Atlantic trade for human cargo in terms of the white man's barbaric cannibalism.[1]

To Africans newly arrived on the coast and still in shock from the trauma of capture and the harsh march to the sea, their sale to men rumored to be cannibals was more than simply strange and frightening; it was literally horrifying. So strong was the fear of being eaten that the new slaves had to be watched closely for signs they might prefer suicide to the unspeakable atrocities awaiting them at the hands of the white foreigners. In his autobiography Samuel Ajayi Crowther described a typical reaction in relating how his fear of being sold to the Portuguese drove him into shock, depression, and, eventually, thoughts of self-destruction: "My appetite forsook me, and in a few weeks I got the dysentery. . . . I determined with myself that I would not go on . . . ; but would make an end of myself, one way or another. In several nights I attempted strangling myself with my band; but had not courage enough to close the noose tight. . . . I determined next, that I would leap out of the canoe into the river, when we should cross it."[2]

When the European traveler Mungo Park joined a slave coffle making its way down the Gambia River, he discovered for himself that he had become an object of the most morbid curiosity.

They were all very inquisitive, but they viewed me at first with looks of horror, and repeatedly asked if my countrymen were cannibals. They were very desirous to know what became of the slaves after they had crossed the salt water. I told them that they were employed in cultivating the land, but they would not believe me; and one of them, putting his hand upon the ground, said, with great simplicity, "Have you really got such ground as this to set your feet upon?" A deeply rooted idea that the whites purchase Negroes for the purpose of devouring them, or of selling them to others, that they may be devoured hereafter, naturally makes the slaves contemplate a journey towards the coast with great terror.[3]

The fears heightened as the new slaves reached the coast and the strange foreigners were encountered directly. Mahommah Gardo Baquaqua, who had been taken into slavery near Zoogoo, south of the bend of the Niger, recalled his terrible fear of these new but unknown monsters: "I had never seen a ship before, and my idea of it was, that it was some object of worship of the white man. I imagined that we were all to be slaughtered, and were being led there for that purpose. I felt alarmed for my safety, and despondency had almost taken sole possession of me."[4]

When Olaudah Equiano arrived at the coast as an Ibo boy of eleven in 1756 and first boarded a slave ship, his imagination ran wild. He had no doubts as to the meaning of the downcast blacks he saw chained near what seemed a great copper cooking pot. He was to be someone's dinner! In reality such great kettles were not for cooking but instead were used on coastal vessels to keep fires burning as a prophylactic measure to prevent fevers; but Equiano, interpreting what he saw to be proof positive of the barbaric rites to come, fainted dead away from terror. When he was revived, he recalled in his autobiography, he fatalistically asked the local slave merchants aiding in the loading if he were not to be eaten "by these white men with horrible looks, red faces, and loose hair." Although they reassured him that he had not been sold to cannibals, he remained unconvinced, certain along with the rest of the new slaves that ultimately he would be consumed by "these ugly men" who had been showing such disregard for even the basic principles of humanity.[5]

Belief in white cannibalism was especially prominent among the younger slaves, and the horror such beliefs created was well illustrated in the testimony of the African-born slave Augustino to the Select Committee of the House of Lords investigating the abolition of the slave trade: "The young ones," he noted, "had the right of coming on deck, but several of those jumped overboard, for fear they were being fattened to be eaten," not an illogical interpretation considering that new slaves who lost their hunger or their will to eat were often force-fed through funnels wedged into their mouths.[6]

Augustino's English audience, which had a far better opinion of whites than that commonly held in Africa, could not understand what had put the idea into the slaves' heads that they were to be eaten. "Are they eaten in their own country?" asked the British interrogator, as ignorant and suspicious of Africa as the new slaves were of the white world. Augustino replied quite politicly, "They do not know for what object they are taken, and the idea comes into their head that it is from being made food of."[7] Interior peoples did not know what use white slavers made of their cargo; as John Barnes, a former governor of Senegal, explained in 1789: "slaves near the coast know what to expect, but those from the interior are terrified by not knowing the purpose [of the trade]."[8] Short years before, Francis Moore specifically noted how this reasoning process worked among the Fulbe of Bondu in the Senegambia region, who "imagined that all who were sold for slaves were generally eaten or murdered, since none ever returned."[9]

But if the appetites of the slave trade were enormous enough to arouse speculation, why did white cannibalism seem a reasonable explanation? In those years bizarre ideas about foreigners were not particularly unusual; indeed, the belief that aliens had an unhealthy taste for human flesh seems to have been common enough throughout the world.[10] Moreover, rumors that new slaves were sometimes eaten had antecedents in traditional African speculations about distrusted neighboring peoples. As Thomas Winterbottom reported from Sierra Leone, "[The local people] appear struck with horror when they are questioned individually on the subject [of man-eating], though at the same time they make no scruple of accusing other natives at a distance, and whom they barely know by name, of cannibalism."[11]

In the West Indies new slaves continued to accuse other African ethnic groups of eating human flesh. For example, an Ibo slave related that he was told by an old woman captured in war by the Coromantees

that they were cannibals, and, indeed, Thomas Edward Bowdich reported from Africa that he was told that the fetish men of the Ashanti
cut out the hearts of enemy soldiers to use in religious rites so as to pass
the defeated heroes' rigor and courage on to their Ashanti conquer-
ors.[12] Other new slaves in the Caribbean said that the Angolas, Mocoes
[Ibibios], and Gangos were man-eating nations in Africa.[13]

On the west and central coasts such traditional rumors of foreign
cannibalism could have transferred easily to the Europeans who were,
after all, indelibly strange in appearance and behavior and inexplicably
voracious in their hunger for black slaves.[14] This seems to have been
the way that similar rumors of white cannibalism grew up during the
era of so-called blackbird slaving in the Pacific when some South Sea
islanders came to believe that only the white man's need for meat could
explain his ceaseless hunger for exporting local islanders.[15] It is also
quite possible that confused rumors of Carib Indian cannibalism,
which were relatively common in Europe, were carried to the African
coast as sailors' tales, further reinforcing speculations about the horrid
destiny awaiting black immigrants to the Americas.[16]

An additional hypothesis about the continuing strength of stories
about white cannibalism was indirectly offered by John Fountain who
after spending the year 1788 on the Cape Coast warned that inland
slaves should be kept separate from the locals, who might excite them
to run away.[17] Presumably, nearby merchants would incite slaves recently purchased by European traders to run away in order to recapture
them and resell them to new buyers—and what better inducement
would be needed than the myth of white cannibalism?

Terrifying rumors of foreign man-eating may also have been used
by African slave merchants to placate new captives by pointing out that
their present situation was not so bad when compared to the fate they
could suffer among alien masters.[18] This clearly seems to have been the
case when Odumata, an Ashanti general, informed Bowdich in 1817
that if any local slaves misbehaved "they told them they would sell them
to the whites, which made them better."[19] And the rumors still worked
half a continent away when David Livingstone visited the Loembwe
River region of Angola and felt himself "obliged to reprove the women
for making a hobgoblin of the white man, and telling their children that
they would send for him to bite them."[20] Indeed, so strong did the

misapprehension of white cannibalism remain that in the middle of the nineteenth century the intrepid explorer Richard Burton unhappily discovered that using his mouth for kissing was ridiculed by his lady friends in Dahomey as a clear sign of the white man's cannibalistic propensities.[21]

Robert Williams, who had served the African Company for three years on the West Coast, put his knowledge of such beliefs to work when his undermanned slaving vessel was threatened by pirates. "He told the slaves he had picked out, to the number of 50, that the ship in sight . . . would fight them, and if they got the better, would certainly, as they were cannibals, kill and eat them all." The black slaves fought so well it took pirate Captain John Cornelius over ten hours to take the ship.[22] When Joseph Wright, a Yoruba of the Egba Alake, arrived in nineteenth-century Lagos, he was apparently told that the Portuguese were cannibals; but once sold to the Portuguese and placed aboard ship he was informed by his new masters (who had just spotted an English man-of-war patrolling the coast watching for illicit slaving) that it was the English who were in reality the man-eaters, and thus capture by the English meant a fate worse than death.[23]

The same worries haunted Samuel Ajayi Crowther after the English took him from a Brazilian slaver on the African coast. In his new situation he and his companions mistook some hanging pork and nearby cannonballs to be the remaining flesh and heads of fellow shipmates taken earlier from the slaver by the English. Only a close inspection of the items relieved them of their horrible fears.[24] Such bizarre misinterpretations of the ways of the white man were not unusual; Louis M. J. O. de Grandpré reported from the West African coast in 1787 that Africans seeing white sailors drinking wine and eating salt pork feared that they were watching cannibalistic rites, and Jacques Henri Bernardin de Saint-Pierre similarly noted that new slaves in Madagascar also "imagined that the whites wish to eat them, that they make red wine from their blood and cannon powder from their bones."[25]

In many African languages the word for "white" people is more literally translated as "red," and storytellers in mid-eighteenth-century Angola highlighted the sinister significance in such coloration when they spoke about a land of the dead located far to the west across the sea where the blood-red-skinned followers of Mwene Puto, Lord of the

Dead, processed the bodies of black captives, making cooking oil of their fat, wine from their blood, cheese from their brains, and gunpowder from their bones.[26]

Wise slaving captains undertook to dispel these horrifying rumors by having interpreters on the slave ships reassure the new captives that they would be used in labor like that they had known in Africa; otherwise, the growing terror among the new slaves could lead to suicides or rebellion.[27] But fears of cannibalism were not easily assuaged. Thomas King, who sailed nine times to Africa during the late eighteenth century, reported that the slaves were quite often a good while on board before becoming reconciled to the idea that they had truly been purchased as workers rather than as sacrificial food.[28] On Olaudah Equiano's ship such fears remained until after arrival in the West Indies: "There was much dread and trembling among us, and nothing but bitter cries to be heard all night from these apprehensions, insomuch that at last the white people got some old slaves from the land to pacify us. They told us we were not to be eaten but to work, and were soon to go on land where we should see many of our country people. This report much eased us."[29]

Unfortunately, sometimes an old hand among the interpreters thought to have some fun at the expense of the greenhorns from Africa by exploiting their ignorance of the Atlantic trade. Olaudah Equiano experienced this too when shortly after his initial crossing he found himself eastward-bound again aboard an English merchantman. As a newcomer he was considered an easy mark for his shipmates' cruel humor. Some of them seemed to have enjoyed raising his hopes by falsely telling him he was being carried back to his own country, but their thoughtless teasing became far more vicious when the voyage lengthened and rations were running low: "In our extremities," Equiano remembered, "the captain and people told me in jest they would kill and eat me, but I thought them in earnest and was depressed beyond measure."[30]

To scare one new slave was cruel, but to scare many was dangerous. In 1737 when the *Prince of Orange* docked at Saint Christopher a local slave boarded the ship and jokingly told the arriving Africans that they would have their eyes put out and then be eaten. Over a hundred of the men jumped overboard resolved to end their lives; and although most were recovered, thirty-three were lost.[31] Similarly, the famous *Amistad* rebellion off Cuba in 1839 was also instigated after the ship's captives were informed by the captain's slave, who surely knew better, that they eventually were to be eaten by the whites. The horrified and desperate Africans rose in revolt, murdering most of the crew, saving only a few to navigate the ship back to Africa.[32]

The same kind of fears led shipboard "scramble" sales of new slaves to be banned in Jamaica in 1784 because of bad experiences with slaves jumping overboard or running away; as Bryan Edwards reported, "it frequently happened . . . that such crowds of people went on board, and began so disgraceful a scramble as to terrify the poor ignorant Africans with a notion that they were seized on by a herd of cannibals, and to be speedily devoured."[33]

Other Africans arriving in the Americas observed what they considered horrifying confirmation that their new masters had, indeed, a fiendish taste for human food. On two occasions when new slaves in Louisiana and Saint Domingue first saw their masters drinking red wines, they were certain it was blood, leading them in desperation to run away or commit suicide.[34] Even as far north as Middleboro, Massachusetts, a new slave surprised his master by running away after simply seeing a roaring oven; only later when the new slave had learned enough English could he explain that he had expected he was to be roasted and eaten.[35]

Even after the slave trade ended, African suspicions of the strange ways of white people persisted. When the anthropologist W. Arens undertook to gather stories of African man-eating in 1968 all he could collect from his Tanzanian informants were opinions that white men were "blood-suckers" who ate Africans or drained their blood to make the special pills that allowed whites to survive in the tropics. The shock of these charges led Arens to reevaluate his own naive ideas about tales of African cannibalism and then "to appreciate the political symbolism of the narrative, which cast colonial Europeans as the consumers of African vitality."[36]

And here may be the key to the longevity of the white cannibalism myth. It was the symbolic truth about the white man's interaction with Africa, as Africans saw that truth, far more than the continent's ignorance of foreigners that kept tales of white man-eaters credible over the centuries. Africans knew that the voracious labor demands of the white world were consuming millions of their countrymen. And in this belief they were, of course, right. The great Molochs of American slavery and European colonialism consumed generations of African men, women, and children. As a mythopoeic analogy it does not seem farfetched to portray chattel slavery as a kind of economic cannibalism; and in that sense, a mythic sense, stories of white man-eaters were true enough.

The Unfortunate Choice; or, Why God Allowed Slavery and the Slave Trade

Why did God permit the development of racial slavery and the cruel slave trade that characterized the Atlantic world from the sixteenth through the nineteenth century? In the interior of Africa, myths of man-eating white aliens were used as explanations of the insatiable Atlantic demand for slaves, but the more experienced peoples on the coast knew that this was not the case. They understood full well that the foreigners who frequented their markets were, like themselves, simply dealers in human cargo. But such knowledge was no answer for the darker questions that loomed beneath the surface of the trade like man-eating sharks cruising the wakes of vessels outbound from the African coast.

Why were Africans rather than Europeans the ones to be taken away into bondage? Why had God given superior technology and control of the Atlantic commerce to white foreigners rather than to his own children? And why in the new lands to the west did God permit white strangers to profit from black labor? These Job-like questions demanded answers. Both in Africa and in America, blacks had to think about growing inequalities of condition between the races.

For the Europeans and European Americans who were prospering from the African trade, the meaning of the unequal exchange was easier to resolve. With a wonderfully self-serving explanation, the whites contended that God had given them power to dominate the globe so that the message of Christianity could be brought to all the world's peoples. The whites thus saw themselves as liberators, profitably doing God's bidding in justly releasing pagan peoples from the oppressions of idolatry.

However, when black converts began to accept Christianity, the missionary impulse could no longer be used to justify continued oppression. How then could subjugation of Christian slaves in the Americas and Christian subjects in Africa be maintained? The whites who continued to benefit from racial inequalities searched rapidly about for alternative rationalizations. The religious among them found a justification for white supremacy in the doctrine that all blacks, even Christian ones, had been relegated to positions of subservience by the curse against Ham (or Cain). More secular whites later claimed, under the guise of Western science, that it was the "white man's burden" to rule over and uplift those races not yet ready for self-rule.[37]

Such cynical and self-serving arguments are not unusual in the conflict of civilizations, and because the dominant cultures usually write the resultant history, we know far more than we would like about such rationalizations of oppression and nowhere near as much as we could desire about how the victims understood the same issues. Fortunately, in the case of the slave trade, the oral traditions of both Africans and African Americans preserve the evidence we need to reconstruct an alternative vision of that past.

Some black converts to Christianity, it must be admitted, came to accept the missionary defense of the slave trade, at least to the degree that they saw the diaspora to America as part of God's plan. As Phillis Wheatley, the African-born New England poet put it,

> T'was a mercy brought me from my pagan land,
> Taught my benighted soul to understand
> That there's a God—that there's a Savior too;
> Once I redemption neither sought nor knew.[38]

But acceptance of the idea that the Christian God brought a merciful redemption to some of his people through the slave trade did not imply a moral dispensation for the slave traders and slave owners who had sinfully profited from the cruelty and corruptions of bondage. Another African-born New England woman, Chloe Spear, put the African-American position quite bluntly: "[Whites] meant [the slave trade] for evil, but God meant it for good. To his name be the glory."[39]

Moreover, even Christian blacks could not credit the farfetched doctrine about slavery being the curse of Cain or Ham; instead, in both Africa and America people of color turned the tale around, pointing out that, if there were any such curse, surely an unnaturally white skin would be the mark of damnation.[40] The basic African attitude toward white skin reversed European prejudices. After the visiting slaver Theodore Canot was seen undressed by several African women, he records, "An ancient crone, the eldest of the crew, ran her hand roughly across the fairest portion of my bosum, and looking at her fingers with disgust, as if I reeked with leprosy, wiped them on the wall."[41] Thus it is not surprising that M. L. E. Moreau de Saint-Méry was told by blacks in Saint Domingue: "the first man came out black from the Creator's hands and the white is only a negro whose color had deteriorated."[42]

When Father Jean Baptiste Labat tried to inspire greater diligence in the slaves building his church in Macouba, Martinique, he resorted to a lie he thought they might believe. He told them that he had once been a black slave in France, but his hard work and obedience had turned him white. No one dared say anything immediately. Later, when a black carpenter working alongside him was having trouble dovetailing a beam, Father Labat drew some lines with a ruler and told him to cut there. The angle worked. "Now I believe you," said the slave, looking him in the eyes. "No white man could do that."[43] It was a clever response and typical of the way African Americans were forced to answer white delusions of superiority.

For their part, Africans were already developing their own explanations for the strange commerce moving inland from the sub-Saharan coast long before most had heard anything of Christianity or the peculiar white rationalizations for European power. One popular supposition, as we have seen, was that the overseas slave trade was required to supply bloodthirsty white cannibals with an endless supply of sacrificial victims. And given the death rate for new slaves in the Americas, this folk explanation was not that far from the figurative truth. Beyond this, Africans also produced a more philosophical analysis of the growing imbalance between the races and condensed this introspection into an explanatory tale tradition that might be called "God's Gifts to the Races." These latter tales, too, presented the slave trade and the growing imbalance of world power from a black perspective; as the tales saw it, the inequalities between the races were caused not by Europe's strength but, instead, by Africa's own shortsightedness and moral weakness.

William Bosman described the story as it was given to him on the African coast in 1698:

> The Africans tell us that in the beginning God created black as well as white men; thereby not only hinting but endeavoring to prove that their race was as soon in the world as ours; and to bestow a yet greater horror on themselves, they tell us that God, having created these two sorts of men, offered two sorts of gifts, to wit, gold and the knowledge of arts and reading and writing, giving the blacks the first election, who chose the gold and left the knowledge of letters to the white. God granted their request, but being incensed at their avarice resolved that the whites should for ever be their masters and they be obliged to wait on them as their slaves.[44]

A little over a century later, in 1817, Thomas Edward Bowdich noted what he called "the Negro tradition of the book and calabash," which he contended was "familiar to every native [of the Fantee/ Ashanti region], and seems to be the source of their religious opinions." According to Bowdich, who heard the tale from "Odumata and other principal men" of the Ashanti, the region's Africans believed "that the blind avarice of their forefathers inclined all the favour of the supreme God to white men."

> In the beginning of the world, God created three white and three black men, with the same number of women; he resolved, that they might not afterwards complain, to give them their choice of good and evil. A large box or calabash was set on the ground, with a piece of paper, sealed up, on one side of it. God gave the black men first choice, who took the box, expecting it contained every thing, but, on opening it, there appeared only a piece of gold, a piece of iron, and several other metals, of which they did not know the use. The white men opening the paper it told them everything. God left the blacks in the bush, but conducted the whites to the water side ... communicated with them every night, and taught them to build a small ship which carried them to another country, whence they have returned after a long period, with various merchandise to barter with blacks, who might have been the superior people.[45]

When Brodie Cruickshank reported the tale tradition in the middle of the nineteenth century he speculated that the tale was not a founding myth, as he said Dr. John Beecham thought, "the source of those superstitions which enthral millions of the negro race," but a tradition that dated its origin no farther back "than the period of the first acquaintance of the natives with the Europeans," "a theory formed from the observation of the circumstances of their respective conditions."[46]

Evidence from the Flemish trader Pieter de Marees's visit to the Gold Coast in 1602 supports Cruickshank's supposition that the tale resulted from the need to explain the cultural differences between African and European. When Marees asked the local peoples about God, he received an answer that seems to indicate he arrived just as this tale tradition was beginning. Note, for example, in the following quotation the phrase "he told us everything," so similar to Bowdich's "it told them everything." Moreover, if Marees's account is close to factual, he may have contributed himself to the formation of the tale's basic ideology. As Marees recorded it,

> When asked about their God, they said he is black as they are and is not good, but causes them much harm and grief. We answered that our God is white as we are, is good and gives us many blessings; that he came down to earth to bring us salvation and was shamefully killed by another people for our benefit; that when we die, we will go and live with him in Heaven, and will not have to trouble ourselves there about eating and drinking. This much surprised them and they were pleased to hear us talking about it. They concluded that we were God's children and that he told us everything. This made them complain, asking why our God did not tell and give everything to them as he does to us, and why he did not give them Linen, Cloth, Iron, Basins and all sorts of Goods as he does to us. I answered that . . . he does not forget them, although they do not know him, he has given them Gold, Palm wine, Millet, and Maize . . . and other Fruits for their upkeep. But this they were not willing to concede, and they could not understand that such things came from God, saying it was not God who gave them the Gold but rather the earth, in which they seek and find it.[47]

Thus, Marees arrived at the coast at a time when the local peoples were feeling the need to justify to themselves how a black God could have given so much to white strangers. The explanation was found in the idea that the blacks, as favorites, had been given the first choice of

God's gifts. But the ancestors had proved greedy, a traditional failing commonly criticized in West African folktales. The forefathers' selection had been shortsighted, and the choice of gold was proving less valuable than the gifts of technology and writing that gave the whites mastery of the sea and possession of the middleman's more bountiful portion.

It was in this light that in the early eighteenth century an officer of the Dahomean army told the English slaver, Captain William Snelgrave, that the Dahomean high God "might be [the God of the whites] who had communicated so many extraordinary Things to white Men."[48] Similarly, King Holiday of Bonny noted God's exceptional gifts to the white man when he told Hugh Crow in 1807, "God make you sabby book and make big ship. . . . But God make we black and we no sabby book, and we no head for make ship."[49]

In retrospect, we can see how clever an insight this was into what was happening to the Atlantic world. When William Bosman first collected the tale in 1698, mercantilist theory in one form or another ruled much of the world's economic thinking. Thus many West Africans, like the Spanish in the Americas, were being undone by the belief that the accumulation of gold and wealth was the true basis of power. But the tale of God's gifts demonstrates a prescient understanding by others on the African coast that the new realities of the Atlantic trade were suggesting something radically different. The mercantilists were wrong. Power did not come through the dead weight of specie; instead, it was the almost magnetic pull of technology that drew resources to Western Europe and its overseas colonies.

One of the most interesting aspects of the mythic tale of God's gifts is that it did not remain simply an African story. Like the peoples of Africa, it too crossed with the slave ships into the Americas where it found new life as an African-American folktale that offered an explanation as to why in a just world blacks ended up as laborers to white masters.

When Moravian missionaries collected the story in 1804 from the Saramaka Maroons of Surinam, the tale retained its original African emphasis on white technological superiority. Although free, the Saramaka were continually faced with the power of the nearby European settlers, and the Maroons' independence was made precarious by their continued dependence on white resupplies of powder, muskets, and a variety of other goods.[50] Thus the first collected American version of the story reflects this tension.

> A negro from the Upper Country [upriver] called here . . . on his journey to Paramaribo. He said he came to tell us a story he had heard from his parents, and to ask whether it was true. They had an old tradition, that the great God in heaven, after he had created heaven and earth, made two large chests, and placed them near the dwellings of mankind, on the coast. The black people, on discovering the chests, ran immediately to examine them, and found one locked, and the other open. Not thinking it possible to open that which was locked, they contented themselves with the other, which they found quite full of iron ware and tools, such as hoes, axes, and spades, when each seized as much as he could carry, and all returned home. A little while after, the white people came also, and very calmly began to examine the locked chest, and, knowing the way to open it, found it filled with books, and papers which they took and carried away. Upon which God said, "I perceive, that the black people mean to till the ground, and the white people to learn to read and write." The negroes, therefore, believe, that it thus pleased the Almighty to put mankind to the proof; and as the blacks did not show as much sense as the white people, he made them subject to the latter, and decreed, that they should have a troublesome life in this world.[51]

In this particular version, at least as it was recorded, the blacks, although having the first selection, received the lesser gifts because of their shortsighted choice; greed ("each seized as much as he could carry") seems secondary to the story until the final curse of a troublesome life. As in Africa, white superiority clearly comes from their technological competence and especially their literacy. The concept that God's white children were somehow excused from agriculture transferred easily from Africa to South America because on the slave plantations of Surinam whites were seldom seen to work the soil.

Elsewhere in the Americas the emphasis of the tale also shifted with the new perspective of bondage. White technological superiority, which had been of such great significance to Africans and the free Saramaka, was not as important to other African Americans. Among the American slaves, the tale emphasized the moral failings of greed and the inevitable self-destruction that follows the corruptions of avarice. Consider the version collected by James Phillippo in Jamaica in the early 1800s; the blacks of Jamaica, he said,

> believed that at the Creation of the world there were both a *white* and a *black* progenitor, and that the black was originally the favorite. To try their dispositions, the Almighty let down two boxes from Heaven, of unequal dimensions, of which the black men had the preference of choice. Influenced by his propensity to greediness, he chose the largest, and the smallest one consequently fell to the share of the white. "Buckra box," the black people are represented as saying, "was full up wid pen, paper, and whip, and negers' wid hoe and bill, and hoe and bill for neger to dis day."[52]

White literacy remained central to the tale, but in Jamaica literacy, like the whip, was seen as an instrument of power and oppression, not primarily as an economic or technological advantage.

The tale probably crossed to North America in the eighteenth century but made its first recorded appearance in 1823 or 1824 in a Seminole creation myth. That it should first resurface among Native Americans in Florida is not as peculiar as it might seem since the Seminoles incorporated many black runaways into their society and adopted much from African-American folklore.[53] When Chief Neamathla offered up his version of the origin myth, which he contended came from his forefathers, he introduced it with a humorous explanation about how the various races were produced. God's first attempt, he said, was an underdone white man, the second an overcooked black. Only on the third attempt did God get it right, producing the red man:

> In this way the Great Spirit made the white, the black, and the red man. . . . Here they were—but they were very poor. They had no lodges nor horses, no tools to work with, no traps, nor anything with which to kill game. All at once, these three men, looking up, saw three large boxes coming down from the sky. They descended very slowly, but at last reached the ground. . . . The Great Spirit spoke and said, "White man, you are pale and weak, but I made you first, and will give you the first choice; go to the boxes, open them and look in, and choose which you will take for your portion." The white man opened the boxes, looked in, and said, "I will take this." It was filled with pens, and ink, and paper, and compasses, and such things as your people now use. The Great Spirit spoke again and said, "Black man, I made you next, but I do not

like you. You may stand aside. The Red man is my favorite, he shall come forward and take the next choice; Red man, choose your portion of the things of this world." The Red man stepped boldly up and chose a box filled with tomahawks, knives, war clubs, traps, and such things as are useful in war and hunting. The Great Spirit laughed when he saw how well his red son knew how to choose. Then he said to the Negro, "You may have what is left, the third box is for you." That was filled with axes and hoes, with buckets to carry water in, and long whips for driving oxen, which meant that the Negro must work for both the red and white man, and it has been so ever since.[54]

The Seminole used the tale to explain their own position in the world as well as to explain the reason God gave whites their exceptional technological competence and blacks their position of enslavement. In the Indian version, unlike the African and African-American versions, the black man did nothing to deserve his fate.

Among North American blacks themselves, the gifts story was transformed into a new version that could be more accurately called "Why the Black Does All the Hard Work." This change in emphasis is illustrated in a story extremely similar to the Jamaican tale but in this case recorded in Charleston, South Carolina, in 1913 by Henry Davis:

> In de beginnin', God he tuk two bundle an' he place 'em before a nigger an' a white man. An' one bundle he mek berry big, an' one bundle bin berry little. De nigger he bin hab fust choice, an' you know a nigger wid he greedy big eye: he tink the big bundle de best, so he tek dat. Den de white man he tek what was left,—de leetle bundle.
>
> Now, when dey unwrop deys bundle, de white man he fine in e leetle bundle a pen an' a bottle of ink; an' dat's how come he do de writin' ob de worl'. An' de nigger he fin' de hoe an' de plough an' de axe in e bundle; an' dat's how come he hafter do de wuk in de worl'.[55]

Zora Neale Hurston collected a similar Florida version in the early twentieth century:

> God let down two bundles 'bout five miles down de road. So de white man and de nigger raced to see who would git there first. Well, de nigger out-run de white man and grabbed de biggest bundle. He was so skeered de white man would git it away from him he fell on top of de bundle and hollored back: "Oh, Ah got here first and dis biggest bundle is mine." De white man says: "All right, Ah'll take yo' leavings," and

picked up de li'l tee-ninchy bundle layin' in de road. When de nigger opened up his bundle he found a pick and shovel and a hoe and a plow and chop-axe and then de white man opened up his bundle and found a writin'-pen and ink. So ever since then de nigger been out in de hot sun, usin' his tools and de white man been sittin' up figgerin', ought's a ought, figger's a figger; all for de white man, none for de nigger.[56]

In all three African-American versions, from Jamaica, South Carolina, and Florida, the original African themes remain—the primal superiority of the blacks, the price that must be paid for greed, and the advantages of literacy (education) over wealth or strength. But other things have changed.

Experience with American slavery and quasi freedom had sharpened the blacks' critical vision of the white man. The whites may have gained power because greed had led the black ancestors to a foolish choice, but the whites in at least two of the tales were now implicitly falling prey to similar moral and intellectual failures—greed was causing the whites to use the whip and afterward scheme, "figger's a figger; all for de white man, none for de nigger."

The "all for the white man" refrain that appended itself to the myth of God's gifts became a common motif in black folk rhymes and songs of the late nineteenth and early twentieth centuries. In 1891 Gates Thomas collected a verse that went: "Naught's a naught, Figger's a figger, Figger for the white man, Naught for the nigger," and the same theme appeared in a folk rhyme later collected by Thomas Talley: "Naught's a naught, Five's a figger, Five fer de white man, Naught fer de nigger."[57]

The myth likewise appended itself onto other folk rhymes and songs. In 1895 Gates Thomas collected a verse about the relationship between the races that went: "White man goes to college, / Nigger to the field; / White man learns to read and write, / Poor nigger learns to steal." The choices from the "God's gifts" cycle of tales fit easily into this theme, which explains the variation recorded by Lawrence Gellert from a tray boy in an Asheville, North Carolina, sanatorium: "White man go to college, / Nigger to the fiel', / White man learn to read an' write, / Nigger axe to wiel', / Well it makes no diff'rence how you make out yo' time, / White folks sure to bring de nigger out behin'."[58]

It is clear that by the turn of the century the earlier African respect for the white man's literacy had given way to an African-American suspicion about the use to which any white talents might be put. Consider, for example, the discussion of education and work by a South Carolina black named Scip contained in Edward C. L. Adams's *Nigger to Nigger:*

> But I watch de world an' I never see readin' an' writin' go 'long wid work. Ef you git a man use to holdin' a pen in he hand or readin' a book, he done forever wid work. De only thing he do den is to study scheme to work somebody else. . . .
>
> Leff it to God Almighty—He put de pen in de hand dat best suited to handle it, an' He have made He own plan 'bout de best place for de plow. Luh God's work alone.[59]

Florida blacks in the early twentieth century explicitly altered the tale so as to deal with the way that slavery had disvalued work by associating it with bondage. Black men who had turned the art of resisting the oppressive labor of bondage into an ideal of a laid-back lifestyle felt compelled to defend themselves from the attacks of their women, whose family obligations precluded any devotion to the easy life. The men told the sexist new version of the tale:

> Know how it happened? After God got thru makin' de world and de varmints and de folks, he made up a great big bundle and let it down in de middle of de road. It laid dere for thousands of years, then Ole Missus said to Ole Massa: "Go pick up dat box, Ah want to see whut's in it." Ole Massa look at de box and it look so heavy dat he says to de nigger, "Go fetch me dat big ole box out dere in de road." De nigger been stumblin' over de box a long time so he tell his wife:
>
> "'Oman, go git dat box." So de nigger 'oman she runned to git de box. She says:
>
> "Ah always lak to open up a big box 'cause there's nearly always something good in great big boxes." So she run and grabbed a-hold of de box and opened it up and it was full of hard work.
>
> Dat's de reason de sister in black works harder than anybody else in de world. De white man tells de nigger to work and he takes and tells his wife.[60]

In this version we can see that attitudes toward whites have been in a continual process of alteration. Whites once again deserve no credit for coming out on top, but they are no longer God's second choice among the races. Instead, whites have the first chance to act but are too hopelessly lazy to do so. Moreover, the white man for all his power is revealed as in reality henpecked by his woman. Thus, in this cynical tale those in power have no virtues; indeed, everyone in the story would prefer to sit back idly on the veranda, until the black woman, ordered by her man to get the box, is foolish enough to set off willingly to work in the expectation of gain. The tale thus portrays black women as foolish and greedy, naive enough about the value of labor to be deserving of the heavy load they carry. Interestingly, by this time the gifts tale had become more humorous and less explanatory; the African moral universe of the original myth was giving way before the cynical vision of Afro-America.

Nonetheless, the original story is still recognizable in a relatively modern Michigan variant collected by Richard M. Dorson in the 1950s:

> Once there was a colored boy, a Jew, and a plain white man. They all were debating on the best thing through life. So they decided to take the conflict to God. God says, "Gen'mens, as you all wish, I would like to help you all." Then God tells them, "Anything you ax, I'll give it to you. Just come back tomorrow at noon."
>
> Next day at noon they all come back. God had a small package, a medium package, and a large package. He says: "I'm going grant you gen'mens all three of these packages." First thing the Negro run and got the biggest package on the shelf. The white man got the next largest package and the Jew said, "Vell, there's nothing left—I'll take the little bitty package and be thankful." Negro he was just boasting: "I know God thinks more of me than he do of you. See how big my package is and how little your package is!" Oh, he just couldn't wait to tear into his package. When he tore it open out stepped a great big mule, with a brand new plow. And a note on the plow said, "For the rest of your days you shall be a farmer."
>
> So he went back to God and said, "God you didn't treat me fair." God told him: "If you hadn't been so doggish trying to git everything you see at one time you might a got some money too. Don't you know good things come in small packages, you fool?"
>
> The Jew got money, and the white man got wits of knowledge.[61]

Here the black gets the first election but only because of his greed; indeed, the point is made that the black man was bringing on his own downfall by foolishly thinking that God liked him best. But as blacks were entering the urban world of wage labor in the twentieth century, the oppressions of unemployment made getting stuck with all the work seem an unlikely ending for the story. Thus, in the next twenty years, the tale changed again so that when Daryl Dance collected versions of it in Virginia in 1974–75, work was no longer the key: "God was making the worl' and He called de people, you know, de white people to get a bag and de colored people to get a bag. De colored people went to get the little light bag and the white people get the big heavy bag; and the heavy bag was money in it, and the light bag ain't have nothing in it. And they say dat's why us ain't got nothin' today; white people got it all."[62]

Some of the old themes remain in this modern version. Blacks have once again done themselves in by their choice, thereby leaving whites in the better, if undeserved, position. But now things have been turned upside down; black laziness, a stereotype created in America, has replaced greed, an African moral prohibition, as the explanatory failure. Moreover, in tune with American materialism and inner-city values, wealth has replaced education as the key to power, and God has become more of a trickster—giving only one gift instead of two.

During the same period another version of the story was being transformed into a different kind of ethnic tale, but one that remained recognizably related to the African original:

> Once a blessing was given out in Heaven. There was a Jew, a white man, and a Negro man there, and God was going to bless 'em all, give 'em all something they could live by. First he axed the white man what he would rather have most in life. He said, "Common Knowledge." He axed the colored man what would he want. He told God he wanted all the money he could spend, all the cigars he could smoke, a new Cadillac, and a pretty woman. Last he axed the Jew fellow what would he have. He said, "Just give me Sam's address and I'll get all I need."[63]

Malcolm X passed the tale along as reflective of his real-life experiences working as a salesman for a Jewish shopkeeper. Malcolm reported in his *Autobiography* that during the 1964 presidential campaign *Jet* magazine recorded a joke that Senator Barry Goldwater reputedly had made: "It was that a white man, a Negro, and a Jew were given one wish each. The white man asked for securities; the Negro asked for a lot of money; the Jew asked for some imitation jewelry 'and that colored boy's address.' "[64]

It is interesting to note that in these modern versions the white man has become God's favorite, or at least he gets first choice of the gifts. Dance heard a similar variation some twenty years later:

> God called a white man and a Jew and a nigger to come before him, and He told them he would give each one whatever he most desired.
>
> The white man said he wanted knowledge [or property or money].
>
> Then God asked the nigger what he wanted, and he asked for a big car, a big house, and a million dollars. So God granted him his wish.
>
> Then he asked the Jew what he wanted, and the Jew said, "Don't bother about any big gift to me; just give me that nigger's address and I'll get all I need."[65]

These "black, white, and Jew" tales reflect a more urban vision of the realities of life. As in Africa, the black brother still chooses wealth, but he is no longer first to choose; and it is no longer as certain by the 1970s that the white man has gained his position by knowledge. Moreover, the black choice of wealth is no longer viewed as particularly greedy (the white is now making the first selection); it is only short-sighted (as it has always been treated). On the surface the tale makes fun of the black man's inability to hold on to his money in the urban world, but at a deeper level the story remains true to its heritage by criticizing the materialistic values of society and, thereby, implicitly admonishing the white man as much as the black.

This critical assessment of materialism has a long history in a special variant of the tale which emphasized the special gift that God had given to the blacks in return for their temporal weakness. Consider the description of the races given by "Aunt Aggy," a Virginia slave of the 1840s, to her white charge: "No honey! De good Lawd doan giv eberyt'ing to his white chilluns. He's gib 'em de white skin, an' larnin', an' he's made 'em rich an' free. But de brack folks is his chilluns, too, an' he gibs us de brack skin an' no larnin', an' hab make us t' work fo' de white folks. But de good Lawd gibs us eyes t' see t'ings dya doan see."[66]

The South Carolinian ex-slave Sam Polite was explicit on the point: "God done gib de white folks a heap of things, but he ain't forgotten us 'cause He gib us Religion and we have a right to show it out to all de world. De Buckra [the whites], deys got de knowing of whys and hows of religion, but dey ain't never got de feel of it yet. I think God ain't have much respect for no kind of religion without de feeling."[67]

This belief, that blacks have a religious sensibility lacking in whites, also made its appearance in Africa as the juggernaut of white colonialism began rolling over the continent. Thus an Akropong chief of the Akan area of West Africa explained to a Christian missionary, "When God created the world, He made books for the white man and fetishes for the black man."[68] David Livingstone, another missionary harbinger of European expansion, also had explained to him in a version of the gifts-to-the-races tale both what was special about the African and why, nonetheless, Africa was doomed to fall under the political sway of Europe. Livingstone had told the Bakwena people (of what is now Botswana) that to end drought they must pray to God in the name of Jesus rather than using "medicine" to make rain; but a local rain doctor took exception, explaining:

> God told us differently. He made black men first, and did not love us as he did the white men. He made you beautiful, and gave you clothing, and guns, and gunpowder, and horses, and wagons, and many other things about which we know nothing. But towards us he had no heart. He gave us nothing except the assegai and cattle, and rain-making; and he did not give us hearts like yours. We never love each other. Other tribes place medicines about our country to prevent the rain, so that we may be dispossessed by hunger, and go to them, and augment their power. We must dissolve their charms by our medicines. God has given us one little thing which you know nothing of. He has given us the knowledge of certain medicines by which we can make rain. We do not despise those things which you possess, though we are ignorant of them. We don't understand your book, yet we don't despise it. You ought not to despise our little knowledge, though you are ignorant of it.[69]

The Bakwena rain doctor who so diplomatically told this to Livingstone clearly understood several of the main factors that would soon facilitate the imposition of European colonialism in Africa—European technological and military predominance, the ethnic divisions that chronically weakened the African continent, and the droughts and loss of cattle that accompanied the arrival of the white man.[70] But we must not forget that the power to make rain in a dry grasslands was a priceless gift, and this tale was not as self-effacing as it may seem on its face, or at least in its translation.

In a related myth, the Nuer of the Sudan region of the upper Nile say that God offered men a choice between rifles and cattle. The Europeans and Arabs chose the guns, and the Nuer and the Dinka took the cattle.[71] Here again, the whites received the technological advantage, but cattle-raising peoples like the Nuer would not consider their own choice a mistake. As the cattle-keeping Dinka explain, "cattle are what we hold above all things."[72]

In Dinka mythology black people were given the choice by God to take either the cow or something called "What":

> God asked man, "Which one shall I give you, black man; there is the cow and the thing called 'What,' which of the two would you like?"
>
> The man said, "I do not want 'What.'"
>
> Then God said, "But 'What' is better than the cow!"
>
> The man said, "No."
>
> God said, "If you like the cow, you had better taste its milk first before you choose it finally."
>
> The man squeezed some milk into his hand, tasted it, and said, "Let us have the milk and never see 'What.'"[73]

As the Dinka saw it, blacks were "the first to come out" of creation. "Black people came out with their blackness and their spears. The others remained and were later given their own strengths like writing. These are the things that were later given to people who were left behind. But spears were the first given to man."[74]

In West Central Africa the gifts tale seems to have developed other variants. The Kalabari of the Niger Delta explained their trade disadvantages in relation to Bonny as a result of just such a stolen gift. According to Kalabari tradition, Oruyingi, mother of the gods, asked her children what they wanted as a gift for the people over whom they would preside. Owoamekaso, goddess of the Kalabari, asked for a book that would attract the European ships to Elem Kalabari. Unfortunately, Oruyinga Ikuba, god of Bonny, became jealous over her choice and tried to seize the book. The book was torn, but Ikuba carried off the greater portion and thereby insured that the larger European ships would go to Bonny and only the smaller vessels to Elem Kalabari.[75]

Another variant of the basic tale tradition appears in a story noting Africa as the mother continent of mankind collected from the Calabar region at the beginning of the twentieth century:

> Once upon a time the god of all the earth had a wife who bore him twin-children—a male and a female. The male was black and the female white. The mother was very disgusted with them as she felt herself very humiliated by their birth; but the god who knew all things told her not to be angry, as she had already born them and it would be wicked to kill them. The female child having grown up went to live in some other country as she was not loved by her mother. During her lonely journey to that other country she picked up a book which she saw dropped from the sky. When she reached her destination she settled down there and acquired the knowledge that was in the book. She married a young man of that country and had sons and daughters, who resembled herself. Her children became multiplied, and when they were strong, they drove away the black inhabitants of that country by means of the knowledge of the arts of war they had acquired from the book. Thus was created the white race who became very numerous and more learned in everything than the black race, because their black ancestor was more loved by their mother, the wife of the god of all the earth.[76]

Here, as in the original gifts-to-the-races tale tradition, the black child is favored. But by the era of colonialism, God's blessing seemed clearly to have gone to the whites; therefore, in this tale white technological superiority (which is again clearly symbolized by literacy) has been given by God to the whites as compensation for their exile from Mother Africa—not because of black greed.

Far across the continent in Northeast Africa the Dinka tell a series of origin tales that revolve around the same theme:

> When man was created, it was as twins. One was a brown child and one was a black child. The woman would keep the black child to herself, away from the father. Whenever the father came to see the children, she would present the brown child and keep the black child because she loved the black child very much. The man then said, "This child whom you keep away from me, in the future, when [he grows] up, I will not show him my secrets." That has remained a curse on us. It is because of this story which we have been told by our fathers that we have been deprived.

And similarly:

> God made one child white and made one child brown and made one
> child black. This black child, his mother loved most. She would hide
> him from the man. . . .
> "This child of yours whom you hide will one day be the slave of these
> other children." The white child was not really breast fed. He merely
> sucked on the breasts after they had been emptied. So he was the child
> his father took. . . . Yes! This white child, his father thus maintained him;
> he looked after him very well. As he was prevented from sucking, his
> father took good care to feed him.[77]

Such tales differed from earlier West African versions that centered on Africa's love for gold because for most sections of Africa the
gold trade simply was not that important; instead, the explanatory
advantage was that Africans had been too favored by nature, too isolated. And, indeed, this was a perceptive explanation as to why African
technology moved at a slower pace than that of Western Europe. For
those who told the story the moral of the tale also revolved around an
internal social point—the mother's failure to love all her children as
equally as possible. Blacks suffered because they had been loved too
well, not because they had been loved too little.

The idea of divine parental favoritism became central to a series
of tales that helped Africans resolve the inherent questions involved in
understanding the origins of the inequalities that made colonialism
possible. Veronika Gorog-Karady has traced this development in African oral narratives and concludes that the widespread distribution of
parental-favoritism tales across the continent and across time suggests
"an ancient and unique thematic structure" to which was grafted the
biblical story of Jacob and Esau.[78] Consider one of her examples—a
tale from the Limba of coastal West Africa.

> Well, at that time, a man bore two children. . . . One was white, one
> black. But they were full brothers, one mother, one father.
> But [the] . . . mother she loved the European, the white one. That
> pleased her. Now the black one—his father loved the black one. . . .
> [The father] made a book. He wrote everything, how to make a ship,
> aeroplane, money, how to make everything. He wrote it in the book, to
> help the one he loved. He too, he took and made a hoe, he made a

cutlass, he looked for millet, he made groundnuts, he made pepper, he made a garden, oranges, everything. He put them down, he gathered them into a pile. He took the hoe, he took the cutlass, he put them there.

If you see unfairness in bearing children, it is not today it begins. One man with two children—he likes to show unfairness to one.

At that time, well, the man said, "We will hide now, I with you, to see what the children will do." Then the wife said, "What will we leave for the children?" He said, "No, I have got my plan." He was wanting to act unfairly. He was going to take the book and to give it to the black one. The mother wanted to give it to the European, the white one, to give him the book. She said, "What will we do?" . . . He said, "We will bring what we are leaving for the children."

Now their father could not see well. He could not see the children clearly. He said, "Child, you, when you go hunt, do not go very far." He just turned round, he caught a sheep, he killed it. [The white one] came, he said, "Father, I have brought meat. I went to hunt for it." Well, that pleased his father. Because he could not see well, he thought he was lifting down the hoe to give to the white one. Behold it was the book he took. "Take the book for me." The wife took the book. He said, "Give it to the child, the one who brought the meat." He was given it. He was not afraid to peep at it. He started reading it. He started seeing the things, how to make an aeroplane, how to make everything, how to make a ship, he saw it in the book.

The black one came. He said, "Father, greetings. What have you kept for me? I have killed a bird. It is what I have brought." He said, "Ah, my child, you are left as a foolish man. Well, take this hoe. Here is a basket, rice is in it. Millet is in it. Groundnuts are in it. Everything that you use when you go to work is there. But you are likely always to be left behind. He is more than you. Everything, if you want to get it, you have to ask your companion, the white one."

You see us, the black people, we are left in suffering. The unfairness of our birth makes us remain in suffering. That is why they want to send us to learn the writing of the Europeans. But our mother did not agree; she did not love us. She loved the white people. She gave him the book. There they saw how to make everything in happiness [without suffering]. They were able to do that and to surpass us the black people. . . .

We will not know what you know unless we learn from you. We are brothers of the same parents, that is why you learn from books, to teach us black brothers so that we may know. We are alike—we are full brothers.[79]

In this tale, as in the earlier version of the gifts story, the black begins in a favored position—his father plans to give him the superior gifts. But the era of colonialism was a cruel time for Africa, and the tale reflected a more distrustful vision of life wherein trickery (as suggested by the missionaries' biblical tales) had upset the natural order of things.

Here the black brother does not receive the "gift" of hard work because of his own greedy, shortsighted choice; instead, he receives the inferior position because his father, in making the original mistake of favoring one child over another, opened the possibility for a disastrous foul-up. Because of his father's favoritism and near blindness, the dishonest white son is, like the biblical Jacob, able unfairly to trick his black brother out of the birthright his father intended he should receive.

This Limba tale recognizes the power that comes with knowledge and explains why whites possess so much of it and Africans do not. The moral is, once again, not that whites deserve their position in the world or that they received dominance because they were innately superior; rather, the tale points out why it is incumbent on the Europeans to share their knowledge with their African brothers and thereby finally to wipe out the earlier wrongs of favoritism and dishonesty.

Oddly enough, the gifts-to-the-races tale seems to have also made its way back from the Americas, all the way to South Africa where, relatively unscathed, it was recorded in Dugmore Boetie's *Familiarity Is the Kingdom of the Lost:*

> When God said to the Afrikaner, "What is your major wish?", the Afrikaner answered, "All I want, Lord, is strength and fertile soil." The Englishman, when God asked him, replied, "Education, Lord, education!" When he turned to the Jew, the Jew tapped his head and said, "Brains." Before God could say another word, the black man said, "I'm a simple man, Lord, all I want is a pick and a shovel." Then God turned to the Coloured man and said, "Well, what can I do for you, my good man?" His hands in his pockets, the Coloured man turned and looked at the black man. He shrugged his shoulders and said, "I was just keeping him company, Lord."[80]

Boetie was using the tale to disparage the Cape's colored population, but at the same time his use of the tale demonstrates that the story of God's gifts to the races has continued to find at least some usefulness in explaining the inequitable distribution of wealth and power among different groups in South African society.

The tale has also survived to be told from the mulatto's point of view in the French-speaking West Indies. In a tale recorded in the early 1960s, God invites a white, a mulatto, and a black guest to dinner and prepares three gifts; each caller will be given an equal chance to choose:

> In order to be fair, God invited to his table on the same day a black, a white, and a mulatto. He prepared for his guests three gifts: a heavily filled chest, a sealed envelope, and an inkwell with matching pen holder. The white man prepared himself rapidly, and soon proceeded in accord with the invitation, arriving at God's house first. He thus chose the envelope which contained wealth. Before leaving, the mulatto made sure he was dressed in elegant fashion; only then did he set out. On the way, he encountered a pretty young woman and began a flirtation. He arrived at God's house just as the Virgin Saint was serving dessert. After trying to lift the chest which he found far too heavy, he chose the desk set, thus gaining intelligence. The black in his preparations lost track of the time, laughing and cursing about everything, his head in the clouds. He forgot to put on his shoes and so had to return to find them. Then he dawdled on the way stopping to look at a pumpkin, to take a drink at the tavern, and to smoke a pipe. He finally presented himself at God's house, embarrassed and grinning stupidly because the meal was already over. There was nothing left but the chest; nonetheless, he considered himself lucky that his gift was so heavy. The Virgin Saint in consolation offered him a drum. Returning home the black found in the chest tools for the work of the world—spades, hoes, etc.—and he began to cry. The white who was passing by said to him: "Don't cry, I will earn a living off you." The black took up his drum and sang of his despair. And since then the blacks have spent their lives working in the sugar cane.[81]

Here many variants of the old motifs survive. In line with modern African-American precedents the white chooses first and gets riches. The white's priority results not from God's favor but from his own efficiency. The dandified mulatto, a new character, is late but still gets writing and intelligence—traits, as in other modern versions, now associated with sterile laziness instead of productive technology. The black man goofs off and arrives after dinner is over. Once again he receives the world's work after being misled by the large size of the chest, but his foolishness rather than his greed is emphasized. In this West Indian version the black still has a special consolation, this time music rather than religion.

Over the generations, a few basic themes have emerged from the African and African-American tales explaining the origin of inequalities between the races. Black people, most of the narratives tell us, were God's original favorites, but as a consequence of their favored position—being first to choose, and choosing wrongly—they fell under the power of their white brothers, who had been inadvertently and secondarily left with the superior gifts of literacy and technology.

But whereas Africans originally used the gifts stories to merge their traditional admonitions against greed with their new respect for the technology of Europe, African Americans, like later colonial Africans, developed far more cynical variations. Less certain of the favored position of blacks in the original order of things, modern black populations in both Africa and the Americas have often seen white deceit and immorality as causative agents of black oppression, although blacks are seen as also responsible for their own fate. But where Africans continued to see literacy and knowledge as the path to power, African Americans in their tales came to see unearned wealth as the principle behind white control and education as a mark of deceit.

The easy transmission of this series of tales across the African continent and into the African-American New World seems a strong argument that such a thing as a common pan-African world view exists, although the argument should not be pushed too far, given the variety of African and African-American peoples and cultures. In this case the pan-African consciousness behind the tales reflects both a moral ethos and a common experience with the white world.

We have a tendency to underestimate the wisdom of common men and women who lack education and a cosmopolitan world view. But these tales should warn us away from such judgments. From the first, the black folk of Africa understood the basic economic and cultural weaknesses that made them vulnerable to the power of white civilization. Only later did most modern Western theorists of the same

issues come to similar conclusions, even if they were far more con-
cerned with Europe than with Africa. Africans, of course, placed
themselves at the center of the story.

The ability of African kinsmen on both sides of the Atlantic to
understand their own liabilities as well as those of their white exploiters
makes the critical vision of these tales all the more important in understanding the era of black oppression that may just now be beginning to
end. Tossing in the backwash of a runaway world economy, blacks in
both Africa and America readily acknowledged the power of Western
technology while rejecting the materialism it served. At the heart of the
tales of God's gifts to the races was the implication that the tragically
mistaken choice of wealth that originally brought the black race to grief
would inevitably bring down white power as well.

CHAPTER 2

"Das Duh Way Dey Ketch Um"

୧୨ If Africans explained the imbalances of the international slave
୧୨ trade with theories of white cannibalism and myths about God's
gifts to the races, African Americans developed their own legends to
explain to their children and grandchildren how it was that Africans
came to be enslaved. Historians usually tend to see the African victims
of enslavement as pawns in a larger game of greed between white
slavers and African coastal elites. But a series of folk narratives that
came into existence in the southeastern United States and the nearby
Caribbean suggest that earlier generations of African Americans understood their forefathers' misfortune differently. One series of legends
blamed the ancestors for character flaws that made them vulnerable to
enslavement, and another group of tales made it clear that slavery was
the product of a most immoral form of man-stealing.

The Color Red Brought Us Here

As the passing of time transformed individual recollections of enslavement into a less personal but more communal property, a number of
legends grew up that blamed black vulnerability to enslavement on the
African's foolish love of exotic adornment symbolized by the color red.
One of the most interesting versions of this color-red legend was
recalled by a Cuban ex-slave named Esteban Montejo:

> It all started with the scarlet handkerchiefs, the day they crossed the
> wall. There was an old wall in Africa, right around the coast, made of
> palm-bark and magic insects which stung like the devil. For years they
> frightened away all the whites who tried to set foot in Africa. It was the

scarlet which did for the Africans; both the kings and the rest surrendered without a struggle. When the kings saw that the whites—I think
the Portuguese were the first—were taking out these scarlet handkerchiefs as if they were waving, they told the blacks, "Go on then, go and
get a scarlet handkerchief," and the blacks were so excited by the scarlet
they ran down to the ships like sheep and there they were captured. The
Negro has always liked scarlet. It was the fault of this color that they put
them in chains and sent them to Cuba. After that they couldn't go back
to their own country. That is the reason for slavery in Cuba.[1]

Here as in many other tales the figurative truth is the essential
message. Montejo's version symbolically captures both how the protective environment of the West African coast limited early European
intervention and how, nonetheless, European slavers and local elites
often manipulated the irresistible attraction of the international trade to
the detriment of the African people.

In its extreme versions, the tradition was clearly a fable and was
probably not taken seriously as a literal description of enslavement.
One such variation recorded from Paul Smith, an ex-slave from Athens, Georgia, clearly seems to be more a tall tale than a historical
recollection: "Old folkses said dey had done been fetched to dis country on boats. Dem boats was painted red, real bright red, and dey went
plumb to Africa to git de niggers. When dey got dere, dey got off and
left de bright red boats empty for a while. Niggers laks red, and dey
would git on dem boats to see what dem red things was. When de boats
was full of em foolish Niggers, de slave dealers would sail off wid 'em."[2]

The black folklorist Zora Neale Hurston had heard the same
general story all during her youth in Florida. As she recalled it: "[According to] the folklore I had been brought up on . . . the white people
had gone to Africa, waved a red handkerchief at the Africans and lured
them aboard ship and sailed away."[3] And this widely told tale survived
right into the 1970s when Daryl Dance recorded versions in Richmond, Virginia, and South Carolina. As Dance's Richmond informant
told her: "I heard that the colored people one time was all on one side
of the river. And the white people was all on this side. And they had a
red flag, red handkerchief or sumpin'. They took that and kept on
waving it, wavin' it and wavin' it, and that caused them to get those
slaves—by that red flag. That's how they managed to come over here.

They waved and got 'em over here—through the red flag. Yeah! So that's the way the colored people mostly got here—got here through that red handkerchief—that red flag. . . . And when they got over here, see, they kep' 'em."[4]

Yet, though folklorists may see these tales as part of a legendary narrative tradition, many black informants presented their versions as historical accounts of actual enslavement; according to Richard Jones from Union, South Carolina, his African-born grandmother told him that it was historically true that red cloth proved a fatal attraction to those who were enslaved.

> Granny Judith said that in Africa they had very few pretty things, and that they had no red colors in cloth, in fact they had no cloth at all. Some strangers with pale faces come one day and draped a small piece of red flannel down on the ground. All the black folks grabbed for it. Then a larger piece was draped a little further on, and on until the river was reached. Then a large piece was draped in the river and on the other side. They was led on, each one trying to git a piece as it was draped. Finally, when the ship was reached, they draped large pieces on the plank and up into the ship till they got as many blacks on board as they wanted. Then the gate was chained up, and they could not get back. That is the way Granny Judith say they got her to America. Of course, she did not even know that the pieces was red flannel or that she was being enticed away. They just draped red flannel to them like us draps corn to chickens to git them on the roost at night.
>
> When they got on board the ship, they were tied until the ship got to sea; then they were let loose to walk about 'cause they couldn't jump overboard. On the ship they had many strange things to eat, and they liked that. They was give enough red flannel to wrap around themselves. She liked it on the boat.[5]

The same basic story was given to Ed Thorpe of Harris Neck, Georgia, by his African-born grandmother Patience Spaulding: "She say all duh people in Africa loves red. Das how dey ketch um. I mean duh folks wut bring um yuh as slabes. Dey put up a red clawt weah dey would see it. Wen dey git close tuh duh boat, dey grab um an bring um yuh. She say das duh way dey ketch huh."[6] North Carolinian ex-slave Hannah Crasson recalled a similar tale: "Our great grandmother was named Granny Flora. They stole her from Africa with a red pocket handkerchief."[7]

Though the details of these legendary tales are at least one narrator removed from the memories of very old women, it is a fact that slavers in Africa occasionally used red cloth to abet kidnapping, and it was not unknown for country people upriver from major trading centers to be lured into enslavement. Robert W. Harms described how this worked in his study of the slave trade of the Central Zaire Basin: "Sometimes [African] traders arriving in an area for the first time enticed children into their canoes by showing them European goods and then made off with them. This tactic, however, made it impossible for the merchant to visit the same place again, so it was not used by 'respectable' slave traders."[8]

There is no doubt that the attractive power of red cloth in Africa would have made it an ideal lure for the purposes of arousing the country people's interest. As early as 1667 the German missionary Johann Müller was appalled by what he felt were the fashion excesses of upper-class African women of the Gold Coast.[9] Three centuries later conditions were little changed as Henry Stanley noted on his visit to Central Africa: "The natives showed no fixed desire for any specialty but cloth—gaudy red handkerchiefs." And, he reported, the Europeans exploited this interest by openly displaying their wares to attract trade: "The dangling of some bright or gaudy article of barter, the strings of beads of dazzling colour, suspended patiently, the artful speech, the alluring smile and gesture, all were resorted to."[10]

It is certainly worth noting how closely Stanley's description of the trade correspond to that remembered by an American slave like Shack Thomas of South Jacksonville, Florida, who in his old age recalled what his father often told him about his capture in Africa: "Adam was a native of the West Coast of Africa, and when quite a young man was attracted one day to a large ship that had just come near his home. With many others he was attracted aboard by bright red handkerchiefs, shawls and other articles in the hands of seamen. Shortly afterwards he was securely bound in the hold of the ship. . . . 'I guess that's why I can't stand red things now!' he says, 'My Pa hated the sight of it.'"[11]

Similarly, the same general tale of enslavement was recorded by Edward C. L. Adams from the Congaree area near Columbia, South

Carolina, in 1927; according to Adams an old ex-slave named Gullah Joe told his friend Tad:

> When I was a boy, a big vessel come nigh to my home. An' it had white folks on it an' dey hab all er bread an' calico an' red flannel, an' all kind er fancy thing. An' dem white folks gee a heap er thing to de people er my tribe an' entice 'em on de boat. An' dey treat 'em so good for two or three days, till atter while de people ain' been scared. At first start off, ain' but a few on 'em on de boat when dey were invite; but atter de other people see 'em git on an' git off an' come back wid all kind er present, dey git so dey ain' been scared.
>
> An' one day dey hab de boat crowd wid mens an' womens an' chillun, an' when de find dey self, de boat was 'way out to sea.[12]

Another South Carolinian, Henry Brown of Charleston, recalled the same legend in 1937 as he described how it was that his grandparents came to be taken into slavery. "My grandpa an' grandma on pa side come right from Africa. They was stolen an' brought here. They use to tell us of how white men had pretty cloth on boats which they was to exchange for some of their o'nament'. W'en they take the o'nament' to the boat they was carry way down to the bottom an' was lock' in."[13]

Georgia slaves, too, have been recorded passing on similar stories about the origins of enslavement. Tatemville's Rosanna Williams was told that her African-born father Lonnon Dennerson and his father, Golla Dennerson, both fell victim to the trick: "Wen muh pa wuz a lil boy, him an muh grandpa wuz fool away wid a red hankuhchuh."[14] On Saint Simons Island, Ryna Johnson recalled that an old African named William told her "lots bout times in Africa." "He say wen dey come in duh boats tuh ketch em, dey trail a red flag[,] an dey ain use tuh see red an das duh wey dey git duh load."[15] Rosa Grant of Possum Point, Georgia, offered a very similar explanation as to how the Africans were ensnared. As she heard it explained in her grandmother Ryna's tales,

> She say dat duh way she happen tuh come from Africa wuz dat dey wuzn use tuh seein anything red. One day dey see a boat wid a red piece uh clawt flyin on it. Wen dey go up close tuh see it, dey wuz caught. Huh mothuh, Theresa, wuz caught too an dey wuz brought tuh dis country. Attuh dey bin yuh a wile, duh mothuh git to weah she caahn stan it an she wannuh go back tuh Africa. One day muh gran Ryna wuz standin wid uh

in duh fiel. Theresa tun roun—so—. . . . She stretch uh ahms out—
so—an rise right up an fly right back tuh Africa. Muh gran say she wuz
standin right deah wen it happen.[16]

It was not just Central Africans whose memories account for the
historical basis of this legend; Ibo slaves too reported the same deception at work in the river areas of the Niger Delta. According to Phoebe
Gilbert of Sapelo Island, her Ibo grandfather blamed his enslavement
on the color red: "Muh gran Calina tell me how he got heah. He say he
playin on beach in Africa, an big boat neah duh beach. He say, duh
mens on boat take down flag, an put up big piece uh red flannel, an all
chillun dey git close tuh watuh edge tuh see flannel an see wut doin.
Den duh mens comes off boat an ketch um, an wen duh ole folks came
in frum duh fiels dey ain no chillun in village. Dey's all on boat. Den
dey brings um yuh."[17]

Despite the popularity of the color-red legend and the commonness of the tales, it is unlikely most slaves were kidnap victims lured to
their fate by red cloth. It would have been impossible to conduct a trade
lasting centuries on the basis of a continual kidnapping of innocent
coastal peoples. Nor could Europeans have made deception a useful
short-term tactic unless the local African authorities were in on the
ruse. Unfortunately, they may often have been, for African traders
employed such deceptions on their own as well as in collusion with
Europeans—not only to kidnap people in the backcountry but more
often to insure that local slaves remained oblivious of newly struck
bargains that would send them into foreign exile.

Local people bargained into slavery by their own relatives and
chiefs and then sold to Europeans were usually kept in the dark about
such matters until it was too late to put up an effective protest. As the
historian Robert Harms points out, "To keep the slaves as calm as
possible, the traders often resorted to trickery so that the slaves would
not realize what was happening to them."[18]

Such deception was probably the case, for example, with the
young boys who were recalled by an ex-slave in the 1870s, remembering the stories his grandfather had told him, as "hiring" themselves out
to white traders only to find themselves shanghaied: "I often yeardy
[heard] him tell how 'e was bring ober from Africa in a ship when 'e was

a boy. De white man lef' de ship behin' and gone asho' in a small boat; an' when dey meet up wid my gran'daddy an' a whole parcel more, young boys like, all from de same village, dey hire dem wid piece ob red flannel an' ting for to 'long wid dem. But when dey git dem on bo'd de ship dey bring dem ober to dis country an' sell dem for slave."[19]

The boys may well have been sold without their knowledge by the local elite even before they loaded the ship but were not told so as to keep them docile. Even in the United States such deceptions had sometimes to be resorted to in order to sell slaves "*Softly,* that is without [their] consent and knowledge," as James Habersham of Savannah, Georgia, described the process in 1775; slaves who knew they were to be sold might run away or provoke serious resistance.[20]

Aside from the literal truth that slavers sometimes used red cloth to facilitate enslavement and to kidnap innocent victims, a deeper figurative meaning also helped shape the development of this legend. On the symbolic level these narratives reveal an African-American assessment that Africa's desire for the most meretricious of Western goods made the continent vulnerable to exploitation and opened the way to tragedy. As W. E. B. Du Bois put it: "Behind this thought lurks the afterthought of force and dominion—the making of brown men to delve when the temptation of beads and red calico cloys."[21]

In these tales the role of African slave traders simply disappeared as inconsequential, and African involvement in the enslavement process was perceived not so much malevolent as simply foolish and naive. Yet, ironically, if African Americans did not blame Africans for their predicament, they did in part admonish themselves. Psychologically, it seems nearly impossible for victims not to impute to themselves some responsibility for the undeserved pummelings of fate. Small children commonly blame themselves for their parents' divorces, and mighty nations conclude that the droughts and diseases that plague them must be God's judgments on their own sinful lifestyles. To do otherwise is to become powerless, hostage to the vagaries of an alien will.

When African Americans said that Africans had fallen victim to the ploys of white slavers, they put their own twist on this psychological need to understand unjustified oppression as partly deserved. In the legends white slavers were clever tricksters who used their victims' own exaggerated love of personal adornment and foreign fashion to entice them into bondage. The legends about the color red blamed enslavement not so much on the white man's alien ways or technological superiority, although they acknowledged his cunning, as on the black man's vanity as revealed in his weakness for gaudy colors.

The choice of the color red as the lure was not necessarily symbolic since in real life red cloth was valued in Africa for its rarity, and the color continued to maintain a powerful attraction for African-American populations as well. It was, as Solomon Northup explained, the southern slaves' favorite color: "As a general thing, the women wear handkerchiefs tied about their heads, but if chance has thrown their way a fiery red ribbon . . . it is sure to be worn on such occasions. Red— the deep blood red—is decidedly the favorite color among the enslaved damsels of my acquaintance. If a red ribbon does not encircle the neck, you will be certain to find all the hair of their wooly heads tied up with red strings of one sort or another."[22]

But the choice of the color red probably also had symbolic overtones, for red was also an almost universal "fetish color" in Afro-America. Among black populations of the Americas as in Africa, red was a color symbolizing danger and power.[23] Thus its choice served both historical reality and figurative truth. An ill-advised greed for the imported luxuries of Atlantic commerce had lured many an African into foolishly becoming part of a monstrous trade in human beings. In recognizing Africa's responsibility, African Americans were renouncing the vanity and greed that had made them vulnerable to exploitation. But as to the exploitation they had no doubts.

Stolen Away from Africa

If legends of the red handkerchiefs suggest that the Africans' naive and "foolish" love of bright colors made them vulnerable to the white man's cunning, they also make it clear that the enslavement process itself was man-stealing, not reputable business. This folk perception is especially important because it comes from the African-American point of view and offers a generally different interpretation of the slave trade than that stressed in contemporary Western histories, which center on the demography and economics of the Atlantic commerce. Over a century ago Frederick Douglass offered the black perspective most explicitly: "I was led to abhor and detest my enslavers. I could regard them in no other light than a band of successful robbers, who had left their homes, and gone to Africa, and stolen us from our homes."[24]

Historians of the transatlantic slave trade, on the other hand, believe only a minority of Africans became enslaved as a result of kidnapping and, of those, most were captured not by Europeans but by Africans who passed their victims along through at least several "legitimate" intermediaries before they were finally sold on the coast.[25] European traders were rarely permitted to venture inland and were far too weak as a group to pursue a long-term commerce based on kidnapping.

Occasionally, unsavory slaving captains who did not expect to return to Africa tried to make a profit by kidnapping (or panyaring, as it was known) an unsuspecting local just before sailing, or by sailing off with the hostages held to insure honest dealings or the last trading party still on board. But because Africans were wary of such misconduct, white kidnapping remained at most incidental to the main trade. Moreover, because Europeans who adopted such tactics put continued commerce in jeopardy for their countrymen, there was resistance to man-stealing even among such an amoral group as the slave traders themselves.

After an incident of panyaring, Africans would take revenge on the next whites to arrive. In the early eighteenth century Nicholas Owen and his brother unhappily discovered how this policy worked when they went blithely ashore to trade and found themselves arrested, stripped of their clothing, and placed in irons. As punishment for the crime of an earlier Dutch trader, the Owen brothers lost both their ship and its cargo, but their lives were spared because they were Englishmen and not Dutch.[26] After another incident of panyaring, Captain Bernard Ladman went so far as to warn his fellows that, unless such kidnapping ceased, "our English colonies will be of no use to us for the negroes study revenge and are resolved to seize upon what they can" and thus would destroy the slave trade.[27]

Captain Ladman was not exaggerating by much; white men simply could not grab Africans off the coast with impunity because until the end of the nineteenth century most African states were far too able to defend themselves and their people. As John Newton put it in his *Thoughts upon the African Slave Trade,* "With regard to the natives, to steal a free man or woman, and to sell them on board a ship would, I think, be a more difficult and more dangerous attempt in Sherbro than in London. But I have no doubt that the traders who come from the interior parts of Africa, at a great distance, find opportunity, in the course of their journey, to pick up stragglers, whom they may meet in their way."[28]

Nonetheless, despite what we know about the probable origins of new slaves and the unlikelihood of European kidnapping as a major source of new bondsmen, African-American folk legends tell a different tale. Typical is Hagar Merriman's autobiography: "My grandparents were brought from . . . Madagascar, caught while running on the sand banks, searching for gold. When taken they had bands of gold on their wrists and ankles."[29]

Black folk in their family histories tended to emphasize not only white kidnapping but especially the theft of innocent black children. Thus Susie Branch of White Bluff, Georgia, recalled a typical family legend that told what "dey" did to her great-grandmother: "Dey steal muh great-great-gran, uh name wuz Sukey, from off duh beach in Africa wen she wuz a young miss. I dunno wut paht of Africa she come from."[30] From nearby Sapelo Island Julia Grovernor, who remembered hearing the old stories about Africa, told a similar but far more developed, poignant, and fanciful tale about the enslavement of her Ibo grandmother Hannah: "Hannah, she wid huh ahnt who wuz diggin peanuts in duh fiel, wid uh baby strop on uh back. Out uh duh brush two white mens come an spit in huh ahnt eye. She blinded an wen she wip uh eye, duh white mens done loose duh baby from huh back, an took Hannah too. Dey done ketched an tie up in sacks. Duh baby an Hannah wuz tie up in sacks lak duh udduhs an Hannah nebuh saw huh ahnt agen an nebuh saw duh baby agen. Wen she wuz let out uh duh sack, she wuz on boat an nebuh saw Africa agen."[31]

Similarly, the New York slave Belinda Lucas recalled her own kidnapping in Africa: "When I was a small child in Africa, being one day at play in the woods, and some people came along; one of whom catched me, and throwing me over his shoulder, ran away with me. After he had gone some distance, he put me down and whipped me to make me run. When we came to the water, they put me into the ship and carried me to Antigua."[32]

Interestingly, this tale closely resembles the enslavement of the Ibo boy Olaudah Equiano as he later described it in his autobiography, except that Equiano's kidnappers were fellow Africans:

> One day, when all our people were gone out to their works as usual, and only I and my dear sister were left to mind the house, two men and a woman got over our walls, and in a moment seized us both; and, without giving us time to cry out, or make resistance, they stopped our mouths, and ran off with us into the nearest wood. . . . For a long time we had kept the woods, but at last we came into a road which I believed I knew. I had now some hopes of being delivered; for we had advanced but a little way before I discovered some people at a distance, on which I began to cry out for their assistance; but my cries had no other effect than to make them tie me faster and stop my mouth, and then they put me into a large sack.[33]

Over the years there was a probable tendency for all slavers in these remembered tales to become whites because that is how the American audience would have interpreted references to slavers and because the tale-tellers themselves were more interested in making a moral point than they were in recording what we might call "scientific" history. The Africans wanted their children and the children of their white masters as well to know that from its very origins American slavery was morally rotten, based on the theft of one person's freedom by another.

The same legendary theme made an appearance in black folk songs as well. Jamaican slaves sang out lyrics that were at once a lamentation and an accusation:

> If me want to go in a Ebo,
> Me can't go there!
> Since dem tief me from a Guinea,
> Me can't go there!
> If we want for go in a Congo,
> Me can't go there!
> Since dem tief me from my tatta,
> Me can't go there![34]

The black abolitionist Henry Highland Garnet saw the moral force in such songs and used the man-stealing theme effectively before an English audience when he sang to them the "Song of the Coffle

Gang," a favorite antislavery tune dealing with the selling of American slaves southward. The song was popular precisely because it drew on well-known legends of enslavement by kidnapping to evoke both empathy and moral indignation:

> See these poor souls from Africa
> Transported to America.
> We are stolen and sold to Georgia;
> Will you go along with me?
> We are stolen, and sold to Georgia;
> Come sound the jubilee![35]

The topic of man-stealing was even well enough known to be picked up by white performers and used on the minstrelsy stage. Early in the nineteenth century Thomas Dibdin's popular song "Negro and Buckra Man" began with the slave's plight:

> Great way off at sea,
> When at home I benee,
> Buckra man steal me,
> From the coast of Guinea;[36]

In 1767 when famed New England poet Phillis Wheatley published her first verse at the age of fourteen, she was some six years and, it would seem, a culture removed from her African homeland, for she described her enslavement in terms of Christian enlightenment:

> 'Twas but e'en now I left my native shore
> The sable Land of error's darkest night. . . .
> Parent of mercy, 'twas thy Powerful hand
> Brought me in safety from the dark abode.

But five years later, after more contact with fellow African Americans, she reinterpreted her past in tune with the legends of man-stealing so as to point out correspondences between the plight of a slave and the position of the American colonies:

> I, young in life, by seeming cruel fate
> Was snatch'd from *Afric's* fancy'd happy seat:
> What pangs excruciating must molest,
> What sorrows labour in my parent's breast?

> Steel'd was that soul and by no misery mov'd
> That from a father seiz'd his babe belov'd.
> Such, such my case. And can I then but pray
> Others may never feel tyrannic sway?[37]

The man-stealing message was further developed in the nine-teenth-century local histories of New England, many of which recalled that a Yankee slave held in their town had been "stolen from Africa when a child." John Tower, for example, was recorded as remembering in old age how his family's bondsman, the African-born Cuffee Jos-selyn, looked as he told of his childhood, of playing innocently in the surf of his homeland while his mother watched so that no harm would befall him. Without warning, sailors from a large ship seized the boy "while his mother stood on the shore wringing her hands and scream-ing for her little boy that she was never to see again."[38]

In a similar tale a North American slave told the minister who interviewed him that he had been "a very little boy" in Africa when the white men made a slave of him: "I left father and mother one day at home to go get shells by the sea-shore; and, as I was stooping down to gather them up, some white sailors came out of a boat and took me away [to Jamaica]. I never see father nor mother again." The ending to this tale of enslavement was a classic motif, and its refrain is echoed by New England's Jin Cole, who similarly finished her narrative with the mournful reflection "and we nebber see our mudders any more."[39]

Actually, few slaves could have been so easily stolen off the African coasts since white slavers approaching through the surf in a rowboat would not have had the benefit of surprise. But the theme was crucial to the legend and well enough known by whites to form the basis of "The African Servant's Prayer," a poem collected by Lindley Mur-ray in his *Narratives of Colored Americans:*

> I was a helpless negro boy,
>   And wandered on the shore;
> Men took me from my parents' arms,
>   I never saw them more.
> But yet my lot, which seemed so hard,
>   Quite otherwise did prove;

For I was carried far from home,
    To learn a Savior's love.[40]

In a well-developed narrative typical of the man-stealing genre, the New England slave Jeremiah Asher remembered listening "with feelings of unmingled grief when grandfather related the story of his capture,—stolen away as he was, from father, mother, brother and sister, never more to see them, and hurried on board of a slaver, to be consigned to perpetual bondage." While quite young, Asher's grandfather accompanied his older brother to his father's rice fields to drive off any feeding birds. When the older boy saw two white men come out of the bush, he immediately understood the danger, grabbed his brother, and ran:

> The white men immediately gave chase. My grandfather says that it was some time before his brother could make him sensible of his danger. He says that he took hold of him and turned him around, so that he might see his pursuers. Then he became so alarmed that he ran as fast and as long as he could, when at last failing in strength, he gave out. Then his brother took him up on his back, and continued to make all possible speed; but finding their pursuers were gaining upon them so fast, he was obliged to give him up and escape for his own life.
>
> The men-stealers soon reached my grandfather, gagged him, and took him up and put him on board the vessel, when they attempted to comfort him by telling him that they were going to take him home.
>
> The brother made his escape to bear the melancholy tidings to his heart-stricken parents, that their darling little boy was stolen, and they would see him no more.
>
> It was twilight when they brought him on board. He saw that, although a large number of men, women and children who had been also thus stolen, he did not recognize one of them. He was, therefore, very lonely and distressed.[41]

This portion of Asher's account of his grandfather's early history is worth considering at some length because it reflects the themes of so many such enslavement tales. Asher recalls his grandfather's experiences with sufficient historical detail to make the narrative generally believable; but, as in the third paragraph quoted above, we can see there has also been an artistic reworking; in recalling a scene his grandfather could not have witnessed, Asher was driving home the tale's moral outrage. On the other hand, when Asher notes in the second paragraph that the kidnappers attempted to comfort the boy by telling him they would take him home, the likelihood becomes stronger that the original kidnappers of his grandfather were African rather than the white aliens who give the grandson's story so much of its dramatic effect.

The Asher tale emphasizes several motifs central to the man-stealing legend: the captured slave was taken as a child, usually from the shore, stolen almost literally from the arms of his family, never to see his parents again. Perhaps the best known of the legend's incarnations came in Alex Haley's bestseller and television blockbuster *Roots* whose hero Kunta Kinte was kidnapped by slavers while innocently looking for drum wood along the Gambia River: "In a blur, rushing at him, he saw a white face, a club upraised; heard heavy footfalls behind him. *Toubob!*"[42] Considering that the historic Juffure, home of Kunta Kinte, was a major trading factory along a section of the Gambia heavily involved in slaving for over a century before the time of Kunta's capture, Haley's emphasis on kidnapping is probably historically misleading, but as a novelist he would doubtless point out it was morally true.[43]

Indeed, in most of these legends about man-stealing as the cause of enslavement, the intent of the tale was not to relate what we might call narrative history. Folklore is not required to be precisely factual, and common people are not expected to be historians. What the black narrators of these legends were after was not a narrow, literal truth about enslavement but a wider, figurative truth about the institution of bondage. African-American bondage was from its origins based upon the theft of one person's freedom and labor by another. No matter what the legal system of the master class might say, the slave understood this basic reality and related it over and over again to youngsters both black and white. In one way or another the freedom of the children of Africa had been stolen by the white masters of America. At its core the legend was true.

The tales of white cannibalism, God's unequal gifts to the races, the enticements of the color red, and white man-stealing all present a mythopoeic rendering of the slave trade era as it was understood by the Africans and the African Americans who were its victims. Today, bogged down in the welter of historical detail, we too often know what happened before we understand what it means. The blacks who told these tales were different. They were not particularly worried about the factual details of what happened—they knew too many of them first-hand—it was the meaning of events that interested them, the moral truths that the experiences illuminated. The legendary narrative traditions about white man-stealing that they passed on to us are an important part of their legacy precisely because of their moral insight; they contain the victims' last words on the meaning of enslavement.

PART II

NO SIMPLE

BLACK

FOLK HERE

CHAPTER 3

A Resistance Too Civilized to Notice

Just as African Americans used African-style oral narratives to develop a communal understanding of the enslavement process and its meanings, so too they maintained patterns of aggressive humor which had been used in Africa to defuse hostility and check antisocial behavior. Across the Americas the shortcomings and abuses of the powerful were lampooned in song just as they had been in Africa. Of course, in America, it was whites in general and oppressive masters in particular that became the favorite targets of this satire.

Too often in the history of American slavery we assume acts of effective resistance are best defined by organized violence because rebellion and revolution are thought by American culture to be the highest, most worthy, most manly forms of protest. But such a vision is far too narrow for African-American studies since traditional African cultures held different values based on differing forms of political science. Indeed, in some ways it might be said that the institutions of traditional African politics were sometimes simply too civilized to be understood by Western categorization.

Most African political systems, for example, did not recognize the right to violent revolution. Instead, African political and social systems depended on a series of built-in control mechanisms designed to head off problems before they became irreconcilable. These social controls usually involved public criticism of abuses of power or deviant behavior and were expressed overtly in institutionalized forms of satiric commentary. Therefore, when African Americans attempted similar controls, it should not immediately suggest a secondary stratagem developed by those too weak for more violent tactics, for African Americans came out of a tradition too sophisticated to regard violence as the primary mode of social and political reconciliation.

Thus it was that, through derisive and satirical songs performed directly before the eyes and ears of their socially dominant targets, black bondsmen were able to release some of their own anger and frustration while redirecting white behavior toward lines more in accord with African-American expectations.[1] The sophistication of this form of resistance is the more remarkable because the whites being held over the satiric grill could not help smacking their lips over the satire even while being roasted with the message. However, this manner of resistance proved too subtle and too civil for our own cruder, more violence-laden culture to recognize, and so satiric song has been generally overlooked as an important countervailing institution. A more African perspective, on the other hand, would permit us to understand that the black bondsmen intended their musical satire as a basic and primary weapon in their arsenal of resistance against oppression.

African Uses of Satire

In Africa social associations, work groups, master singers, and individual villagers all traditionally wielded satirical songs against abuses by neighbors, relatives, great men, and rulers. As the traveler Richard Burton explained, "The [West African] people are fond of singing, and compose extempore, whilst playing, dancing, or working,—the African can do nothing without a chant,—short songs, often highly satirical and much relished by the listeners."[2] The songs were especially useful in fostering social harmony because they permitted socially approved criticism without fostering unpleasant and dangerous personal, face-to-face confrontations. Since these satiric songs carried the propriety of custom and good manners, private slights were not allowed to fester, nor were the great and powerful permitted to remain immune from the complaints of the weak; instead, grievances and frustrations could be aired before the bar of public opinion where they could be controlled and dealt with by social pressure and communal wisdom.

Africans used such satire to reduce both social and personal stress; in fact, it was a kind of communal psychological medicine, as a high priest of the Ashanti explained to R. S. Rattray:

You know that every one has a *sunsum* [soul] that may get hurt or knocked about or become sick, and so make the body ill. Very often, although there may be other causes, e.g. witchcraft, ill health is caused by the evil and hate that another has in his head against you. Again, you too may have hatred in your head against another, because of something that person has done to you, and that, too, causes your *sunsum* to fret and become sick. Our forbears knew this to be the case, and so they ordained a time, once every year, when every man and woman, free man and slave, should have freedom to speak out just what was in their head, to tell their neighbors just what they thought of them, and of their actions, and not only their neighbors, but also the king or chief. When a man has spoken freely thus, he will feel his *sunsum* cool and quieted, and the *sunsum* of the other person against whom he has now openly spoken will be quieted also. The King of Ashanti may have killed your children, and you hate him. This has made him ill, and you ill, too; when you are allowed to say before his face what you think, you both benefit. That was why the King of Ashanti in ancient times, when he fell sick, would send for the Queen of Nkoranza to insult him, even though the time for the ceremony had not yet come round. It made him live longer and did him good.[3]

Suggestively, in terms of the African-American experience, Africans used precisely this kind of satire to resist European colonialism. The satiric form of the criticism, as Leroy Vail and Landeg White discovered, legitimized the content: "This 'free expression' is in many African societies not only tolerated but openly welcomed as a major channel of communication between the powerless and the powerful, the client and the patron, the ruled and the ruler."[4]

A victim of African public ridicule was obliged to grin and bear the mocking allusions in somewhat the same manner that in Western society a man is expected to be able to take a joke at his expense whereas he would be justified in avenging an insult. As an informant explained about a song directed against the field manager of a Mozambican sugar estate, "You could swear at him [in the song] and he just smiled." To say the same things outside the song "would be just insulting him . . . , just provoking him," but sung criticism permitted no retaliation—"there will be no case."[5]

Some African societies limited most of their political satire to holiday festivals or special situations, but satiric songs of more personal gossip and recrimination were a part of daily life. Such satire was especially refined by the bardic *griots* who were renowned for their praise songs but equally feared for the sharp, deflating barbs of their wit.

Throughout much of Africa, songs used for social control traditionally made fun of the pompous and condemned those who neglected their duties or were cruel and overbearing. "One can well imagine," explained Hugh Tracey in his study of Chopi musicians, "the forcefulness of the reprimand conveyed to a wrong doer when he finds his misdeeds sung . . . before all the people of a village, or the blow to the pride of an overweening petty official who has to grin and bear it while the young men jeer to music at his pretentiousness."[6] What better sanction, he wondered, against those who outrage the ethics of a community than to know they will be pilloried by the barbs of a master singer and the general laughter of the public. In such songs, cleverly veiled but pointed references to the sources of social injustice were broadcast throughout the marketplace to the widespread enjoyment and satisfaction of the public.[7]

Among the Ashanti such satire was directly institutionalized in the traditional *Apo* rites and similar ceremonies, where ridicule of authority was especially sanctioned and encouraged for a limited period.[8] During such occasions a ruler would be reminded of his vulnerability to social criticism:

> All is well to-day
> We know that a Brong man eats rats,
> But we never knew that one of royal blood eats rats.
> But to-day we have seen our master, Ansah, eating rats.
> To-day all is well and we may say so, say so, say so.
> At other times we may not say so, say so, say so.[9]

Such satiric traditions also characterized the Africa of the slaving era. William Bosman, for example, observed just such an annual festival at Axim on the Gold Coast at the beginning of the eighteenth century, where, he reported, for eight days perfect liberty of lampooning was allowed; indeed, he said, "scandal is so highly exalted, that they may freely sing of all the faults, villainies, and frauds of their superiors as well as inferiors, without punishment, or so much as the least interruption; and the only way to stop their mouths is to ply them lustily with drink, which alters their tone immediately, and turns their satirical

ballads into commendatory songs on the good qualities of him who
hath so nobly treated them."[10]

The satire was not only political. John Atkins noted in 1721 that
as part of the diversion of evening entertainments the inhabitants of
Sierra Leone would gather in an open part of town to form "all round in
a circle laughing, and with uncouth notes, blame or praise somebody in
the company."[11] Africans used satiric song to burlesque domestic quar-
rels and neighborly disputes as well as to hew villagers to the line of
proper social conduct. As Brodie Cruickshank observed from the Gold
Coast in the nineteenth century, such songs were often improvised by
singers who were "very expert in adapting the subjects of [their] songs
to current events, and [who] indulge in mocking ridicule, in biting
sarcasm, in fulsome flattery, or in just praise of men and things,
according as circumstances seem to demand." As Cruickshank explained, "This habit of publishing the praise, or shame of individuals in
spontaneous song, exercises no little influence upon conduct."[12] Africans, like all men, were susceptible to flattery and in dread of public
ridicule. And as the press is feared and courted in modern America, so
too were the improvisational singers who served as the organs of public
opinion in traditional African society.

In Africa as in Afro-America, work songs were a favorite vehicle
for satire. For this reason visitors to Sierra Leone in the eighteenth and
nineteenth centuries found the songs of native boatmen particularly
entertaining. To the stroke of the oars a lead singer among the rowers
would boom out an impromptu couplet, and his crew would respond in
a general chorus. The songs boasted the exploits of the rowers and
lampooned females of their acquaintance; they also broadcast the news
of the coast and added gossipy satires of current events. Sometimes the
sarcasm of the crew was more pointedly directed at their employers or
the important men of their society. As Thomas Winterbottom observed
in the 1790s, the songs were often "of a satirical cast lashing the vices of
the neighboring head men."[13] Though it may have been safer to crit-
icize neighboring leaders, the allusions were of unmistakably wider
application. Subtlety and wry indirection were the requirements of
African verbal wit, and the demonstration of verbal skill demanded
satire by allusion. The rowers were not afraid to be more direct in their
comments; as Winterbottom noted, the impromptu songs of the boat-

men "frequently describe the passengers in a strain of praise or of the most pointed ridicule."[14]

Satire functioned in African society as an important way of releasing frustrations that would otherwise have been repressed. The satiric functions of the "amusing spirits" of the Poro society of Sierra Leone, the topical satire of the Egungun cult, and the humorous pantomime of the Ogo society of the Yoruba and Igbo peoples of Nigeria all show marked similarity to African-American examples.[15] Likewise, the satiric commentary of secret society maskers in Sierra Leone and Hausa praise-singers in northern Nigeria parallel African-American holiday songs used by slaves to win gifts from a master. The songs of both areas display a quality of social blackmail, since the persons honored by the attentions of the singers had to come up with a gift to avoid being publicly mimed or ridiculed. Yet, because great generosity to the spirits or praise-singers was the expected behavior, the gifts were regarded not as a response to extortion but, rather, as a worthwhile display of the victim's social prestige, which the singers naturally reciprocated with fitting songs of praise.[16]

Work-song texts from a coffee and quinine plantation in the Kiv area of the then Belgian Congo are particularly suggestive in showing the transition from praise to satire that also characterized New World plantation work songs. Young Bashi women directed their songs at the owner of their plantation, who was also serving as interpreter of the texts. He had recently stopped giving rations of salt and oil because he had raised wages. The singers began by praising the plantation and its owner until in the fourth song the question of the salt and oil rations was raised. By the fifth and final song the women were threatening to take jobs elsewhere if the rations were not reinstated. The songs informed the owner of a discontent that he had not realized existed among his workers. The young women had not complained directly, but through the medium and progression of their songs they had been able politely but pointedly to express their unhappiness.[17]

Whites had been favorite targets of African satire and mimicry since early Portuguese and French missionaries on the slave coast found themselves and their services mocked in local frolics led by their best catechism pupils.[18] In the same way, Thomas Edward Bowdich and his junior officers found their alien idiosyncrasies a source of contemptuous amusement to the Ashanti war captains who were pledging their loyalty to the king before setting out to battle the Fantees: "Each captain made the oath impressive in his own peculiar manner; some seriously, some by ridicule, at our expense, and that of the Fantees, pointing at our heads and ears, and endeavouring to intimidate us by the most insolent action and gesture." The king's troop of small boys also considered the white men figures to be mocked, Bowdich reports, and "used to entertain themselves with mimicking our common expressions and our actions, which they did inimitably."[19]

European traders fared just as badly, for they too were universal targets of local humor. Brodie Cruickshank noted that on the Gold Coast any passing white man was soon caricatured by the improvisational talents of local songsters: "They would quickly seize some peculiarity of his character whether good or bad, and celebrated it aloud, amidst the unrestrained merriment of the bystanders."[20] A. B. Ellis explained the same situation later in the nineteenth century, noting that "it is not uncommon for singers to note the peculiarities of persons who pass, and improvise at their expense. This is particularly the case when the strangers are European, as the latter do not . . . understand Tshi, and the singers can allow themselves greater latitude than would be the case if their remarks were understood."[21]

Almost everything the white man did was funny to his African observers, as Captain Hugh Clapperton discovered while visiting the Yoruba in 1826 when a special series of plays was given in honor of his arrival. The third act featured a "white devil" which, Clapperton reports, "went through the motions of taking snuff, and rubbing its hands; when it walked, it was with the most awkward gait, treading as the most tender-footed white man would do in walking barefoot, for the first time over new frozen ground. The spectators often appealed to us, as to the excellence of the performance. . . . I pretended to be fully as pleased with this caricature of a white man as they could be, and certainly the actor burlesqued the part to admiration."[22]

In 1827 René Caillié found himself a special favorite of the Mandingo women of Tieme: "They ridiculed my gestures and my words, and went about the village mimicking me and repeating what I had said. . . . My sore foot was the object of their ridicule, and the difficulty I experienced in walking excited their immoderate laughter."[23]

Similarly, in the 1860s Richard Burton found his note-taking to be an object of mime and satire by the jesters of Dahomey.[24] Such traditions continued into colonialism when companies recording tunes sung by African laborers in European ports discovered that the songs sold well in West Africa precisely for their biting satire of white society.[25]

Satiric Resistance in the Americas

Given the use of satiric song in Africa, it should not be surprising that throughout the New World during the slaving era African-American bondsmen also displayed a genius for improvising songs lampooning the foibles of their masters and advertising harsh or unfair treatment for the general censure of society. Bryan Edwards observed that blacks in the eighteenth-century West Indies adopted a special genre of improvised ballad for their "Merry meetings and midnight festivals," where they gave "full scope to a talent for ridicule and derision, . . . exercised not only against each other, but also, not infrequently, at the expense of their owner or employers."[26] James Phillippo noted at the beginning of the nineteenth century that in Jamaica such songs "had usually a ludicrous reference to the white people, and were generally suggested by some recent occurrence."[27] As Richard R. Madden explained in 1835, the African-American facility for extemporaneous song-making and sarcastic mimicry was extraordinary: "They are naturally shrewd and quick observers, fond of imitation, and wonderfully successful in practicing it. I think they have the best perception of the ridiculous of any people I ever met."[28]

On the British island of Saint Christopher, Clement Caines recorded that "the Negroes dress every occurence in rhyme, and give it a metre, rude indeed, but well adapted to the purposes of raillery or sarcasm." Caines had personal experience of the matter when he discovered he himself had been the subject of a young slave girl who had been "singing her master" all over his estate for failing to give her a promised coin. Apparently, she kept it up until Caines's wife gave her a hearing.[29]

Sometimes the satire was as cruel as it was humorous; one of the most interesting examples was recorded in British Jamaica at the beginning of the nineteenth century. Robert Renny reports that Europeans arriving at the dock in Port Royal were met by a boatfull of black women selling fresh fruits and singing what seems to me the strangest advertising jingle on record:

> New-come buckra [white man],
>   He get sick,
> He take fever,
>   He be die.
>   He be die.
> New-come buckra,
>   He get sick.[30]

Since fever was a real and terrifying danger for newly arrived Europeans, the song was sharply pointed indeed. Mocking arriving Europeans was also a favorite pastime in mid-nineteenth-century Rio de Janeiro where, according to the German traveler Ernst von Bibra, blacks welcomed incoming vessels by sticking out their tongues and yelling curses and obscenities.[31]

Jamaican slaves used satiric song to commemorate the infamous conduct of a local master who threw his critically ill slaves into a gully to die after stripping them of their belongings. One of the slaves recovered and fled to Kingston where he was later discovered by his master, who immediately reclaimed him. But when the full story came out, it was the master who was driven from Kingston, with the event becoming the inspiration for what became a well-known song:

> Take him to the Gulley! Take him to the Gulley!
>   But bringee back the frock and board.—
> Oh! Massa, Maasa! me no deadee yet!—
> Take him to the Gulley! Take him to the Gulley!
>   Carry him along.[32]

Similar satires were found on the French islands where, as Jean Baptiste Dutertre noted in the seventeenth century, the Africans were "satirists who reveal even the slightest faults of our Frenchmen [who] cannot do the least reprehensible thing without [the blacks] making it the subject of amusement among themselves. In their worksongs, they repeat all their masters or overseers have done to them, good or bad."[33] Father Jean Baptiste Labat had observed the same characteristics on his travels. The blacks, he reported, were "satirical to excess, and few people apply themselves with greater success to knowing the defects of people and above all of the whites, to mock among themselves."[34]

As in Africa, African-American ridicule and censure gained force through musical presentation. Much like proverbs set to music, improvisational lampoons of the moment were transformed into pieces of traditional folk wisdom and entertainment, enjoyed and remembered in good part for the melodies connected to them. As Lafcadio Hearn noted in late-nineteenth-century Martinique, "vile as may be the motive, the satire, the malice, these chants are preserved for generations by the singular beauty of the air, and the victim of a carnival song need never hope that his failings or his wrong will be forgotten; it will be sung long after he is in his grave."[35]

In Spanish Cuba, J. G. F. Wurdemann observed that such songs were often combined with dancing, and he reported that "in their native dialects [the slaves] ridicule their owners before their faces enjoying with much glee their happy ignorance of the burden of their songs."[36]

But generally it does not seem to have mattered if the victims of the songs understood that they were being burlesqued. In fact, Edward Long reported from eighteenth-century Jamaica that having a nearby overseer listen to the derision directed at him "only serves to add poignancy to their satire, and heightens the fun."[37] Thus, on the Haitian island of La Gonave, when the leading citizen landowner—a mulatto named Constant Polynice—hosted a Congo dance, a guest lampooned him with a song:

> Polynice the tax collector
> Rides at night on his white horse.
> We will drive him away with stones,
> And a misfortune will strike him.

Despite the lyrics, Polynice was generally well liked, and he apparently accepted the song without malice, smiling as if he would have been hurt not to have been so honored.[38]

Slave gangs often used their work songs to comment on their own foibles as well as those of their masters, overseers, and slave drivers— sometimes, as in Brazil, it was in the riddle form of a *jongo* under the direction of a master singer who would disguise his allusions where necessary with African words and by transforming his targets metaphorically into animals or trees.[39]

At other times the New World satires became openly insurrectionary. In 1805 Trinidad a Mr. de Gannes de la Chancellerie was bathing in the river that ran through his plantation when twelve black women, balancing plantain baskets on their heads, came by on the path. Swaying their hips to the rhythm of the chac-chac pods they carried, the chorus of women offered up what was to him a bloodcurdling threat:

> Pain c'est viande beque [Bread is white man's flesh]
> Vin c'est sang beque [Wine is white man's blood]
>   San Domingo! [a reference to the recent revolt]
> Nous va boire sang beque [We will drink white blood]
>   San Domingo!

After other Trinidadian whites heard the same or similar songs foreshadowing an impending slave revolt, an inquiry was begun that resulted in both executions and severe punishments for the accused rebel leaders.[40]

Mrs. A. C. Carmichael heard another type of insubordinate "funny song" on the same island in the early 1830s, which ridiculed the whites' inability to stop the fires set by Maroons in the hillside sugarcane:

> Fire in de mountain
> Nobody for out him [No one will put it out]
> Take me daddy's bo tick [dandy stick]
> And make a monkey out him
> Poor John! Nobody for out him. [Poor John Bull][41]

In North America, too, slaves used a variety of forms of satiric resistance. Among themselves, bondsmen especially enjoyed parodying their owners in both mime and music. A South Carolina white was scandalized when he secretly beheld a Saturday night country dance of the blacks near Charleston in 1772. "The entertainment," he reported, "was opened by the men copying (or taking off) the manners of their masters, and the women those of their mistresses, and relating some highly curious anecdotes, to the inexpressible diversion of that company."[42] South Carolina slaves continued to parody their masters well into the nineteenth century. A "street girl" from Beaufort explained in the 1840s that "us slaves watched the white folks' parties when the guests danced a minuet and then paraded in a grand march. . . . Then we'd do it, too, but we used to mock 'em, every step. Sometimes the white folks noticed it but they seemed to like it. I guess they thought we couldn't dance any better."[43]

Whites usually seemed slightly flattered by what they interpreted as "awkward" attempts by black society to duplicate their manners. Typical of white obtuseness was the report of Peter Marsden in the 1780s that Jamaican slaves during Christmas holidays danced "minuets with the mulattoes and other brown women, imitating the motion and steps of the English but with a degree of affectation that renders the whole truly laughable and ridiculous."[44] Several decades later another Jamaican, James Stewart, once again overlooked the obvious: "Scenes were exhibited in which his Lordship, with several other distinguished characters, were personated by negroes in full costume, [but] . . . they had lost sight of one grand requisite to complete the resemblance, viz.—ease of manner, and consequently their deportment [was] strangely at variance with that of their originals, rendering such mimic actions truly amusing."[45]

If masters refused to realize there was more than one dimension to such slave foolishness, the black audience knew better. As Shepard Edmunds explained when describing Tennessee slaves doing a cakewalk, "The slaves both young and old would dress up in hand-me-down finery to do a high-kicking, prancing walk-around. They did a take-off on the high manners of the white folks in the 'big house,' but their masters, who gathered around to watch the fun, missed the point."[46]

In late-eighteenth-century New England, black election day celebrations were marked by a grand parade and training of troops by the newly elected black leaders. Whites always found ludicrous the consummate dignity of the black officials; it seemed even more ridiculous when the black troops would take the command "Fire and fall off" literally—tumbling from their horses onto the common field. Such parodies were considered fun, and it was reported that masters did not interfere until "the utmost verge of decency had been reached, good-naturedly submitting to the hard hits leveled against themselves, and possibly profiting a little by some shrewd allusion."[47] Similar satiric parodies were found in South Carolina where in 1843 William Cullen Bryant described a mock military parade by the blacks as "a sort of burlesque of our militia trainings, in which the words of command and the evolutions were extremely ludicrous," and corresponding satiric parades were also common in Haiti during Mardi Gras celebrations.[48]

The "foolishness" of the slaves in their pastimes reflects the traditional wisdom of the jester that satire is safer and more effective when veiled as coming from a clown. Charles William Day noted how, during carnival in nineteenth-century Trinidad, black celebrants lampooned the slave condition to the general enjoyment of black and white.[49] But James Phillippo observed how Jamaican blacks used this self-parody and feigned ignorance to their own advantage: "The lowest and most unintelligent of the tribes are Mungolas. Their stupidity, however, has often been more feigned than real; thus, when attracting the gaze of the multitudes at their annual carnivals by their grotesque appearance and ridiculous gambols, they have often been known to indulge in the keenest satire and merriment at their own expense, repeating in chorus, 'Buckra tink Mungola nigger fool make him tan so.' "[50]

A satire of a master did not seem so dangerous when it followed on the heels of a self-parody of the slave condition or a series of praise songs flattering the master's vanity. Consider the progression of a Louisiana slave song:

> Negro cannot walk without corn in his pocket,
>   It is to steal chickens.
> Mulatto cannot walk without rope in his pocket,
>   It is to steal horses.
> White man cannot walk without money in his pocket,
>   It is to steal girls.[51]

The preceding song is also interesting because it approached the topic of the white man's access to black women, an access that black men were often powerless to prevent. That whites could use their wealth and power to "steal girls" must have been a source of constant irritation, if not humiliation, for black men who were allowed neither equal opportunities of their own nor even normal social defenses for their women. One way to strike back and to release frustration was through satiric song.

Consider an example of this genre recorded during a John Canoe festival in early-nineteenth-century Kingston, Jamaica; again, an African-like song progression satirizes white male attitudes about sex and race. To the tune of "Guinea Corn" the John Canoe performer sang and tumbled before a white man in his audience to bring forth humorously the theme of the inevitable conversion of white men to the superiority of women of color.

> But Massa Buccra have white love,
> Soft and silken like one dove.
> To brown girl—him barely shivel—
> To black girl—oh, Lord, de Devil!
> But when him once two tree year here,
> Him tink white lady wery great boder;
> De coloured peoples, never fear,
> Ah him lob him de morest nor any oder.
> But top—one time bad fever catch him,
> Colour'd peoples kindly watch him—
> In sick room, nurse voice like music—
> From him hand taste sweet de physic.
> So alway come—in two tree year,
> And so wid you, massa—never fear
> Brown girl for cook—for wife—for nurse;
> Buccra lady—poo—no wort a curse.[52]

"Get away, you scandalous scoundrel," Michael Scott reports himself as having responded to this comic challenge. The song had clearly been offered in jest, and not without a touch of flattery about the sexual opportunities open to the white massa. But also embedded in the lyrics were sly innuendoes about the deadly fevers when whites would lie helplessly dependent on their servants, and a reverse kind of sexual argument that white wandering resulted because no man would reasonably choose a white woman over a woman of color. If that were true, then the unequal access by men of different races to each other's women seemed less unsettling; also if that were true, black men faced competition not so much because they were weak but because their women were so much more desirable.

A far more personal and more pointed song on the same theme comes from Saint Kitts, where a slave singer named Cubenna recalls in a kind of calypso air how his master sent him off on an overnight journey to the capital carrying a note to Doctor Thompson. Cubenna, however, met the doctor on the road and was told he could return home at once; the doctor would send an answer the next day. The overjoyed slave ran home to be with his wife:

> Heart been so glad now. Ey-ey-a-a-eye
> Ya mee do run, man, ya mee dig, man . . .
> I run na mi house, man!
> I call 'pon mi wife, man!
> I push-um [the door]—I shove um:
> [S]he won't gie no hanswer;
>
> I wake um at las', man,
> I tell um 'bout someting,
> Someting de waalk de [there]
> He walk to mi chamber.
> [S]he tell me: 'he b'lieve say de Jumbee [spirit].
>   Ey-ey-a-a-eye etc.
>
> I look for me bow'tick [heavy walking stick]
> Ya mi da lick wi' [which I beat with]
> I lick 'way 'pon Jumbee,
> Jumbee de bawl de'—Ey-ey-a-a-eye.
> He jump na de back-door;
>
> I meet Uncle Quacoo,
> I tell um 'bout Jumbee;
> Jumbee bin waalk de',
> He waalk de wi' shoe on!
>
> He tell me, since be bin barn now,
> He never bin hearee,
> Jumbee could waalk de, and walk wi' de shoe on.
> He tell me, he b'lieve say: "Da, Massa!"
>   Ey-ey-a-a-eye.
> Massa go killa me—oh![53]

Here the difficult topic of a white master's access to a black man's woman is confronted directly. On the surface the black man has been cuckolded by his devious master and played for a fool by his unfaithful wife, but Cubenna clearly gets his revenge by beating upon the massa who his wife claims is only a noisy spirit. It must be noted, however, that the singer is also a realist who understands that such revenge would inevitably have its own costs. Here in a satiric song aired before the general public a black singer humorously tried to come to terms with a problem that struck to the very core of black male life.

Since in satire the slaves were able to use their own weakness to advantage, the satiric resistance of bondsmen in the Americas was seldom repressed. Blacks used an African-style improvisation that permitted them to move toward either praise or ridicule, flattery or criticism, so as to influence the behavior of those in power. As Nicholas Cresswell reported in 1774, the blacks of Nanjemoy, Maryland, sang to their banjos a "very droll music indeed. In their songs they generally relate the usage they have received from their masters or mistresses in a very satirical style and manner."[54] William Faux noted this same propensity a half-century later in 1819 while listening to the work songs of a chorus of galley slaves in Charleston but saw where the songs were heading: "The verse was their own, and abounding in praise or satire, intended for kind or unkind masters."[55]

This ability to transform songs of praise into songs of recrimination was especially important in using improvisational tunes to countervail a master's domination or to win a reward. Black oarsmen in eighteenth-century Louisiana were no different from the Krumen of eighteenth-century Sierra Leone or the oarsmen of nineteenth-century Charleston in alternating praise with sarcasm to create a self-fulfilling prophecy:

> Sing lads; our master bids us sing
> For master cry out loud and strong
> The water with long oar strike
> Sing, lads, and let us haste along. . . .
>
> See! See! The town! Hurrah! Hurrah!
> Master returns in pleasant mood.
> He's going to treat his boys all 'round.
> Hurrah! Hurrah for master good.[56]

The hint that a good master treats his slaves could hardly be missed, for as John Lambert explained about a similar "nonsense" rowing song he heard on the Savannah River in the early nineteenth century, "I however remarked that brandy was very frequently mentioned, and it was understood as a hint to the passengers to give [the slave rowers] a dram."[57]

When patriarchal southern masters permitted their servants an entertainment, as at Christmas or corn-shucking time, they would often indulge their bondspeople's desire to sing for them. And, as with similar entertainments in Africa, the singers required a treat for their efforts. Sometimes the slaves went from plantation to plantation, like the John Canoers of North Carolina and Jamaica, singing satiric frolic and praise songs before demanding small rewards.[58] A master who failed to offer the expected treat would be derided by a song like the following:

> Poor massa, so dey say;
> Down in de heel, so dey say;
> Got no money, so dey say;
> Not one shillin, so dey say;
> Got A'mighty bless you, so dey say.[59]

At other times, the subject of recompense was approached indirectly but still through a use of humor. As Robert Shepherd recalled, the slaves at a corn shucking sang, "Oh! My head, my poor head. Oh! My poor head is affected!" But as Shepherd explained, "Dere weren't nothing wrong with our heads. Dat was just our way of lettin' our overseer know us wanted some liquor. Purty soon he would come 'round with a big horn of whiskey, and dat made de poor head well, but it weren't long before it got worse again, and den us got another horn of whiskey."[60] Sometimes a master might forget (or try to evade) what was expected of him; but he would be quickly reminded of his failure by a pointed improvised verse in the ongoing corn song:

> Young Tim Barnet no great thing,
>   Oh! Jenny gone away!
> Never say, come take a dram.
>   Oh! Jenny gone away!
> Master gi's us plenty meat,
>   Oh! Jenny gone away!
> Might apt to fo'git de drink.
>   Oh! Jenny gone away![61]

Later, as the victorious team in a corn shucking carried the master or overseer around on their shoulders, they crowned him with a garland of praise songs, but a perceptive master might have noticed even then that some of the leaves were the poison ivy of sarcasm:

> Oh, Mr. Reid iz er mighty fine man,—
> Er mighty fine man indeed;
> He plants all de taters,
> He plows all de corn,
> He weighs all de cotton,
> An' blows de dinner horn;
> Mr. Reid iz er mighty fine man.[62]

Slaves with relatively decent masters encouraged their kindness by emphasizing their masters' best traits through flattering songs of praise; but always there was the implicit threat to turn this praise around. As one slave sang,

> Massa's nigger am slick and fat,
>   Oh! Oh! Oh!
> Shine jes like a new beaver hat,
>   Oh! Oh! Oh! . . .
> Jones' niggers am lean an po'
>   Oh! Oh! Oh!
> Don't know whether they git 'nough ter eat or no,
>   Oh! Oh! Oh![63]

Few masters could resist comments on fellow whites (even knowing they should not have been permitted) when they came as part of such gratifying praise. But neither should they have missed the implications about the public censure of slave owners who neglected the needs of their bondsmen. Slaves might report the derelictions of ol' Massa Jones when they had a master nearer to home in mind, just as Africans in Sierra Leone couched their criticisms in complaints about neighboring headmen and the blacks of Trinidad disguised theirs in the process of ridiculing the governments of neighboring islands.[64]

Masters, of course, loved the songs of praise and blocked out the impropriety of slaves judging their owners when the comments seemed positive. Consider, for example, the black oarsmen who sang of the physical attractions of their white mistress, Fanny Kemble; she loved every romantic minute of it:

> There is one privilege which I enjoy here which I think few Cockneyesses have ever had experience of, that of hearing my own extemporaneous praises chanted bard-fashion by our Negroes. . . . Rowing yesterday evening through a beautiful moonrise, my two sable boatmen entertained themselves and me with alternate strophe and antistrophe of poetical description of my personal attractions, in which my "wire waist" recurred repeatedly, to my intense amusement . . . ; and I suppose that the fine round natural proportions of the uncompressed waists of the sable beauties of these regions appear less symmetical to eyes accustomed to them than our stay-cased figures.[65]

Whether the bondsmen were using the moonlight to croon smoothly of Ms. Kemble's many charms or were softly making fun of her corseted figure that was far too narrow by African tastes, what was happening was that black men were openly commenting on the physical attractions of a white woman, moreover, on the physical attractions of the woman who was Massa's wife.

Of course, not all slave owners got off easily with songs of praise or veiled allusions. Frederick Douglass records that bitter derision also appeared. It was clear enough in a frolic song he recorded when the slaves sang:

> We raise de wheat,
> Dey gib us de corn;
>
> We bake de bread,
> Dey gib us de crust;
>
> We sif de meal,
> Dey gib us de huss;
>
> We peel de meat,
> Dey gib us de skin;
>
> And dat's de way,
> Dey take us in;
>
> Dey skim de pot
> Dey gib us de liquor,
> And say dat's good enough for nigger.[66]

Even a well-thought-of master had to be careful of his behavior or face ridicule. When Ned Lipscomb, described by one of his slaves as "de best massa in de whole country," ran off to avoid Sherman's army during the Civil War, his slaves fitted him into a song then making the rounds, which began:

> White folks, have you seed old massa
> Up the road, with he mustache on?
> He pick up he hat and he leave real sudden
> And I believe he's up and gone.
>
> Old massa run away
> And us darkies stay at home.
> It must be now dat Kingdom's comin'
> And de year of Jubilee.[67]

During the same era, Thomas Wentworth Higginson, a white officer greatly respected by his black troops, discovered their remarkable propensity for satire; though they did not lampoon him, they did satirize white enlisted men who were to receive higher wages than corresponding black troops: "My presence apparently checked the performance of another verse, beginning, 'De buckra 'list for money,' apparently in reference to the controversy about the pay question, then just beginning, and to the more mercenary and less noble aims they attributed to the white soldiers."[68]

Thus it was that throughout the era of slavery African Americans across the New World used satiric songs to resist white oppression. When, under the interdictions of bondage, blacks found themselves unable to develop formal methods of social regulation, they fought back with the informal controls that in Africa had accompanied public satire, praise, and ridicule. By cleverly intermixing criticism of their masters with flattery, and by combining their praise and criticism with corresponding lampoons of black behavior, African-American bondsmen desensitized the seeming impropriety of black slaves satirizing the society of their white owners. Thus, in their songs slaves were able cleverly to voice many of their grievances before their masters and openly vent their frustrations and disdain as well.

By commenting on the virtues and foibles of white society, the slaves were sometimes able to improve their own situations, for few masters preferred the barbs of ridicule to the enticements of praise and flattery. That it did not work better on European Americans is unfortunate but understandable since the whites lacked well-developed similar institutions of their own; nonetheless, such satire still worked more effectively in most cases than desperate acts of violence or running away—both of which usually only resulted in severe punishments and hardened attitudes. Moreover, the songs were emotionally healing to the singers themselves. If slavery could not be overcome, it could be withstood. The soul would survive.

We have long known that slaves adept at dissembling behavior relished "puttin' on Ole Massa," as it was known, but clearly there was more to African wit than the clever lie and more to African-American resistance than flight or suicidal violence. In the satire of song and pantomime slaves not only put Ole Massa on, they put him down as well, and put him down directly, in public, to his face.

CHAPTER 4

The Aristocratic Heritage
of Black America

Normally, when we think of African immigrants to the New World, we consider them in terms of their ascribed social status as slaves; indeed, not long ago historians did not even refer to African arrivals as "immigrants." But slavery was a caste position most Africans acquired only because of the existence of servitude in the Americas. In Africa, these same bondsmen had usually been free,[1] and many were of aristocratic or elite heritage. Indeed, an elite of African headmen, chiefs, nobles, and royalty came to the Americas in considerable numbers along with their families.

Unlike emigrants from Europe and Asia, who were most often the flotsam and jetsam of their homelands, Africa's forced migrants were not the "teeming refuse" of their native shores; instead, many of the enslaved Africans were a true people of class—a reality almost antithetical to the stereotyping of slaves as simple "black folk." The commonly held notion that the population of the United States is derived from lower- or middle-class origins may be true enough for whites and Asians, but it is often not true for African Americans. Given the wide-branching nature of inheritance, by now a majority of black Americans may have the blue blood of African royalty and aristocracy mixed in their veins.[2]

The nobles of Africa did not forget their heritage upon arrival in the Americas; if a bitter fate had made them other men's servants, they nonetheless continued to feel the innate superiority of their inherited status and elite upbringing.[3] Moreover, their pride was reinforced by the esteem of fellow countrymen who loyally continued to hold them in highest regard. Even the whites of the master class, who, after all, lacked nobility of their own, were impressed to have among their servants patricians, men and women of royal blood or noble birth.[4]

Because of the hundreds of African societies from which slaves were taken, the multitude of political units involved, and the large size of polygynous African families, there were many more Africans of prestigious rank vulnerable to enslavement than we might, as Westerners, suppose. Consider, for example, T. E. Bowdich's description of the Gabon region: "Kings are numerous in Gaboon. . . . The greatest trader, or the richest man of almost every small village assumes the title." In the twentieth century the anthropologist Melville Herskovits commented on the same phenomena along the west coast generally, where historically many states had been no larger than a few hundred square miles: "To this day, in a small village, one may be introduced to its 'king' by a loyal follower of this petty, powerless potentate; and the village will likewise be designated a 'kingdom.' . . . These reflect identifications which, earlier, were to independent states."[5]

Moreover, noblemen from the upper classes were especially liable to be enslaved for reasons of political intrigue, for as Mahommah Gardo Baquaqua reported, "when any person [gave] evidence of gaining an eminent position in the country, he [was] immediately envied, and means [were] taken to put him out of the way." The African elite were also often victimized by the internecine wars fostered by the international slave trade. Nobles from the losing sides of battles were too dangerous to keep as local servants in Africa's less restrictive bondage; instead, they were killed or sent into exile in the Americas.[6]

As one such prince explained to John G. Stedman in eighteenth-century Surinam, "My father . . . was a king, and treacherously murdered by the sons of a neighbouring prince. To revenge his death, I daily went a hunting with some men, in hopes of retaliating upon his assassins; but I had the misfortune to be surprized, taken, and bound; hence these ignoble scars [around his wrists and ankles]. I was afterward sold to your European countrymen on the coast of Guiana—a punishment which was deemed greater than instant death."[7]

The importance of African royalty in the New World first struck me when I was researching the black community of eighteenth-century New England. Far more often than I would have expected, the town histories would note one of the town's slaves as a prince or princess of royal African blood: in Massachusetts King Pompey, Shilbogee Turry-Werry, Prince Youngey, Prince Freeman, and Jin Cole were slaves said to be of royal birth; in Rhode Island Queen Abigail, Prince Robinson, Venture Smith, and Senegambia were likewise remembered as royals, as were Prince and Cuffee Whipple in Portsmouth, New Hampshire. In Connecticut, Bilah Freedom of Litchfield and Tobiah and his son Eben Tobias of Derby were all recognized in local histories to have been of majestic ancestry.[8]

Because the black population of early New England was small and Yankee slaves usually lived as part of their masters' families, the heritage of the bondsmen was well known by the master class—so much so that in her novel of local color, *Oldtown Folks*, Harriet Beecher Stowe made use of the royal stereotype by casting her fictional character Boston Foodah as of princely blood.[9] Both white and black New Englanders were prone to brag about the royal heritage of certain local bondsmen, and both races shuddered over the cruelty of a fate that would cast princes into endless servitude in an alien land.

As early as 1638, John Josselyn had been disturbed by an incident he observed in the new Massachusetts Bay Colony while he was the guest of Samuel Maverick. Maverick held a female slave he intended to mate with a male bondsman. She was, however, of royal heritage—a point Maverick must have recognized well enough since she kept as a maid a fellow bondswoman whom, according to Josselyn, used "a very humble and dutiful garb . . . toward her." The former queen held the idea of sleeping with a commoner in utter disdain and threw the impudent fellow from her bed; the next morning she created a major scene, crying out before her master and his guest against the barbarism of trying to force a queen into becoming the breed mare of slaves.[10]

Maverick's anguished queen was not the only slave noble in the New World who kept personal attendants. Toussaint L'Ouverture's son, Isaac, reported that his grandfather, a son of the chief of the Aradas in Dahomey, was captured by a plundering expedition and eventually transported to Haiti, where he found among his fellow slaves countrymen by whom he was recognized and from whom he received the tokens of respect they judged due his rank. Moreover, the plantation's overseer gave Toussaint's father, Gaou-Guinou, full liberty on the estates and allowed him five slaves to cultivate a portion of land assigned him in honor of his rank.[11]

Most likely Gaou-Guinou was a plantation slave driver; masters in the West Indies commonly gave favors of rank to their foremen whom they often chose on the basis of African chiefly lineage. These aristocrats from among the slaves were given the most extensive provision grounds, the largest houses, the best clothing and food, and the rights to several wives. These special black men could, as a matter of course, command other bondsmen to cultivate their fields, tend their stock, and sell their produce at the island markets.[12]

Whites had long recognized the good sense in trying to use African-born or elected New World black royalty to effect a kind of indirect rule over the Negro community. As early as 1475, Juan de Valldolid had been appointed "Chief and Judge" over the black population, free and slave, of Seville in Spain by virtue of his "noble lineage among Negroes."[13] The idea carried over to the Americas where in Brazil, Cuba, Jamaica, Maryland, Saint Lucia, New England, and, no doubt, elsewhere black kings, chiefs, and governors were expected to check, and even punish, misbehavior in the local black communities.[14] However, the whites did not institute the recognition of black royalty among the slaves; instead, the masters were simply showing common sense by parasitically trying to exploit governing institutions the blacks had already developed to honor the royalty and nobility among themselves.

African slave merchants had long made a distinction between royals and commoners; they preferred to purchase bondsmen who had been peasants or slaves from their infancy, noting that they made better, stronger, and more docile servants than upper-class Africans. Hugh Jones of Virginia agreed, explaining, "those Negroes make the best slaves that have been slaves in their own country; for they that have been kings and great men there are generally lazy, haughty, and obstinate; whereas the others are sharper, better humored, and more laborious." Upper-class Africans, the Barbados Assembly complained in 1693, were people "nursed up in luxury and ease, and wholly unaccustomed to work." This observation finds support in the testimony of an ex-slave recaptive in Sierra Leone: "I was a gentleman's son in my country, and they do nothing but eat, sleep, and make war." Thus, when Ayuba Suleiman Ibrahima [Diallo], the merchant son of a high priest of Bondu, arrived at a tobacco plantation in Maryland in 1731, he was too softened by his comfortable Old World life to be physically capable of the harsh toil of slavery.[15]

Many Africans of royal birth or high status naturally believed common labor beneath their dignity; so, like a Jamaican slave who had been "a great man in his own country," some simply refused to be a slave for any man, preferring suicide to the humiliations of bondage.[16] As Captain John Stedman noted in eighteenth-century Surinam, "I have seen some instances of newly-imported Negroes refusing to work, nor could promises, threats, rewards nor even blows, prevail: but those had been princes or people of the first rank in their native country . . . whose heroic sentiments still preferred instant death to the business and miseries of servitude."[17]

When, in Cuba, a former prince of the Luccomees (a Yoruba people) was forced to lie down to be flogged, Fredericka Bremer reports, his attendants, in order to reduce the shame, lay down too, "likewise requesting to be allowed to share his punishment." John Stedman discovered a similar situation in Surinam. When African princes refused to perform their labor, he reports, "I have seen the other slaves fall upon their knees, and entreat the master to permit them to do the work required, in addition to their own tasks; which being sometimes granted, they continued to shew the same respect for the captive prince that he had been accustomed to receive in his own country." The early-nineteenth-century travel writer James Smith reported the story of a planter in Demerara, British Guiana, who unknowingly became the owner of an African queen when he purchased a lot of Africans from on board a slave ship. "For some considerable time they were observed to pay great deference to one of the females of their number, and to endeavor, upon every occasion, to screen her from severe labor. Upon inquiry, it was found that she was the queen of their nation, and had been taken prisoner and enslaved with the rest of them. And what is remarkable, this deference is said to have continued until her death."[18]

Thus, for fellow countrymen the crossing to America did not end the fealty due African nobility. As Fredericka Bremer explained from

Cuba in the middle of the nineteenth century, "Many of the slaves . . . who are brought to Cuba have been princes and chiefs of their tribes, and such of their race as have accompanied them into slavery on the plantations always show them respect and obedience." At the end of the eighteenth century in Haiti, Moreau de Saint-Méry observed, Mina Negroes (slaves from the Gold Coast port of Elmina) recognized "princes of their country . . . prostrating themselves at their feet and rendering homage." In Brazil it was said that on chance meetings in the streets, African dignitaries were "saluted respectfully, their hands kissed, and a blessing requested of them." Even some masters were reported to have paid their royals considerable respect.[19]

Generally, whites tended to regard slaves more favorably if they were reported to be of noble blood. Class attitudes in Natchez, Mississippi, were still strong enough in 1828 to shape Colonel Andrew Marschalk's respect for his royal bondsman Abd Rahman Ibrahima: "I did not look upon Prince, or Ibrahim, as a mere biped slave but as a dignified captive, a man born to command, unjustly deprived of his liberty." Similarly, when in 1817 the German traveler J. G. Flugel was informed of the royal lineage of several New Orleans slaves, he immediately saw qualities of innate nobility rather than servility: "Gildemeister of Bremen . . . told me that three of the negroes in the group closest to us were formerly kings or chiefs in Congo. I perceive in them a more genteel address. They are richly ornamented and dance extremely well." In the same vein, Elizabeth Allston Pringle recalled that on her father's rice plantation in nineteenth-century South Carolina were "three quite remarkable, tall, fine-looking, and very intelligent Africans who had been brought . . . to this country. Tom, Prince, and Maria . . . had been of a royal family in their own land, and had been taken in battle by an enemy tribe with which they were at war, and sold to a slave ship. No one ever doubted their claim to royal blood, for they were so superior to the ordinary Africans brought out. They were skilled in the arts of their own country and had artistic taste and clever hands."[20]

Having recognized the "superior" qualities of their royal bondsmen, masters then were willing to acknowledge some of the distinctions given to the captive princes by their own people. Thus William Gray reported from coastal Texas in 1831 that among some recently imported Guinea slaves shipped from Cuba there was a fourteen- or fifteen-year-old boy, who, Gray noted, "is acknowledged to be a prince, and deference is shown him. He claims the prerogatives of five wives, and flogs them at his pleasure."[21]

But not all masters were so understanding regarding their royal slaves. A woman of royal birth who had been exiled from Cabinda for adultery arrived as a slave in Sibiro, Brazil, with the homage of her shipmates and her arms and legs still decorated with bracelets of gold-plated copper. Like others of her class, this monarch in exile, who became known in Brazil as Teresa the Queen, was imperious, refusing to work. But in this case, as in probably many others, Teresa was broken by force; in the end, she chose to live as a slave, rather than die as a royal martyr.[22] Ann Parker recalled that her mother in North Carolina kept her royal status secret from the white slaveholders: "Yes, she wuz a queen, an' when she tol' dem niggers dat she wuz dey bowed down ter her. She tol' dem not ter tell hit an' dey doan tell, but when dey is out of sight of de white folks dey bows down ter her an' does what she says."[23]

But since the black community often demonstrated its respect for African nobility in concrete terms, whites could not completely over-look such relationships, even if they thought them unseemly for bonds-people. Thus, in mid-nineteenth-century Rio de Janeiro, Thomas Ewbank could report there was a Mina black called "The Prince" whose Negro subjects honored his royal blood and high position by working long hours to purchase his freedom from the combined savings of their own labors.[24]

Jin Cole of Deerfield, Massachusetts, like many Africans of high birth, was said to have never been content as a slave because she was unwilling to forget her days as the daughter of a king of the Congo region. Sometimes this unhappiness with the New World, with bond-age, and with white masters also came to include a disdain for the commoners among fellow bondsmen like that mentioned earlier in regard to Samuel Maverick's slave woman. Ex-slave Ann Parker ex-plained it this way: "I ain't had no daddy case queens down marry an' my mammy, Junny, wuz a queen in Africa. Dey kidnaps her an' steals her 'way from her throne an' fetches her hyar ter Wake County in slavery." The Reverend Robert Boucher Nicholls reported to the

House of Commons that an African princess in Barbados refused for twenty years either to eat or to converse with fellow slaves whom she regarded as beneath her status. And from the American South, Charles Ball noted a lesser version of this same class consciousness, remarking that his paternal grandfather, to whom he was very close, "always expressed contempt for his fellow slaves, for when young, he was an African of rank in his native land."[25]

William Gray apparently misinterpreted a similar type of class distinction in Texas where he observed an African girl who would not lower herself to interacting with her inferiors. He explained it thusly: "One girl sat apart and held no converse with the crowd. She is said to belong to a different tribe from the rest, and to stand on her dignity."[26]

It was more usual, however, for noteworthy Africans to serve as community leaders and symbols of the African heritage. Thus it was that the founders of the Casa das Minas of coastal Brazil were descended from the royal family of Dahomey.[27] Likewise, in the eighteenth century when the king of a small African state was brought to the mines of Villa Rica in Minas Geraes, Brazil, he was honored by his countrymen as Chico Rei (Little King). Once there, Chico Rei consolidated his former subjects into an African-style mutual aid society whose communal savings were used to buy its members out of slavery. They then began to perform a similar service for other tribal groups among the bondsmen. According to the historian Arthur Ramos,

> Francisco was proclaimed king of this little community and hence passed into legend as Chico Rei, Little King. With his second wife, whom he took in Brazil, his son and daughter-in-law, he formed a royal family in Villa Rica. His wife was popularly accorded the designation of queen and his son and daughter-in-law, prince and princess respectively. Legend has it that the "nation" which Chico Rei created bought the rich mines of Encardideira and Palacio Velho. With the gold which these mines produced, Chico Rei widened the scope of his plan, freeing more and more Negroes. The "nation" chose as its patron saint, Saint Ephigenia, under whose auspices a fraternity of the same name was founded. The members constructed the magnificent Church of the Rosary which is still to be seen in Ouro Preto.[28]

In New England, as in most of the rest of the New World, the black communities during the slavery era elected kings and governors to preside over their yearly celebrations. Men of royal African heritage were logical candidates. Thus, in Rhode Island, when Prince Robinson of Narragansett was elected governor of the black community, we might suspect that his mother's royal status was one of the deciding factors.[29] Similarly, even the whites in Derby, Connecticut, knew that local black governors Tobiah and his son Eben Tobias were the direct descendants of an African prince.[30] Likewise, in Lynn, Massachusetts, a prince from the Gambia region served as the master of ceremonies for black holiday celebrations in the mid-eighteenth century, where along the Saugus River, it was said, maidens gathered flowers to crown their king and the men reminisced over happy hours they had known in Africa.[31]

Similarly, in Albany, New York, Old King Charley, a prince from central Africa, was leader of the blacks celebrating Pinkster. As king, Charley set the beat of the drum and led off the dance; moreover, as a "Guinea man" and prince, Charley was said to have possessed autocratic power over the Albany black community. Robert Walsh reported an analogous situation in Rio de Janeiro in the 1820s, where he noted that there was a stone at the corner of the Travessa de S. Antonio that had served for many years as the throne of an African prince from Angola.[32]

The famed voodoo practitioner Doctor John of New Orleans claimed his father was a great king in Senegal and pointed to his facial scars as proof.[33] Olaudah Equiano's more specific claim to a "noble" heritage explained how this worked among the Ibo:

> My father was one of those elders or chiefs I have spoken of and was styled *Embrenche*, a term as I remember importing the highest distinction, and signifying in our language a mark of grandeur. This mark is conferred on the person entitled to it by cutting the skin across at the top of the forehead and drawing it down to the eyebrows, and while it is in this situation applying a warm hand and rubbing it until it shrinks up into a thick weal across the lower part of the forehead. Most of the judges and senators were thus marked; my father had long borne it. I had seen it conferred on one of my brothers, and I was also destined to receive it by my parents.[34]

A Georgia slave remembered in his youth being impressed by the markings on a war chief's son taken into slavery in Saint Marys: "Patty he wuz the chief son an he have three straight mahks slantin down on he right cheek an that wuz a bran tuh show who he wuz. He was the waw chief son and doze mahks tell whut tribe he belong tuh." In the 1840s, J. B. Cobb similarly noted that in Georgia four native Africans with facial tattooing "were treated with marked respect by all the other Negroes for miles and miles around," presumably because of their aristocratic heritage.[35]

Whites were also impressed by the indelible nobility of their royal slaves. Thomas Thistlewood, a Jamaican overseer, noted in 1751 that Jenny, his "favorite," was a Nago (Yoruba) whose face and belly were covered with tribal markings and who claimed to have been "a grand Man's Pickininny [child]: and that he had a horse, cattle and slaves of his own, and that she was stole[n] when he was not at home." Florida planter and slave trader Zephaniah Kingsby was so taken with Anna Madgigene Jai, the daughter of an African chief, he married her and gave their children European educations, but he was frustrated from doing more by Florida's laws against free blacks holding property.[36]

Henry Ravenel of South Carolina was one of several writers in the United States who recalled a childhood fondness for the "old country" tales of native Africans, some of whom, as Ravenel remembered, showed "the 'tattoo' marks of royalty seared upon their faces and bodies." Fanny Saltar, too, vividly recalled her Philadelphia family's servant, Daddy Caesar: "He was a prince in his native country and as a mark of that distinction his forehead and cheeks were deeply slashed with lines."[37]

Many of Africa's nobility had suffered exile as prisoners of war. An early compilation of sources at the Vatican Library illustrates this process in sixteenth-century Kongo: "Since the Isle of Horses, where the king had taken refuge was small and the number of fugitives very great, most of them soon died of plague and starvation. They sold one another. Fathers were seen selling their sons. The Portuguese of Sao Tome bought them and took them to Portugal. Among them were members of the royal family and the first families of the kingdom." Thus we can appreciate why the 1736 arrival in Rio de Janeiro of a slave claiming to be a son of the king of the Kongo was immediately reported to Dom Joao V in Portugal.[38]

It should not be surprising that throughout the Americas members of the African aristocracy often served to crystalize rebellious sentiments into well-led slave rebellions since the powerful loyalty given African leaders made them natural leaders. Ralph Vigil has explained how this worked in a sixteenth-century slave rebellion in Panama:

> All the rebels respected, obeyed, and revered King Bayamo as their *senor y rey* natural, and in their veneration of the king they mixed those rites and ceremonies they had performed before their monarchs and chieftains in Guinea with the respect they had seen Spaniards display before their judges and superiors. Thus, Bayamo, the *ladino* chieftain of the colony of 300 maroons, governed in the manner of a barbaric magistrate and defended the colony from the Spaniards who wished to destroy it.[39]

Given the respect shown African leaders, it is not surprising that in the first half of the seventeenth century a former African monarch named Domingo Bioho led a group of thirty Colombian Maroons to freedom and then fortified their independence by building an African-style village defended by open trenches and palisades. Bioho's settlement soon expanded its power by raiding the surrounding regions and developed into the famous Palenque de San Basilio. Bioho, known as King Benkos, was ceded certain rights by Spanish authorities—including the right to wear Spanish clothes and to carry a golden sword and dagger—although he was eventually executed during another insurrection.[40] Such experiences with African leadership explain why in 1647 Spanish authorities in Santiago, Chile, took the precaution of executing a royal African simply because they feared that his 400 slave followers might rebel in the aftermath of a local earthquake.[41]

During the same era a Maroon settlement in Mexico came under the rule of just such an African leader. "This Yanga was a Negro of the Bron nation [Brong or Abron, an Akan culture], of whom it is said that if they had not captured him, he would have been king in his own land. . . . He had been the first maroon to flee his master and for thirty years had gone free in the mountains, and he united others who held him as chief." In a pan-African gesture of solidarity, Yanga gave the command of his armies to a black from Angola, while he reserved for himself the civil administration of the rebel state.[42]

The situation was similar in Brazil where rebel settlements known as *quilombos* were commonly ruled by black royalty.[43] Some of these rulers may have been elected solely on the basis of competence, but others like Carunkango, an African prince from Mozambique, took power from their African heritage. Carunkango's quilombo eventually developed a subsistence economy that allowed its 200 Maroons to terrorize the region around Campos, Brazil, for many years in the nineteenth century.[44]

In a like manner, Court (called Tackey after the Akan word for chief), the rebel leader of the Saint Marys, Jamaica, slave rebellion of 1760, was a young "Koromantyn," who was said to have been a chieftain in the Gold Coast.[45] And although in reality he may have only been from an important family, he styled himself a great man, for it was reported by English officials that he "endeavoured to put on a Port and Mien Suitable to his affected Dignity of King."[46]

Royal African women were also recognized in the New World; and some of those elected queens of black communities in the Americas, like Luiza Mahin, the central figure of the Hausa revolts (or jihads) of Bahia, Brazil, in 1835, held power in good part because of their African heritage.[47]

African royals were always potentially dangerous in this regard. When a severe caterpillar plague struck the upper James River in Virginia in 1728–29, a number of slaves took advantage of the disorder to flee into the wilderness under an African prince to build a Maroon colony near the location of present-day Lexington. According to the historian T. E. Campbell: "They built a town of boughs and grass houses in the manner of the homes of their native land, and set up a tribal government under a chief, who had been a prince among his own people before slave traders brought him across the Atlantic. . . . The whites located them and the next year military men mustered from all sections of the colony moved on their settlement, killed the chief, and returned his followers to their masters."[48]

Le Page du Pratz was appalled to discover that the commander of a slave revolt in Louisiana had been a resistance leader in Africa, exiled to their American colonies by the French.

> I learnt that Samba had in his own country been at the head of the revolt by which the French lost Fort Arguin; and when it was recovered . . . , one of the principal articles of the peace was, that this negro should be condemned to slavery in America; that Samba, on his passage, had laid a

scheme to murder the crew, in order to become master of the ship; but that being discovered, he was put in irons, in which he continued till he landed in Louisiana.

I drew up a memorial of all this; which was read before Samba by the Judge Criminal; who, threatening him again with torture, . . . upon which Samba directly owned all of the circumstances.[49]

In seventeenth-century Lima, Peru, the marqués de Guadalcazar reported a rumor that the Dutch had specifically reared two sons of African kings for the purpose of rallying the Peruvian slaves to the cause of Holland. If true, nothing seems to have come of this particular threat, but the Spaniards' worries were understandable.[50]

The same traits of courage and nobility that made African aristocrats leaders of New World black communities, rebel as well as bond, made them heroic characters in European literature and art. The noble Coromantee prince and war captain, Oroonoko, first appeared in Aphra Behn's novelette of 1688 as the prototype captive slave-king, whom she claimed to have known personally. The story was soon dramatized for the English stage by Thomas Southerne, John Hawkesworth, and Francis Gentleman, and in the translations of Antoine de La Place and the Abbé le Blanc the book became one of the nine most-read volumes in eighteenth-century France. At least some American masters may have been aware of the tale; a letter of James Habersham of Savannah, Georgia, written in 1764 gives the name of one of his male slaves as Oronoko.[51]

The literary Oroonoko, although the leader of an antiwhite slave revolt in Surinam, was described effusively by Behn as inherently noble, possessing "that real Greatness of Soul, those refined notions of True Honour, that absolute Generosity, and that Softness, that was capable of the highest Passions of Love and Gallantry."[52] Many similarly fictionalized accounts of enslaved African princes of noble character, like Jean François de Saint-Lambert's Zimeo, followed in the literature of France, England, and the United States.[53]

An especially well-developed example is the tragic character Pierrot (or Bug-Jargal) in Victor Hugo's novel about the Haitian Revolution. Bug-Jargal, the enslaved son of the king of KaKongo, is portrayed as a natural leader whose recognition by his fellow slaves gave him a leadership role in the San Domingo revolt. The noble slave twice saved the white heroine he loved from afar and even saved the white hero before sacrificing his own life for his fellow black revolutionaries; still, the narrator, Captain D'Auverney, was slow to make the connection between slave and prince. Nonetheless, D'Auverney could not help but suspect that within the mistreated slave lay a different man:

> I remembered, not without surprise, the look of rough majesty imprinted on his face,—the shining eyes, the white teeth against the shining black skin, the wide forehead, especially surprising in a negro, the scornful curl which gave to his thick lips and nostrils a haughty and powerful look, the dignity of his bearing, the beauty of his form, which, although thin and worn from the fatigues of daily labor, still showed Herculean development. I recalled the imposing apearance of the slave, and said to myself that he was well fitted for a king.[54]

European poets and painters were especially taken with the tragic theme of the enslaved African princess. In 1788 the poet William Collins inspired George Morland's painting *Execrable Human Traffic; or, The Affectionate Slaves* with a verse about a noble African woman taken in bondage by brutish white slavers. In Collins's poem, the woman, Ulkna, and her child were torn from the arms of her helpless husband and sold on the coast:

> Two British captains with their barges came,
>   And quickly made a purchase of the young;
> But one was struck with Ulkna, void of shame,
>   And tore her from the husband where she clung.
> Her faithful Chief, tho' stern in rugged war,
>   Seeing his Ulkna by a White caress'd,
> To part with her, "and little son Tengarr!"
>   His gentler feelings could not be supprest. . . .
> With hands uplifted, he with sighs besought
>   The wretch that held a bludgeon o'er his head,
> And those who dragg'd him, would have pity taught
>   By his dumb signs, to strike him instant dead.
> While his dear Ulkna's sad entreating mien,
>   Did but increase the brute's unchaste desire;
> He vaunting bears her off, her sobs are vain,
>   They part the man and wife whom all admire.[55]

A similar poem written in 1827 by the wife of African traveler Thomas Edward Bowdich described a chief's daughter who was abducted by African slave traders and taken to the coast. There she escaped and was found by British settlers who made her a servant and Christianized her. Later freed and reunited with her family, she married a neighboring prince and effected a "little reformation" by convincing both her new husband and her royal brother to decrease their use of human sacrifices.[56] The enslavement of this noblewoman was illustrated in Henry Thomson's painting *The Booroom Slave* of 1827, which showed her as a new slave, sunk on one knee, praying for divine deliverance from her plight.

European literature's romantic interest in enslaved royalty was reinforced by the appearance of reputed African kings brought to Europe on slave ships. As early as 1455 "a black king" from Sierra Leone was reported to have sung at the Portuguese wedding of the Infanta D. Joana; he was later freed to appear at the courts of France and England.[57] Another such prince, Peter Panah, the son of the king of Mesurado, after being kidnapped and sold into bondage was recognized on the London docks around 1788 by Carl Bernhard Wadström, a Swede who had recently traveled to Africa. Wadström bought and freed the slave-prince and made him his protégé until the prince's death two years later. This relationship, which was of course flattering to at least part of white civilization, became the subject of the 1789 painting by Carl Fredrik von Breda, *Portrait of Carl Bernhard Wadström Instructing a Negro Prince, Peter Panah.*[58]

Another celebrated African who appeared at the English court was a slave from Maryland named Job (Ayuba Suleiman Ibrahima Diallo). Ayuba was a Fulbe born into an important clerical family from Bondu, where he studied alongside the future king of his people. Ayuba had become a successful merchant when he was taken into slavery. Recognized for the important personage he claimed to be, Ayuba was freed and taken to England where he was honored with a gold watch presented by the queen.[59]

In the reign of Louis XIV of France two boys, said to be the sons of an African prince, were brought to court and educated by a Jesuit appointed to the task by the king. Years later one of the young men was insulted and threatened with dishonor unless he fought a duel. Forced into action, he bested his opponent without injury to either party, but this departure from his tutor's moral guidance so disillusioned the noble African with the hypocrisies of Europe that he was said to have tearfully departed France saying that he could not live with such contradictions, for how could Christianity be of any use to the French if it did not influence their actions? In his homeland, he said, men were never dishonored for acting according to the principles of their religion.[60]

In the same era "Prince Aniaba" from Assini of the present-day Ivory Coast was received at the French court with such enthusiasm that King Louis XIV became his godfather. Louis gave his new godson instruction in Christianity and European manners and then sent his supposed brother monarch back home to Africa where he was said to have unaccountably reverted to African ways. However, Aniaba was not really a prince at all but only a shrewd impostor named Lewis Hannibal, the slave of a coastal caboceer, who saw how to take advantage of Europe's interest in enslaved princes.[61] In much the same way, another black of lesser origins who had been raised as an interpreter and sent to Europe with a white prisoner released by the king of Dahomey eventually appeared in England, where he was celebrated in local papers as Prince Adomo Oroonoko Tomo, ambassador to King George.[62] When a slave girl presented to British naval officer Lieutenant Forbes of the *Bonetta* married a Sierra Leone merchant in Brighton it was a grand social occasion because the bride was presented by Forbes as a royal princess, a rank which it later turned out may have been an exaggeration.[63]

Such fraud and confusion were all the more possible because lesser princes in Africa were known to have been sent to Europe for educations only to be enslaved by treacherous white captains. As the famous Dr. Johnson explained to Boswell, "Princes have been sold by wretches to whose care they were entrusted, that they might have an European education. But once they were brought to a market in the plantations, little would avail either their dignity or their wrongs." Johnson's reference was presumably in regard to two sons of a king of Anomabu on the Gold Coast who were panyared and then ransomed from the West Indies by the British government and presented to King George in 1749. Intriguingly, the newly freed princes were taken to Covent Garden to see the play *Oroonoko*, where it was reported one of the royal visitors became so moved he had to leave and the other was reduced to tears.[64]

In 1762 an African prince of Amabou (Anomabu on the Gold Coast) sent one of his sons abroad for an education. When the boy returned four years later, the ruler permitted a younger son and a nephew, both about ten years of age, to follow. But this time the slaving captain reneged on his bargain and sold the boys, later known as Prince and Cuffee Whipple, into perpetual slavery in Portsmouth, New Hampshire; and although the history of this transaction was known locally, the boys were never returned home.[65]

The same fate also could befall noble children such as those who were often held hostage to insure the security and honesty of African traders. As a committee of the House of Lords explained in 1788, "It has always been the practice of merchants and commanders of ships to Africa, to encourage the natives to send their children to England; as it not only conciliates their friendship, and softens their manners, but adds greatly to the security of the trader."[66] Thus Grandy King George of Old Town complained in a letter to a Liverpool merchant: "Other Captains may say what they please about my doing them any bad thing, for what I did was their own faults, for you may think, sir, that it was very vexing to have my sons carried off by Capt. Jackson and Robin's sons and the King of Qua's son—their names is Otto, Imbass, Egshiom, Ogen, Acandom, Ebetham, Ephiyoung, Aset."[67]

Whites who were generally unbothered by slavery were, nonetheless, fascinated by the tragic fate of noble Africans who fell into bondage. Thus the religious autobiography of the ex-slave Akawsaw Granwasa, or James Albert, sold well in Europe and America more because Albert claimed to be the enslaved grandson of the king of Bournou (Bornu?) than for his account of his Christian conversion—the nominal topic of the piece.[68]

Richard Madden explained his own respect for a slave of a Mr. Anderson of Kingston, Jamaica, in terms of the slave's former nobility and offers us insight into his motivation when he tried to make his English audience empathize with the fallen African:

> By what name, under heaven, . . . must that system be called, which sanctioned the stealing away of a person like this, as much a nobleman in

his own country as any titled chief is in ours, and in his way, without disparagement to the English noble, as suitably educated for his rank? Fancy Sir, one of the scions of our nobility, a son of one of our war-chiefs—Lord Londonderry's, for example, educated at Oxford, and, in the course of his subsequent travels, unfortunately falling into the hands of African robbers, and being carried into bondage. Fancy the poor youth marched in the common slave coffle to the first market-place on the coast. He is exposed for sale: nobody inquires whether he is a patrician or a plebian: nobody cares whether he is ignorant or enlight-ened: it is enough that he has thews and sinews for a life of labour without reward.[69]

Even in the most racist region of the United States, the American South, local literature was penetrated by the legends of enslaved noble Africans. When George W. Cable published the story of the rebel Bras Coupe in *The Grandissimes,* his 1880 novel of Creole New Orleans, he included most of the legendary motifs that characterize the stories of captured African royalty.[70]

In this case the African was described as a powerfully built giant of a man, a prince of the Jaloff captured in war and taken in slavery to New Orleans. He could accept bondage as a fortune of war, but he violently rejected physical labor as beneath his station. Thus, according to Cable's story, Bras Coupe came to the attention of his master: "The dauntless captive and fearless master stood looking into each other's eyes until each recognized in the other his peer in physical courage, and each was struck with an admiration for the other which no after difference was sufficient entirely to destroy." Since a king could not be a field hand, the solution was to make Bras Coupe a driver, and an excellent driver he became.

Tragically, however, on his wedding day Bras Coupe drank alco-hol for the first time and consequently struck his master in an argument about getting more to drink. Before running off as a Maroon to the great swamp, the black prince condemned his owner with a voodoo curse. Finally recaptured, the noble slave was lashed and lamed; but the punishments were of no consolation to his former owner who soon died, ruined by the African's powerful magic. Bras Coupe too was dying, but once again he demonstrated his nobility by releasing his master's wife and infant son from the curse. When asked by a priest if he knew where he was going, the dying prince "lifted his hand, and with an ecstatic, upward smile, whispered, 'To—Africa'—and was gone."[71]

Despite the elite literary tradition of doomed but noble resistance, New World slave masters in their own folk narratives understandably preferred not to celebrate the rebels among their royal slaves; instead, they chose to memorialize those whose nobility was manifested in loyal service. Typical was the memorial to the model slave, Iambo, published in the *Gazette of the United States* in 1789:

> An African prince subdued in battle, capitulated his bow and quiver—a bauble bought his life. A British merchant sent him to South Carolina, where he was used as a slave. A placid countenance, and submissive manners, marked his resignation; and preserved him in all situations, the possession of his arms—the only companions he had left—the sole objects of his affections. His stateliness and strength recommended him to Colonel Mott, a humane master, in whose service he died, in steadfast faith of a certain resurrection in his native state.
>
> The bow and quiver were preserved as relics of a faithful slave, in the Colonel's family, who gratefully remember the services, the fortitude, and fidelity of the trusty, the gentle, Iambo.[72]

Near Columbia, Tennessee, there is a monument erected "in memory and appreciation of the loyalty and service of the slaves owned by the early settlers of Zion Community." Buried among them was Daddy Ben, a prince of Africa owned by Colonel Scott. The stone records: "His loyalty to his master won for him the award of a gold eagle from a British officer. He was hung three times, still he refused to tell where he had hidden his master."[73]

In early-eighteenth-century Jamaica, Sir Charles Price was reviewing some newly purchased slaves when he was said to have noted one among them looking especially troubled. A female interpreter could not get the sullen bondsman to speak, but a fellow countryman of the sufferer then spoke in explanation. The silent man was a caboceer, or village chief, on the Gold Coast and had owned many slaves, the informant explained; in fact he himself had been among them. Sir Charles was said to have been so "touched with the vicissitude of fortune" which had reduced a fellow nobleman to bondage alongside one of his former slaves that, after having the story checked, he manumitted the unfortunate caboceer, offering him a return to Africa or a place of relative comfort in Jamaica. According to the tale, the former chief not only chose to stay and marry a young slave woman; he also eventually returned the favor of his master by restraining Price's slaves, who were mostly his countrymen, from joining in the Black Rebellion of 1769.[74]

In the United States, two Fulbe princes, Ayuba Suleiman Diallo and Abd Rahman Ibrahima, are known to have been given their freedom, and both eventually returned to Africa. Martin Delany and Bishop Henry McNeal Turner also told similar stories of royal ancestors being freed. Delany said his maternal grandfather, Shango, was freed because of his royal birth and returned to Africa, while his royal grandmother, who was similarly emancipated, chose to remain in America. Turner likewise recalled that his royal grandfather, David Greer, won his freedom and decided to stay in the New World.[75]

The African slaver Captain Canot told of meeting a princess of Galinas who returned home to Africa to the country of her father, King Shiakar, from whom she had been separated for twenty-four years after being taken into Cuban slavery as a fifteen-year-old girl. Canot says she only stayed ten days, considering the court of her elder brother sadly deficient in decency since the men were not wearing trousers.[76] New England whites told a somewhat similar story of a slave woman named Queen Abigail, who persuaded her owner, Roland Robinson, to finance a return trip to Africa for her so that she could recover her son, whom she brought back with her to Rhode Island.[77]

As already noted, black families had their own traditions about the royal slaves. Senegambia, a slave from Narragansett, Rhode Island, was said never to have tired of telling stories of the wealth of his father, a Gambian king who maintained a large trading fleet and had a "gold-iron" dog-shaped knocker on the door to his entrance hall.[78] Hannah Crasson of North Carolina remembered her "aunt" as "a royal slave" of dignified bearing and exquisite posture who "could sure tote herself. I always loved to see her come to church," said Crasson. "She sure could tote herself."[79]

Other slaves may occasionally have been a little jealous of these royal claims. Elias Dawkins, an ex-slave and a commoner by heritage, reported: "Ciller was de daughter of a king in Africa, but dat story been

traveling ever since she got to dese shores and it still a-gwine." Whatever the case of Ciller, most blacks and whites of her era believed the
tales of royal birth. As Joseph Cobb noted from Mississippi, the slaves
"boast that the blood of royalty flowed through their veins, and there is
no doubt of the fact." Indeed, in the 1950s Nell Grayden reported that
many of the blacks of Edisto Island, South Carolina, were still proud of
their descent from an African king brought to the island as a captive in
the early days of slavery.[80]

Many famous black Americans have claimed descent from royal
African forebears. The noted mathematician and scientist Benjamin
Banneker, for example, was the grandson of an African prince who was
at first too imperious to work as a slave. He must have come to the
attention of his white mistress and impressed her mightily because she
eventually married him.[81]

As noted earlier, the early black nationalist leader Martin R.
Delany claimed African aristocracy on both sides of his family: His
mother's parents, Graci Peace and Shango, were both of royal lineage;
his father, Samuel Delany, was the son of a Golah chieftain captured
with his family during a local war. Both Delany and his parents believed
he was destined for a leadership role by virtue of his heritage.[82]

Likewise, two famous American emigrationists were reported to
be of royal African birth. The minister and abolitionist Alexander
Crummell was the grandson of a chieftain from Timanee, Sierra
Leone. And according to the descendants of Thomas Peters, their
forebear, a member of the royal family of the Egba Yoruba, was kidnapped in the 1760s aboard the slave ship *Henri Quatre* and taken to
Louisiana, where he proved a rebellious slave; later sold to Wilming-
ton, North Carolina, Peters won his freedom as a sergeant with Lord
Dunmore's black regiment, and after the African-American loyalists
who fought for their freedom were abandoned by the British in Nova
Scotia, Peters led the fight for immigration to Sierra Leone.[83]

The black abolitionist Henry Highland Garnet was descended
from a Mandingo chief who had been taken as a prisoner of war and
sold to American slave traders. Garnet recalled that, because of his
grandfather's moral and religious power and his absolute integrity of
character, the chief had been made a trusty on a plantation at New

Market, Maryland. Robert Russa Moton, who succeeded Booker T. Washington at Tuskegee Institute, claimed to be related to a young African prince who, after selling some war prisoners to a European slave dealer, was tricked aboard ship and drugged, only to end eventually at a slave auction in Richmond, Virginia. He never was a contented slave; but his faithfulness was such that his master permitted him three special holidays each year with the shipmates of his crossing to America.[84]

America's greatest black Shakespearean actor, Ira Aldridge, claimed to be as royal of blood as the character Oroonoko he first played on the London stage. One often repeated account says that Aldridge's father was born of princely descent in Senegal. According to the tale, a missionary converted the boy, who was then sent to America to study at Schenectady College in New York. There he became a minister and married before returning to Senegal after an opposing chief died. The struggle for succession that followed denied him political power, but Aldridge's son Ira was said to have been born while the family was still in Senegal. Sometime around 1816 the family returned to the United States where Ira began his formal education. The story could, of course, be press agentry well suited to an actor who began his career playing a royal African slave. But, if so, it is only further reflection of the attraction that the legends of Guinea's captive kings held for Europe.[85]

Later in the nineteenth century three other successful black men—C. C. Antoine (a lieutenant governor in Reconstruction Louisiana), Henry McNeal Turner (a Georgia legislator and bishop of the A.M.E. church), and the Reverend London Terrill, the accomplished second pastor of the First Baptist Church of Lexington, Kentucky, described themselves as descended from royal Africans who passed on to them traits of intellect, industry, discretion, greatness, and benevolence.[86] On the distaff side, Ella Sheppard Moore, student leader of the original Fisk Jubilee Singers, noted of her heritage that "My great-grandmother was the daughter of an Indian chief and married my great-grandfather, the son of an African chief."[87]

Pride in royal ancestry diminished only slowly. When William Seabrook attended a ball in Port-au-Prince, Haiti, in the 1920s, he met the young Maurice de Joie who was, Seabrook says, "Proud as Satan of a descent traced back . . . to one of the great African princely families on the southern edge of the Sahara."[88]

In the early twentieth century such family pride was still found in the United States. William Sanders Scarborough, the president of Wilberforce University (1908–20), remembered that he was the great-grandson of an African chief.[89] Mary Church Terrell, famous for her work in the women's movement and in civil rights, traced her ancestry on her father's side back to her great-grandmother Lucy, who was said to have been a beautiful "Malay" princess who had been enslaved when her family fell from power.[90] Similarly, Richard Robert Wright, Sr., an important educator, politician, editor, and banker, recalled that his maternal grandmother Lucy was a Mandingo princess who landed at Havre de Grace, Maryland, during the late eighteenth century.[91]

The American sociologist E. Franklin Frazier observed a late-twentieth-century skepticism about such traditions, which by then seemed far removed from the reality of everyday life for black Americans:

> The Wrights [Richard Robert and Richard Robert, Jr.], who for two generations have achieved distinction as educators, claim descent from a Mandingo chief. George Schuyler, who holds a unique place among Negro journalists and authors, traces his ancestry on his mother's side to Madagascar. With his characteristic skepticism, he remarks that the claim that she was a princess was "probably a lie." A physician in Charleston, South Carolina, traces the African origin of his family to his father's grandmother, the daughter of a chief in Madagascar, who was taken by missionaries to France to be educated but was stolen and sent to America, where an unsuccessful attempt was made to enslave her. . . . A physician in [Chicago] tells of a great-grandfather of royal blood who was purchased and freed by Quakers after he refused to be enslaved.[92]

Despite his mistrust of such family histories, Frazier easily collected similar stories from his own students when he asked them about their heritages—such as the following example:

> In the year 1771 somewhere in the heart of Africa, there was born to an African king a baby boy by the name of Lewis; this baby boy was destined to be one of my ancestors. This baby had a brother by the name of Hosea. Very little is known of Lewis' early days, and of his life in Africa,

for at a very early age his father sent him to France with two bachelors who were Frenchman. Here in France, Lewis was to receive his education and learn the ways of the French people. Lewis had no sir name [*sic*], thus he took the name of the two bachelors, who were brothers and is now Lewis De Benyard. After staying in France for only a short while these Frenchmen turned their faces towards America, and it was thus that Lewis De Benyard found himself in America. At the age of about 15 Lewis landed in America on St. Simons' Islands. He was reared on Jeckle Island [*sic*] and having received a rather good education was made overseer of a set of slaves in that district.[93]

Such traditions were also received with skepticism by the social historian J. C. Furnas, who nevertheless registered their commonness when in 1956 he suggested that claims of black Americans to mixed ancestry may have been exaggerated because, as he sarcastically put it, "the Indian appears as often as the African king in Negro fantasy about lineage." Willard Gatewood, in his study of the turn-of-the-twentieth-century black elite, effectively both noted and then disregarded the connections of the elite to African aristocracy by commenting: "As in the case of their white ancestors, they tended to endow the African branches of the family tree with a prominence they did not always possess. Their genealogical charts contained a disproportionate number of African 'kings' and Madagascan 'princesses.' "[94]

There is probably some truth to the charge that not all the noble African ancestors who were claimed as kings, queens, princes, and princesses by their American progeny really held such exalted rank. But on the other hand, there is no doubt that hundreds if not thousands of noble Africans arrived on American shores. Indeed, when compared to European Americans with their middling and lower ancestry, Americans of African heritage truly are a noble people. It would be a pity if history were to forget black America's royal heritage.

Prior to our own times, each new generation of African Americans had found its own meaning in the experiences of the captive kings and queens of Guinea. Usually they found strength; as Kathryn Morgan of Philadelphia put it in 1966, "I was taught to believe that my 'aristocratic' blood would help me overcome any insult or hardship I might encounter. . . . I never questioned the implication that my African ancestors were kings and queens and my white ancestors were 'quality' whites."[95] In the same way educator Mary McLeod Bethune used her African royal heritage as a source of inspiration, dedication, and feminism: "Mother," she wrote, "was of royal African blood, of a tribe ruled by matriarchs. . . . Throughout all her bitter years of slavery she had managed to preserve a queenlike dignity." In the history of her proud mother, Bethune found the moral strength to become a leader of her people and a champion in the struggle for human dignity in America. "For I am my mother's daughter, and the drums of Africa still beat in my heart. They will not let me rest while there is a single Negro boy or girl without a chance to prove his worth."[96]

We, too, should remember America's only royal immigrants— men and women from Africa whose enslavement was only part of their story. Otherwise, we are all too likely to read the present back into the past and misunderstand our nation's early history. Instead, we should recall what Mary McLeod Bethune's mother taught her daughter to pass on to others—that our nation's African forebears would want us to remember who they were, that their majestic heritage and regal dignity were as important as the misfortunes of their bondage.

CHAPTER 5

"Duh Root Doctuh Wuz All We Needed"

Far too often we accept the stereotype of new African slaves as unskilled laborers, but there was much more to them than hard work and physical strength. The Africans who came to the New World during the era of slavery also brought with them several varieties of intellectual expertise. African medical knowledge is one example of the many skills that were carried across the ocean to make a major impact on American lives. Unfortunately, because African medicine was non-Western and nonwhite, early black medical practitioners, when considered historically, have usually been characterized as folk doctors and their medicine stigmatized as root work or superstition.

Granted that black medicine in the antebellum Americas was not particularly scientific, but the same could be said about most of the medical arts practiced by the era's white doctors. African practitioners were, in fact, no less skillful than their European counterparts, and in many ways black medical practice was superior to that offered by the white practitioners who were typically recognized as the era's only legitimate doctors. The transference of African medical knowledge permitted black Americans not only to tend to their own medical needs but to contribute to the improvement of American health as a whole.

Africans had a broader, more psychologically sophisticated conception of disease causation and control than did early emigrants from Europe. In the American colonial era, European theorists like the "vitalists," "iatrochemists," and "iatrophysicists" argued in various ways that illness was the result of a maladjustment of the general system of the body.[1] African practitioners also searched for the maladjustment of a general system, but in their case it was a wider social system that they thought was disturbed.

African medicine was holistic; the African medical specialist was interested not so much in the immediate pathology of a malady as in answering a more philosophical or sociological question: Why did this particular patient fall ill at this particular time? Since the final explanation of illness was often given as witchcraft, sorcery, unhappy ancestors, or improper conduct, African specialists treated illness in its psychological as well as physiological manifestations, offering not only medical treatment for the physical ailment but also advice as to proper rites and behavior that might also be needed to effect a cure of the underlying spiritual malaise.[2]

This holistic emphasis carried over to the New World. When, for example, James L. Smith's father fell seriously ill on a Lancaster County, Virginia, plantation in the early 1820s, the white doctor sent for by Smith's master was of no avail. It was then that the master was told of a more specialized black doctor some ten miles distant. This old practitioner proved more successful. Looking at his divining cards, the black healer diagnosed "poisoning," telling the master that his slave woman Cella had committed the foul deed in revenge after losing her job of running the plantation to Smith's father. After medicine was given and Cella beaten and shipped off to Norfolk, Smith's father slowly recovered. Curing the illness, in accord with African ideas, had required both physiological and sociological/religious attention.[3]

Such traditional Africanized health care was too wide-reaching to fit into modern Western definitions, which differentiate medicine from magical or religiously oriented curing rites. African Americans, however, took a long time to make a separation between religious specialist and physician in the medical care they offered one another. As Frederick Douglass explained in regard to a slave called "Uncle" Isaac Copper by whites and blacks in nineteenth-century Maryland: "When the [title] 'Uncle' was dropped, he was called Doctor Copper. He was both our Doctor of Medicine and our Doctor of Divinity."[4]

Without debating the cultural limitations of modern Western definitions of medical care, it is quite possible to study the many physiologically based medical practices that Africans brought with them to the New World. These alone, although only a part of African-American medical tradition, contributed much to early American health care.

Although the general theories of medical practice differed between Europe and Africa, the immediate physical routines of doctoring were basically similar. This was noted by the slaver Hugh Crow during an Atlantic crossing with a cargo of slaves in the late eighteenth century: "The Eboes," he said, "were very subject to headache, and in order to relieve them we sometimes resorted to cupping. They were not strangers to the operation, but told us it was a remedy often had recourse to in their own country."[5] Nonetheless, when physical procedures proved unsuccessful in the noisome pestholes which were the slave ships, Africans turned with confidence to the spiritual skills of their own doctors. According to Hugh Crow, "One of these, who seemed to partake of the priestly character who I had on board during a sickness in the ship, begged strenuously for a male fowl, and on receiving it he killed it cutting its throat. He then threw himself into many strange postures, and while muttering some incantations over the sick men, he sprinkled the blood on their heads. They were mightily pleased with the ceremony, although they were in a dying state."[6]

European observers rejected such rites as loathsome superstition or devil worship and closed their minds to the possibility that they could learn from African practitioners. Such rejection is ironic since not only were essentials of physical diagnosis and treatment—auscultation, drawing blood by cupping and leeching, scarifying, sweating, purgation, certain surgical procedures, bonesetting, and the administration of herbal medicine—common to both areas of the world, but belief that prayers and religious rituals added to the potency of a cure was also an article of faith among both groups.[7]

Cotton Mather, a Puritan minister in eighteenth-century Massachusetts, publicized to his own credit a major New World adaptation of African medical practice when he advocated inoculation as a method of reducing the seriousness of the smallpox epidemics then scourging the Atlantic world. Mather was informed as to the usefulness of this treatment by his "Guramantee" servant. The man was probably Coromantee, a generalized ethnic term for peoples shipped from the Gold Coast fort at Kormantin. As Mather reported, "I have since met with a considerable number of these Africans, who all agree in one story: that in their country grandy-many die of the small-pox. But now they learn this way; people take juice of small-pox; and cutty-skin and put in a drop; then by and by a little sicky-sicky, then very few little things like small-pox; and no body die of it; and no body have small-pox any more."[8]

Though knowledge of variolation seems to have been common among some of the blacks, the ethnocentric whites had at first paid no attention, for as Cadwallader Colden of New York explained in 1753, "It is not to be wondered at, since we seldom converse with our Negroes, especially with those who were not born among us; and though I learned this but lately when the smallpox was among us last spring, by some discourse being accidentally overheard among the Negroes themselves, I have had the same Negroes above 20 years about my house, without knowing it before this time."[9] Condescension toward African culture had almost cost white America a major breakthrough against the dreaded smallpox.

Elsewhere whites continued to misperceive the intent and effectiveness of African-style variolation. For example, James Stewart, an eighteenth-century historian of the West Indies, mistakenly believed that Negro mothers in Jamaica "willfully infected their children with yaws that they might be released for a time from their labour."[10] But a more inquisitive observer, the eighteenth-century historian Bryan Edwards, listened to one of his Akan slave women explain that variolation was a medical technique used on the Gold Coast to inoculate children with infectious matter from the yaws to give them a mild case of the disease and provide resistance later in life. And, indeed, the anthropologist R. S. Rattray reported that variolation for smallpox was practiced "from time immemorial" by the tribes of the Ashanti hinterland. Similarly, Mungo Park during his travels on the Windward Coast at the end of the eighteenth century was told by a European doctor stationed there that people in the Gambia region practiced variolation for smallpox in what may also have been a traditional procedure.[11]

Another misunderstanding revolved around the strong predisposition of African-born slaves to eat clay. White doctors and many slave owners fought the custom as pernicious and even suicidal, but their black slaves continued to consume claylike soils in spite of the opposition. Indeed, earth cakes were commonly sold in both West Indian and African markets, a custom that has led modern researchers to suggest that Africans and African Americans practiced geophagy as a remedy for nutritional deficiencies such as lack of iron; given the slaves' diet, white attempts to prohibit geophagy probably did more harm than good.[12]

Some white Americans discovered they could profit from the advice of black medical practitioners. Lieutenant Governor William Gooch of Virginia reported in 1729 that he had "met with a Negro [named Papan], a very old man who has performed many wonderful cures of diseases. For the sake of his freedom, he has revealed the medicine, a concoction of roots and bark." Because of its use in reputedly curing yaws and syphilis, the black doctor was freed from slavery at a cost of sixty pounds.[13] Similarly, in eighteenth-century Surinam the sorcerer and herbal doctor Graman Quassi, renowned for having discovered the quassia root used in Europe as a bitters and in Surinam as a febrifuge, was honored by the prince of Orange with a fine uniform, a medal, and a silver-headed cane.[14] When eighteenth-century historian Le Page du Pratz of Louisiana opened himself to new medical ideas from black immigrants, he learned remedies for yaws, scurvy, and female "distempers."[15]

The African interest in herbs and barks used to reduce fevers may have also been involved in the discovery of quinine treatment for malaria. The first recorded white use of quinine came at the Viceregal Palace in Lima, Peru, in 1638 when the illness of the Countess Cinchon became so severe that, it was said, the court physician risked a desperate, last-chance remedy with a medicine he had heard was used for fever in the unhealthy gold-mining district of Loja to the north. What is interesting is that the *quinquina* bark he ordered was not a traditional Indian cure for fever; indeed, it seems to have gone against basic principles of the region's Native American medicine, and many local Indians continued to refuse to use it as late as 1890. The native peoples had no traditional medicine against malaria because the malady had not even been known in the region until after the arrival of the Europeans and Africans.[16]

Of the three population groups in the region—Africans, Europeans, and Indians—the Africans had the best medical background to have discovered the new curative powers of the bark. Thousands of African slaves had been settled in the audiencias of Lima and Quito since the mid-1500s; and although there were only a few in Loja proper, Africans were common in the upland plantations area. They resided in even larger numbers in the cities, where skilled blacks commonly practiced medicine and dispensed their own drugs. Noteworthy in regard to the Cinchon story is that African cures were generally regarded as alien and dangerous by the white authorities, so that in 1572 the Lima city council forbade blacks to prepare or dispense drugs in the local apothecary shops on the grounds they replaced "healthful medicines" with their own deleterious ones.[17] Nonetheless, fearing the otherwise certain death of his mistress, it is quite possible the white court physician, Dr. Juan de Vega, might have tried such an African remedy as a last resort. If so, an African contribution to the discovery of quinine is not at all unlikely.

Certainly, it was not unusual for white doctors to be interested in African-based cures. In Jamaica Dr. Richard R. Madden openly recorded his interest in learning from the African-born doctor Benjamin Cockran (Gorah Condran), who practiced medicine successfully enough to apply for membership in the Kingston College of Physicians in 1834. As Madden explained, Dr. Cockran "was in the habit of coming to me on Sundays, to give me information about the medical plants and popular medicine of the country; and a more intelligent and respectable person, in every sense of the word, I do not know. . . . His skill as a negro doctor, one of the English physicians of Kingston assured me was considerable." In this instance Dr. Madden even offered us some information on the empirical training of his black colleague, who had begun his medical career in Africa, "in Mandingo country:—nobody taught him first"; he started by observing which vegetation harmed cattle and which plants cattle ate when they were sick; only later did the young man move on to the study of the effects of herbal medicine on humans and, perhaps, formal study.[18]

Throughout the Americas, the African experience with yaws made treatment of that malady a black specialty; as Dr. William Hillary of Barbados explained, "the Negroes have by long observation and experience found out a method of curing this disease." Dr. George

Pinckard, commenting on the same proficiency, noted that the "Negro doctors of the estates justly vie with [local white practitioners] in medical knowledge," and as Dr. Hillary observed, "they sometimes perform notable cures, both in [yaws] and some other diseases."[19]

Likewise, because of the Africans' greater experience with poisonous snakes, it is not surprising that the handling of snake bites was another black medical specialty.[20] In South Carolina, knowledge of antidotes for poison won a slave named Caesar a hundred-pound pension; his decoction of plantain, hoarhound, and goldenrod roots compounded with rum and lye added to an application of tobacco leaves soaked in rum was highly regarded for rattlesnake bite.[21]

Africans skilled in bloodletting brought their leeches and horns with them into their New World practice. As Thomas Ewbank explained, "Another, belonging to the same family, was taken sick, when one of his associates cupped him—a favorite African remedy; many negroes are not less expert in applying than in removing disease by it. The operator scratches the skin with a flint, places the wide end of a sheep's horn over it, and sucks out the air. Negro chirugeons uniformly prefer bleeding their patients in sunshine, insisting that the effect is then most beneficial."[22]

Black women as well as men practiced the leeching and cupping trade, as can be seen by examining the account book of Richmond's Phebe Jackson.[23] The black barber-surgeons of Brazil sometimes signed on as doctors for slaving vessels where their transcultural medical skills could win the confidence of both crew and cargo.[24] And similar African skills in bloodletting may help explain why so many New World barbers were Negro.

Black bloodletters also expanded their practice into other areas of medicine and dentistry. In antebellum Georgia, Daddy Jack transferred his surgical skills to dentistry when he cut around aching teeth with his lancet and cauterized inflamed nerves with a red-hot nail; similarly, a runaway New Jersey slave named Simon was advertised in the *Pennsylvania Gazette* in 1740 as able to "bleed and draw teeth, pretending to be a great doctor." Evidence from nineteenth-century Virginia suggests that such skills were handed down in families; the black preacher Peter Hawkins and his son followed the trades of both dentistry and bloodletting in early-nineteenth-century Richmond, and a photograph from the 1890s shows "Aunt Sophia" and her daughter extracting teeth in front of a slave cabin at the Rorer Iron Mines.[25]

Despite black dental skills, in the colonial era African Americans had less need of dentists than did Europeans since Africans traditionally practiced better oral hygiene. Thus Pieter de Marees reported from the Gold Coast in 1602 that local citizens "generally pride themselves on having beautiful, shiny white teeth, for they always go around picking their teeth (with a certain kind of stick), with which they manage to scrub and rub them so that they shine as white as Ivory."[26] It was the same in the early Americas, where blacks commonly used small twigs as brushes to clean their teeth and sweeten their breath. As Moreau de Saint-Méry reported from Saint Domingue, "[The Africans] wash their hands and particularly the mouth with extreme care. The women especially. . . . It is rather common to see them carrying at the end of a soapy vine a small piece of wood which they first crush with their teeth so as to form a sort of brush with which several times during the day they clean their teeth."[27]

West Indian–born Robert Campbell made the immediate connection between African and African-American oral hygiene practices when he visited the Akus of Yoruba country in 1859: "They pay great attention to the teeth, using the chewed ends of certain roots for the purposes of brushes, as do the people of the West-Indies, where the custom was doubtless introduced by Africans."[28]

In contrast, Europeans and European Americans of the era practiced little in the way of dental hygiene besides an occasional mouth rinse and suffered greatly from rotting, discolored teeth.[29] It seems possible that European Americans, who stereotyped black Americans as having shining white teeth, may have been influenced to adopt tooth brushing in part because of their realization of the efficacy of African-American dental hygiene. Unfortunately, as Africans took up American diets high in carbohydrates and sugar they, too, began to suffer tooth decay.[30]

The largest contribution of African medical knowledge in the New World came in the daily medical care given to black slaves by African and African-American practitioners. J. G. Stedman, for example, estimated there were some 800 black surgeons or "dressy" Negroes on the plantations of Surinam in the 1770s.[31] White doctors were too few and too expensive to play an important role in slave medical care; even had such doctors been available, their treatments were often worse than ineffective.[32] Indeed, their lack of success in the few cases they did see produced little confidence in white medical ability within the black community. South Carolina slaves had a proverb that explained it: "Black people rule sickness with magic, but white people get sick and die."[33]

When in the middle of the nineteenth century South Carolina plantation owner James Henry Hammond found white doctors ineffectual, he asked friends for advice, then prepared his own treatments designed to produce vomiting and diarrhea. When purges, cathartics, and emetics were not successful enough, he replaced them with painfully hot steam baths. Is it any wonder, then, that he later discovered that his slaves not only had been avoiding reporting their illnesses to him but had been using their own doctors and medicines whenever they could? He, of course, did not see it that way. Instead, in African-American medicine he found an explanation for his medical failures. Thus he reported to his diary, "Traced out the negro Doctors . . . who have been giving out medicine for years here & have killed I think most of those that have died. Punished them & also their patients very severely."[34]

Other planters likewise noticed the slaves' preference for their own doctors. William Dawson, a Potomac planter, told Robert Carter of Virginia, "the black people have more faith in [Brother Tom, Carter's coachman] than any white doctor."[35] The same disposition was the rule in Jamaica, leading Dr. W. J. Titford, who studied local cures there with the assistance of a "negro doctress," to report that "[her] fame was great in the Red Hills, and [her] knowledge, in the opinion of the negroes, was far superior to that of [white] physicians."[36] Rebecca Hooks similarly recalled that on the Georgia plantation where she had been a slave the white doctor was not nearly so popular as the "granny" or midwife who brewed medicines for every ailment.[37] This explains why the white physician hired by Henry Ravenal, a South Carolina planter, complained that his prescriptions were thrown out of the window while the decoctions of Old March, the root doctor, were taken in their stead.[38]

Interestingly, black women became more important folk medical practitioners in the United States than did black men; as Newbell Niles Puckett noted in the early twentieth century, "The great mass of folk medicine is in the hands of women rather than in the hands of men. The women are the great practitioners, the folk-doctors—the old Granny with her 'yarbs an' intmints' does much to keep alive these folk cures and to make these beliefs in general much more a feminine possession than the context would seem to indicate."[39]

This emphasis on women's commitment to health care had begun in Africa where, for example, among the Ashanti, Thomas Edward Bowdich reported, "The fetish women [are] generally preferred for medical aid, as they possess a thorough knowledge of barks and herbs, deleterious and sanitive."[40]

Female doctoring continued in the New World as African women passed on knowledge of herbal medicine to their children and grandchildren. As Preely Colman of Alton, Texas, said of her mother, "My mammy learned me a lots of doctorin', what she learnt from old folkses from Africy." "All dese doctorin' taings come clear from Africy, and dey allurs worked for mammy and for me too."[41] In a Jamaica healing center studied by Leonard E. Barrett, such African traditions survived for over a century, transmitted through the female line across three generations.[42]

Boys also learned the old traditions from women. Root doctor Jack Waldburg's teacher in Georgia was his African-born grandmother: "She duh one wut lun me tuh make medicine from root. She a midwife an tell me duh kine tuh use."[43] Similarly, in Texas, Old Dr. Jones used root medicine, and according to Patsy Moses, "he learned them in the piney woods from his old granny. He didn't cast spells like the voodoo doctor, but used roots."[44] Other cures were also passed along; in nineteenth-century Georgia, for example, Rosa Grant was taught by her African-born grandmother that a "misery" in the arm or leg could be cured by splitting a black chicken and applying it to the painful area.[45]

In the African-American community gender roles were defined quite differently than in the surrounding white society. No tight sexist lines were drawn between the role of doctor and nurse, and black women were respected for the full extent of their medical knowledge.

African-born women, as well as their daughters and granddaughters, were commonly recognized by both the slave community and the master class as proficient doctors. Uncle Bacchus White, a former slave from Fredericksburg, Virginia, expressed it simply: "Aunt Judy uster tend us when we uns were sick and anything Aunt Judy couldn't do hit won't wurth doin'."[46]

When Robert Carter's slave Sukey was "greatly affected with fits" in 1781, another bondsman on the plantation suggested that Carter send for Bennett Real's "Black Hannah," who traveled "great distances from home to visit sick people." A century later in 1860 John Hamilton of Williamsport, Louisiana, recommended that his brother avoid white physicians for his slaves, noting, "We doctor upon the old woman slave and have first-rate luck." Ex-slave Bob Mobley noted that, though there was a doctor on the Georgia plantation where he was raised, his "mother was a kind of doctor too." She would "ride horseback all over the place an' see how they was gettin' along. She'd make a tea out of herbs for them who had fever an' sometimes she gave them water from slippery elms."[47]

If black women were often consulted by whites only as a last resort, they still seemed to have had an impressive record of successful cures. Thomas Ewbank reported from Brazil:

> My friend the vicar had a lad long troubled with a bruised leg. The sore resisted all his attempts to heal it. As a last resource, a colored "wise woman" was consulted. She raised a smoke of dried herbs, muttered over the wound, made motions as if stitching its lips up, put on a cataplasm of herbs, sent him home, and in a week he was well. Another young slave had a diseased foot; nothing seemed to do it good; and at length his owner gave him leave to visit a dark sorceress, who talked to it, made signs over it, rubbed it with oil, covered it with a plaster, and in a few days he was sound too.[48]

It was common in the Americas for African, African-American, and African-Indian herb women like "Doctoress Phillis" of Barrington, Rhode Island, to help support themselves by gathering, selling, and dispensing herbal medicine.[49] In the West Indies where such women were known as weedwomen, the names of the plants they have used—such as jumbee bead, jumbee pepperbush, Congo root, and quassia (bitterwood)—illustrate the early African connection.[50] During the nineteenth century white doctors in the southern United States often adopted herbal cures first developed by black specialists.[51] We should note, of course, that in many of these herbal cures there was probably a passing of Native American medical knowledge, especially about local plants, into what became the African-American herbal expertise.

The usefulness of herbal therapy, though not approaching modern medical techniques, was superior to most of the other treatments used prior to the twentieth century. As Edward Long noted of Africa in 1774, "The chief medicaments among the Negroes are lime juice, cardamoms, the roots, branches, leaves, bark, and gums of trees, and about thirty different herbs. The latter have been experienced in many cases wonderfully powerful, and have subdued diseases incident to their climate, which have foiled the art of European surgeons at the factories."[52]

Most Africans had enough herbal knowledge to practice some simple folk medicine, and after experimenting with the new plants and any new Indian techniques they had learned, they passed this medical lore on to their children in the New World.[53] Unfortunately for African-American health care, many paternalistic masters tried to prohibit use of the herbal medicines, preferring to offer instead their own or a local white doctor's purges, emetics, tonics, or ointments.[54]

Despite the responsibility taken by masters and mistresses for the proper health care of their servants, most of the daily medical attention given in larger plantation sickrooms and hospitals was under the supervision of black nurses.[55] As R. W. Gibbs, a South Carolina planter and physician explained it in 1858, "On every plantation the sick nurse, or doctor woman, is usually the most intelligent female on the place; and she has full authority under the physician over the sick."[56] More precisely, the best of these nurses were really doctors in their own right, a reality recognized on the Worthy Park plantation in Jamaica, for example, with the honorary title "Doctoress."[57]

In Brazil, African women skilled in nursing or midwifery were the region's primary medical "professionals," having, it was said, "the respect and consideration of all."[58] As early as 1551 in colonial Peru, the African women who sold foodstuffs in the city of Lima also offered medical therapy such as treating buboes by using sarsaparilla, a native

American root.[59] Such an early date suggests the medical knowledge and interest in herbal medicine African women brought with them from their homelands and reinforces speculation that it was African Americans who first developed medical treatments based on quinine and sarsaparilla.

Black midwifes were extremely important throughout the Americas, handling, for example, some 90 percent of black deliveries in the American South and many white ones as well.[60] Alexander Telfair of Savannah, Georgia, was not alone when he instructed his overseer that his slave "be allowed to serve as a midwife for both black and white in the neighborhood."[61] The plantation midwife won recognition even in a racist world because, as Fanny Kemble explained, she was "an important personage both to master and slave, as to her unassisted skill and science the ushering in of all young Negroes into their existence . . . is entrusted." Kemble did not always approve of these black midwifes or their techniques; but even when she noted one southern infirmary under the control of an "ignorant old Negress, who was the sole matron, midwife, nurse, physician, surgeon, and servant," she was describing the range of medical and nursing skills expected of the black women who oversaw the basic health needs of larger plantations.[62]

If white doctors sometimes, due to professional jealousy or for cause, also criticized these midwifes for unsanitary and dangerous practices, it should be noted that in the antebellum United States black women under the care of black midwifes experienced a lower mortality rate in childbearing than did southern white women with their expensive white practitioners.[63] Similarly, the herbal cures black practitioners offered to their clients throughout the New World were safer and more effective than the violent purges and emetics offered by the master class.[64] The skill of the black midwifes was based on common African educational practice where girls were instructed in both herbal medicine and midwifery.[65]

In aspects of public health, African immigrants made several contributions. In general, it seems, they improved the nutritional habits of many of their masters by paying more attention to the production, consumption, and cooking of vegetables as a principal part of the diet.[66] A slave doctor in Louisiana had a cure for scurvy using lemon juice some thirteen years before the first European physician advocated a similar remedy, but his work was neglected. Unfortunately, cultural influences ran both ways, and in diet as in personal hygiene, when Africans became more acculturated, their lives became more European-American and less healthy.[67]

Coming from a tropical climate, Africans were originally far more aware of basic body cleanliness than European Americans, who seldom bathed. Pieter de Marees, an early Dutch visitor to the Gold Coast, found such hygienic practices a peculiar notion: "[The Africans] are very curious to keep their bodies clean, and often wash and scour them"; and two centuries later Europeans like T. E. Bowdich were still marveling that among the Africans "both men and women are particularly cleanly in their persons, the latter washing themselves, and the former being washed by them daily on rising, from head to foot, with warm water and Portuguese soap."[68] African arrivals carried the same concerns to the Americas, as Moreau de Saint-Méry observed from Haiti: "Body cleanliness is characteristic of blacks, especially the women, . . . who regularly take a plunging bath in a lively running stream unless they are reduced to making do with rainwater they have collected."[69]

Unfortunately, it was a rare European who adopted African bathing routines, although J. G. Stedman claimed he survived military duty in Surinam only because of the excellent nursing care of his slaves and because he followed the advice of an old black man who told him to swim twice daily and wear loose clothing as it would "not only serve for exercise . . . but [it] keeps [the] skin clean and cool, and the pores being open, . . . [allows] free perspiration. Without this, by imperceptible filth, the pores are shut, the juices stagnate, and disease must inevitably follow."[70] At the time Stedman took this advice, the best European medical theorists were only just coming to the same conclusions, but frequent bathing remained extremely unusual among whites.[71] Thus in 1775 Moravian missionaries in Surinam were scandalized when they came upon two young black Saramaka women bathing a sick newborn child in cool water; the white missionaries' reaction was all the more ironically misguided by their own lack of experience—they neither bathed nor had children of their own.[72]

Later, in the colder climate of North America, whites would accuse blacks of being dirty, smelly, and uninterested in personal cleanliness. By 1860 a Georgia physician went so far as to say, "so notoriously filthy are negroes," that they constituted "a people allied to hogs in their nature and habits." What truth there was in such accusations followed from the Africans' enculturation into more European-American ways and from the hard labor and poor housing given to slaves by their white masters. Even the Georgia planter who found blacks so dirty suspected the truth: "the filthiness of negroes is, perhaps, as much due to the indifference and mismanagement of owners, as to a natural fondness of the African race for dirt."[73]

African Americans also brought from Africa techniques that reduced the danger from disease-carrying insects. Many black laborers in the Americas kept fires constantly burning in their homes and at work in the fields to protect them against both insects and chills—an African practice that often drew the sarcasm of white observers who did not understand its usefulness.[74] The West Indian historian Edward Long, however, suspected that such fires might give Jamaican blacks added protection from disease: "The custom of the Negroes in this respect, perhaps, may conduce as much as anything to their enjoying health in such marshy soils, when white persons are affected by the malignant effluvia, and contract sickness."[75] And, indeed, European ships on the African coast soon adopted the practice, keeping fires constantly burning in kettles on their decks.

In general, African Americans seem to have maintained a better sense of group responsibility for community health. After most white authority had fled Philadelphia during the great yellow fever epidemic of 1793, Richard Allen and Absolom Jones, leaders of the Free African Society of Philadelphia, won a place in the history of public medicine by organizing a large segment of the black community to nurse the sick and bury the dead.[76] Although many Philadelphia whites later proved ungrateful for, and disrespectful of, the skill and concern of black nurses, Benjamin Harrison of Petersburg, Virginia, in similar circumstances, did not; he manumitted his bondswoman Jensey in January 1825 for "several acts of extraordinary merit performed . . . during the last year, in nursing, and at the imminent risk of her own health and safety, exercising the most unexampled patience and attention in watching over the sick beds of several individuals of this town." His faith in African-American competence was rewarded, for after emancipation Jensey Snow opened a much needed local hospital in Petersburg.[77]

Free women of color commonly served Europeans as nurses throughout the Caribbean area, winning great respect; Lieutenant Thomas Phipps Howard, who served in Haiti from 1796 to 1798, for one, was deeply appreciative: "Their attention & tenderness to the sick is really meritorious to the highest degree in the World. . . . I myself have twice experienced this from their Hands, & am happy in giving them as some small Return for the extreme Care of me the full Tribute of my Praise."[78]

Black men, like their women, were also important practitioners of medicine. Virginia's Doctor Lewis, Brazil's Master Torquato, New York's Peter Santomee, and Connecticut's Doctor Primus Manumit were typical of noted African-American practitioners during the period of slavery; the latter three trained under white doctors and served white as well as black patients.[79] Even the restrictions of a racist society could not stop General Pinckney in nineteenth-century South Carolina from giving over the medical care on his plantation to a black doctor and nurse, and many other planters seemed to have used black male practitioners at least some of the time.[80]

Specialists in herbal remedies, like the Haitian revolutionary Toussaint L'Ouverture, gained a wide reputation for the practical (and sometimes supernatural) effects of their medicine.[81] But status as a skilled doctor could prove dangerous for a slave, since the herbal knowledge that could cure was confused by European Americans with the more esoteric skills of conjure, which whites considered a form of poisoning.

Fear of poisoning often led in its turn to repressive legislation against black medical practitioners. In South Carolina and Georgia, for example, after 1750 the law warned that, if "any slave shall teach or instruct another slave in the knowledge of any poisonous root, plant, herb, or other sort of poison," the death penalty would result.[82] Similarly, black doctors were common enough in Virginia that in 1748 the colonial legislature felt it necessary to prohibit all slaves, on pain of death, from administering medicine without the consent of the owners of both the doctor and the prospective patient. In 1792 the law was modified to permit acquittal of those slaves who administered medication with good intention and effect, but the burden of failure was still potentially prohibitive to formal black medical practice.[83] In colonial South Carolina and Georgia local laws provided that "no Negroes or other slaves (commonly called doctors) should hereafter be suffered or permitted to administer any medicine, or pretended medicine, to any other slave; but at the instance or by the direction of some white person."[84]

These laws were probably not well enforced, however, as is indicated by the 1797 runaway advertisement in the *Charleston City Gazette and Daily Advertiser* for Pero who, it was said, "passes for a Doctor among people of his color." Not all penalties were based on formal ordinances; informal censures were used as well. This was done in October 1832 when the Welsh Neck Baptist Church of South Carolina excluded Cupid, the black man of a Mrs. McCullough, for lying, and "giving medicine of his own to a sick Negro woman, and visiting the plantation contrary to the orders of the owners."[85]

On the other hand, where white doctors were scarce, as in eighteenth-century Surinam, European Americans sometimes tried to pressure blacks renowned as healers before their conversion to Christianity to return to practicing medicine.[86] As a general rule, black doctors were too important to do away with altogether; but under threat of various penalties black medicine was seriously inhibited in the Americas.[87] Thomas Roughley was probably typical of many white Americans in his observations; though he distrusted black practitioners as "a most fearful fraternity," he had to admit that their medicine, nonetheless, did "a great deal of good."[88]

The powerful Western bias toward "scientific medicine" continues to color modern appreciation of the skills of early black practitioners, who were somehow successful despite their lack of university training. Consider a recent rather patronizing assessment of slave midwifes: "Whites employed slave midwifes rather than doctors as a means of cutting operating expenses. Midwifes were often relatively competent but some of their techniques, such as their placement of an ax under the delivery mattress to 'cut' the pain of childbirth, were based more on superstition than on proven medical science."[89]

Rather than rejecting such practices as simple "superstition," we should note that the "relatively competent" slave midwifes knew from long experience that their holistic and magical folk medicine was effective in easing the pains of delivery, even if we would say the effects were psychosomatic rather than magical.[90] Slave women, when given the choice, chose black midwifes because they were better than the alternatives, and masters usually wisely followed along—no matter how they rationalized their actions.

Nonetheless, over the long run Christian masters and, later, slaves came to depreciate the sophisticated sociological and psychological aspects of traditional African and African-American medicine as superstition because such practices were magical and religious at base. Even black practitioners slowly came to see their practice in a Western cultural framework. This transfer from a holistic (and magical) African perspective to a technological (and Christian) Western viewpoint was caught by the Cuban ex-slave Esteban Montejo in his explanation of herbal medicine in Cuba: "It was the nurses who were half witches who cured people with their homemade remedies. They often cured illnesses the doctors couldn't understand. The solution doesn't lie in feeling you and pinching your tongue; the secret is to trust the plants and herbs, which are the mother of medicine. Africans from the other side, across the sea, are never sick because they have the necessary plants at hand."[91]

Although he emphasized pharmacology rather than psychology, Montejo illuminated a larger truth: African medicine worked in the black community because African Americans respected the skill and knowledge of the African men and women who brought traditional medicine with them to the New World. As William Newkirk of Tatemville, Georgia, explained, "Well, duh root doctuh wuz all we needed. Dey wuz bettuh dan duh doctuhs now-a-days. Deah wuzn all uh dis yuh cuttin an wen yuh sick, duh root doctuh would make some tea an gib yuh aw sumpm tuh rub wid an das all. Den fo yuh know it, yuh wuz all right. He would fix tings fuh yuh ef somebody done put sumpm down fuh yuh. Deah wuz many ways tuh wuk it. Sometime he would gib yuh sumpm tuh weah wid yuh aw sumpm tuh take."[92]

Within the black community a good part of the superiority of African-American practitioners to white doctors came from their ability to treat the social and psychological illnesses associated with belief in conjure. As Henry Clay Bruce recalled after his emancipation from slavery, "There have been cases where Colored people took sick from some cause, and imagined themselves tricked or poisoned by someone, and the white doctor, unable to do them any good, gave up the case, and the patients believing themselves poisoned and therefore incurable, have died, when they might have been saved, if the white doctor had only . . . announced himself a conjurer, and proceeded to doctor the patient's mind."[93]

Similarly, in the early nineteenth century the older brother of a slave patient of Dr. A. D. Galt of Williamsburg, Virginia, observed to the doctor that his white medicines were useless because Gabriel "had been tricked" and "must have a Negro doctor."[94] But since illness described as a result of evil spells (rather than unknown causes) seemed like superstition to European Americans, black doctors rarely received any credit from whites for their ability to treat the whole patient, despite the fact that a patient's spirits were usually raised by the knowledge that the malady was treatable.

The repression of black medicine during the era of slavery has likewise obscured the important role African medical knowledge played in colonizing the New World. Throughout the Americas, the primary health care for black Americans was under the direction of African Americans adept in diagnosis, nursing, herbal and holistic medicine, midwifery, bonesetting, bloodletting, minor surgery, psychology, and other African medical skills. Not only did these early practitioners care for their own communities; they also contributed to the medical well-being of the wider American society, especially in the use of quinine, smallpox inoculation, herbal remedies (at the same time increasing the American pharmacopoeia stock with the addition of at least seventeen African herbal drugs), and in practical nursing.[95]

These early black immigrants founded a continuing interest in medical knowledge and practice within the black American community. Unfortunately, beginning in the nineteenth century the skills of many male practitioners were atrophied by the legal repressions of racist societies. Women's interest in medical care, on the other hand, remained unabated and contributed directly to the ongoing tradition of nursing and midwifery among black women. We must not be misled into thinking that black medicine started with the entrance of black men and women into white-run medical and nursing schools; instead, we must recognize that black medicine has a long and noteworthy tradition in the Americas and that it was part of the expertise Africans brought to the successful development of the New World.

PART III

NIGGER

IN THE

WOODPILE

CHAPTER 6

The Hidden Heritage of Mardi Gras

New Orleans proudly proclaims its Mardi Gras, one of the great carnival festivals of the Americas, as the scion of a noble line of European holiday traditions, tracing it from the Roman Saturnalia to French festive customs imported during the settlement of Louisiana. Such a lineage seems reasonable enough if we look only toward Europe. But what if we adopt a less Eurocentric perspective?

Elsewhere across the Caribbean basin, major holiday celebrations in the nineteenth century are assumed to have been heavily influenced by African precedents, even if the festival days that gave rise to the occasions were European in origin. Moreover, such celebrations generally followed a regional pattern of Saturnalia featuring raucous parades and masked balls honoring elected black royalty. The noisy and unruly processions commonly were highlighted by colorful competitions between extravagantly costumed African societies; other members of the entourage often included masked "devils" and "Indians" as well as ragged funnymen and other satiric maskers who begged for gifts.

Though the Louisiana Mardi Gras seems to fit the general Caribbean pattern, the New Orleans holiday has been interpreted from a quite different perspective. The Crescent City's Mardi Gras has always been considered European-American rather than African-American in ancestry. It is worth taking a closer look at the New Orleans festivities and retracing the steps historians have followed in developing their theories about the European lineage of this classic American festival, but this time considering the possibility of an African-American influence.

By the 1850s it seemed to the French elite of New Orleans that the graceful Parisian style of the city's Mardi Gras balls and street maskings were being pushed rudely aside by a rabble of flour-throwing African-American and Irish boys whose street brawls and general lower-class impudence had been driving respectable people indoors.[1]

In 1857 the French-language press, following the lead of the city's Creole elite, officially ignored the holiday in hopes that the rowdy celebration would soon die of its own excesses. But, instead, 1857 was the year in which the New Orleans Mardi Gras would be drastically reformed and revitalized by the appearance of a "Mistick Krewe" of revelers featuring the masked god Comus high on a float surrounded by a party of devil-maskers. The Krewe's grand parade was the beginning of a tradition that would last to the present day as the most exciting and characteristic part of the New Orleans Mardi Gras.[2] And it is there historians began their search for the roots of the modern Mardi Gras.

Robert Tallant was among the first to observe that the renewed vitality of the 1857 carnival was not based on French Creole tradition as had long been assumed. Instead, after tracing the origins of the King Comus parade, Tallant boldly hypothesized that the New Orleans style of carnival was of American-Irish or Pennsylvania Dutch (*Deutsch*, i.e. German) heritage. He argued against Creole origins for Comus's Mistick Krewe after he discovered the group had only six French names among its eighty-three players. Instead, he pointed out, the instigators were, as the *New Orleans Bee* complained, not Creoles but rather "swine-eating Saxons."[3] The 1857 celebration had been organized by the American gentlemen of the city, especially several newcomers who had borrowed the idea of a grand parade from Mobile, Alabama, where a group called the Cowbellions de Rakin had been celebrating Christmas and New Year since the 1830s and 1840s with parades, maskers, theme floats, and a masked ball.[4]

Here and nowhere else, thought Tallant, was the clue to the taproot of the modern Mardi Gras. When he discovered the strange Cowbellions de Rakin Society had been organized in Mobile by a native Pennsylvanian named Michael Krafft and a party of his friends in 1830 or 1831, Tallant concluded that the origin of the Mardi Gras parades was, for lack of a better alternative, Pennsylvania Dutch.[5]

More recently, Samuel Kinser, after examining the surrounding milieu of French and African holiday customs present in colonial New Orleans, returned to the first Mistick Krewe of Comus for clues to the original source of the modern holiday. He discovered there were no French families at all represented among the nineteen young men who attended the first organizational meeting, which proved the creative impulse clearly came from newcomers to New Orleans from the nearby port city of Mobile, Alabama. The Crescent City's Mistick Krewe was consciously imitating the popular Cowbellions de Rakin Society of Mobile. Thus Kinser in his search for origins, like Tallant before him, had been led inexorably to the intentions of the Cowbellions' founder, Michael Krafft.[6]

According to legend, the initial Mobile celebration began on Christmas Eve, 1830 or 1831, when the tipsy Michael Krafft, on the way home from a party (perhaps with some friends), tied cowbells to the teeth of a rake that he slung over his shoulders. He wandered through the streets of the city noisily ringing his bells and making a spectacle while proclaiming himself to be "The Cowbellion de Rakin Society." His odd behavior must have seemed fun because on New Year's Day Krafft repeated the performance with a group of more than fifty fellow "Cowbellions."

These were said to be gentlemen of the "better sort" who made themselves up "as weird as they could" and carried hoes, rakes, gongs, and cowbells on their evening carouse. The revelers boisterously roamed the streets of Mobile shouting and singing and making a fantastic and rowdy noise, stopping only to serenade certain important citizens who furnished them with liquid refreshments.[7]

In following years the society sent out an unusually masked forerunner on Christmas Day attended by a Negro guardian. This vanguard, with cow in tow, crossed Mobile ringing an immense cowbell to announce the impending New Year's appearance on the secret Cowbellion Society. By 1840 the revels had been formalized into the first grand parade under a "Heathen Gods and Goddesses" theme.[8]

Professor Kinser concluded that the odd costuming and behavior of Michael Krafft during the Christmas revel were reflective of his German-American heritage, for among German Americans in Nova Scotia and Pennsylvania the Christmas season was marked by the arrival of a "belsnickle," a man disguised as a demonic version of Saint

Nicholas outfitted in a furskin coat or cap. The belsnickle (literally, furry Saint Nick) tradition came from Alpine regions of Switzerland and Austria where a wildman shaking cowbells at his waist and brandishing a whip went quêting from house to house frightening the children before bestowing small gifts.[9] Moreover, Kinser discovered another Pennsylvania parallel in the Philadelphia masking parades of the "fantasticals," such as was reported in 1847 when a "callithumpian band . . . accoutred grotesquely and with blackened faces . . . rams horns, bells, and kettles . . . shocked the very moon with their enactments."[10]

Yet from a more African perspective, looking to Pennsylvania for sources while neglecting more obvious African-American models closer to home seems to be stretching for a connection. Arguably, there are correspondences between Krafft's Christmas display and the belsnickle tradition, but is the association formative? Certainly, it is odd that Krafft did not simply announce himself to be a belsnickle if that was his intent, just as it seems peculiar that he would give such an unusual name as Cowbellion de Rakin Society to a parody of German-American customs.

There may be an important, if coincidental, clue hidden in the reference to the Philadelphia maskers, since in their noise, their cacophony of ringing bells and banging kettles, their shocking antics, "grotesque" dress, and blackened faces, the "fantasticals" seem the very model of a white inversion of the African-American festive style. By the nineteenth century, Philadelphia was as much a city of African-American emigrants from the South as it was a city of German emigrants from Europe. Moreover, by 1847 blackface minstrelsy was sweeping northern cities with its immensely popular white imitations of black entertainment. And, whereas the name Cowbellion de Rakin does not sound at all like Pennsylvania Dutch, Cowbellion de Rakin' could easily represent Krafft's (or his friends') parody of black folk speech—especially since the society spelled "raking" as "rakin"—the dropped *g* being typical of the way whites recorded the era's black speech patterns.[11]

In the same way, many other decisions of the early society suggest whites playing at being blacks. The decision to become a secret society, the choice of idiophonic musical instruments such as cowbells and gongs, the ragged mismatched dress of the maskers, the choice of emblems—hoes, rakes, and cows—identified with the slave class, as well as the decision to "parade" on New Year's Day all reflect the culture of Mobile's black slaves far more than the holiday celebration style of the participating white gentry.

There is no doubt the first Cowbellion Christmas celebration appears to be similar to many of the African-American Christmas and New Year festivities so common in the nearby Caribbean world. Compare, for example, Krafft's holiday inspiration with that of another early-nineteenth-century Christmas funnyman observed in Kingston, Jamaica, by Michael Scott. During the Kingston festivities groups of black tradesmen formed sets that went through town stopping at houses where the celebrants demanded and received treats and small gifts. The revelers of the butcher's party were led by an outlandish funnyman:

> At the wrists of his coat he had tin or white iron frills, with loose pieces attached, which tinkled as he moved, and set off the dingy paws that were stuck through these strange manacles, like black wax tapers in silver candlesticks. His coat was an old blue artillery uniform one, with a small bell hung to the extreme points of the swallow-tailed skirts, and three tarnished epaulets; one on each shoulder and O ye immortal gods! O mars armipotent! the biggest of the three stuck at his rump, the *point d'appui* for a sheep's tail. . . .
>
> The performers were two gigantic men, dressed in calf-skins entire, head, four legs, and tail. The skin of the head was made to fit like a hood, the two fore-feet hung dangling down in front, one over each shoulder while the other two legs, or hind feet, and the tail, trailed behind on the ground; deuce another article had they on in the shape of clothing except a handkerchief, of some flaming pattern, tied round the waist. There were also two flute players in sheep skins, looking still more outlandish from the horns on the animals' heads being preserved; and three stout fellows, who were dressed in the common white frock and trousers, who kept sounding on bullocks' horns.[12]

The Cowbellions' style seems far from the European dress and precision of other, nonsecret, holiday groups made up of white Mobilians. The parade of the German Society of Mobile, for example, was described in 1851 as properly martial: "their band was splendid—

for every German is a musician—and the uniform quite national."[13] Instead, the Cowbellions adopted a form far more in keeping with African-American celebrations such as the one observed in the West Indies by Hans Sloane at the beginning of the eighteenth century: "They have likewise in the Dances Rattles ty'd to their Legs and Wrists, and in their Hands, with which they make a noise, keeping time with one who makes a sound answering it on the mouth of an empty Gourd or Jar with his Hand. . . . They very often tie Cow Tails to their Rumps, and add such other odd things to their Bodies in several places as gives them a very extraordinary appearance."[14]

A similar use of idiophonic accompaniment by festive dancers was found in the Bamboula performances of Haiti and New Orleans where black dancers tied tin rattles to their ankles in the manner of their forefathers and in a way that could well have inspired Michael Krafft's use of tied bells in the first Cowbellion celebration in Mobile.[15]

Black festivals similar to the early Cowbellion performance were also found along the Atlantic coast of the United States in the Christmas custom of "John Kunering." In early-nineteenth-century North Carolina black merrymakers "dressed in their ordinary working clothes" and served "as a guard of honor" to a character called "the rag man" and his assistant, who carried a small cup to collect the presents given the group as they paraded up to the plantation great houses to perform. The house-to-house begging is suggestive of Cowbellion activities, but even more so is the dress of the honor guard and the peculiar get-up of the rag man: "A costume of rags, so arranged that one end of each hangs loose and dangles; two great ox horns, attached to the skin of a raccoon, which is drawn over the head and face, leaving apertures only for the eyes and mouth; sandals of the skin of some wild 'varmint'; several cow or sheep bells or strings of dried goats' horns hanging about their shoulders, and so arranged as to jingle at every moment; and a short stick of seasoned wood, carried in his hands."[16]

The men who reinstituted Mobile's celebrations during Mardi Gras in 1866, after a hiatus caused by the Civil War, seem to have understood the African-American essence of their activities for they called themselves the "Lost Cause Minstrels," a name reflective of blackface minstrelsy.[17] It was said the man among them who made the most noise was considered the best musician—a typical European reaction to African and early African-American music: "In the Negro festivals," said Monk Lewis from Jamaica, "the chief point lies in making as much noise as possible"; similarly, Leon Beauvallet offered from Cuba the typical white complaint about black holiday clamor: "it was enough to drive one mad to hear their weird noises provided by the raucous instruments and their no less raucous voices."[18]

The African nature of the celebration is also suggested by the reaction of the New Orleans press when the Mobile-inspired Cowbellion style arrived in the Crescent City, for the *Bee* punned about the celebrants' "mobile movements," suggesting the reporter intended reference both to an African-American physical style in the celebrants and to the Mistick Krewe's Alabama provenance.[19]

The importance of the single jester in African-American holidays also strikes a chord with Krafft's first Mobile celebration. At Guines in Cuba, "an athletic Negro in fantastic dress accompanied the procession, performing a wild dance and all sorts of contortions."[20] And Charles Day reports that a favorite part of black festivities was a "funny man" who "rattled a small gourd filled with shot against his hand, and screamed a sort of song which gave the initiated much delight."[21]

Typically, in Afro-America as in Mobile, holiday revelers had a custom of visiting various homes to solicit refreshments or gifts. In coastal areas of the American South, black holiday celebrants wearing masks and outlandish costumes, typically under the leadership of their "John Canoe," went "from house to house, tumbling and playing antics to pick up money for themselves."[22] On 27 December 1842, the blacks of Saint Marys, Georgia, paraded during the last day of their feast "with a corps of staff officers with red sashes, mock epaulettes & goose quill feathers, and a band of music." They were followed "by others, some dancing, some walking & some hopping, others singing, all as lively as lively can be." With "music enough to deafen" observers, the black merrymakers went about "levying small contributions on all the whites," who in turn appeared as maskers in their own right on the next day.[23]

The whites probably went along with these customs because they were fun. They would not have seemed particularly alien, since European mumming traditions of men in costume going from house to house begging for money and performing humorous songs and skits were common enough in the Celtic areas of Britain, although they did not transfer to the Americas in the sense that whites remained principal actors.[24] As an appreciative audience for such displays, however, whites were receptive and clearly enjoyed the parallel African-American institutions.

It was the same throughout the Caribbean. In 1840s Antigua, for example, Christmas Day was a black holiday, "ushered in with the sound of fiddles and drums; parties of negroes going round the town about four o'clock in the morning, playing upon their instruments for the purpose of breaking people's rest . . . and then they have the assurance to call at the different houses during the day for payment. . . . a flourish is then given with fiddle and drum, and they march off to distract another quiet household."[25]

In Jamaica such holiday groups brought with them their associated musicians, who behaved more exotically than, but nonetheless much like, the earliest Cowbellions:

> Several companions were associated with him as musicians, beating banjas and tomtoms, blowing cow-horns, shaking a hard round black seed, called Indian shot, in a calabash, and scraping the bones of animals together, which, added to the vociferations of the crowd, filled the air with the most discordant sounds. They were chiefly followed by children and disreputable women, the latter frequently supplying the performers with intoxicating drinks. Being generally encouraged, they paraded the streets, and exhibited themselves in private houses, for whole days and nights successively.[26]

It is quite possible the same tradition helped shape the *Courir de Mardi Gras*, the Running of Mardi Gras, found among the backcountry Cajuns and black Creoles of Louisiana, for many of the black Creole traditions—the group of male maskers with their music, their captain with his whip and flag, the house-to-house begging for gifts, the clowns who tried to scare women and children, the improvised singing and call-and-response chorus[27]—seem more characteristic of African/African-American masking and secret society patterns than they do of French-Canadian ones.

That a parody of African-American culture might have been Krafft's original intention would not be unlikely in 1830s Mobile where half of the port city's population was Negro. There were plenty of opportunities for white Mobilians to become familiar with, and influenced by, the exotic festive style of black societies even if they had not traveled widely. An 1854 letter in the *Alabama Planter*, for example, complained of "all day bacchanalian revels in certain districts" of Mobile, despite the mayor, three years previously, having arrested a dozen slaves for singing and dancing without a license.[28]

Visitors to New Orleans often commented on black celebrations typical of the Gulf region. James Creecy, visiting Congo Square in 1834, noted the "queer, grotesque, fantastic, strange, and merry dancers" and their accoutrements of "fringes, ribbons, little bells, and shells and balls, jingling and flirting about the performers' legs and arms." The best dancer expected small coins to be thrown in appreciation. Whites made up an attentive audience for the "hilarity, fun, and frolic." "Hundred of nurses, with children of all ages, attend," it was said, "and many fathers and mothers, beaux and belles are there to be found. . . . Every stranger should visit . . . once at least."[29] Timothy Flint did visit in the early 1820s and saw blacks dancing "through the streets" following a black king: "All the characters that follow him . . . have their own peculiar dress, and their own contortions. They dance, and their streamers fly, and the bells that they have hung about them tinkle."[30]

Such black festivities seem a more likely model for the first Cowbellions of Mobile than any of the region's European-American festive traditions. Moreover, holiday celebrations highlighting sexual or class role reversals have always been common. In early-nineteenth-century Trinidad, for example, local planters disguised themselves during carnival as estate slaves so that they could dance and parade African-style in humorous processions through the streets in front of other maskers disguised as carnival Indians.[31] Might not the Cowbellions, like the Philadelphia fantasticals, have done the same?

Another basic theme of the Mobile and New Orleans Mardi Gras celebrations after 1870 had also long been common much earlier in African-American festivities. Typically during New World holidays, black brotherhoods honored elected royalty with exotic parades and festival balls. In fact, grand royal parades featuring black kings and their courts escorted by masked dancers and musicians playing a noisy assortment of home-made idiophones were the most common holiday form in the New World. Typically, such holiday festivities also were the occasion for the parading of the maskers of the African secret societies.

Such African-American festivals date back to the seventeenth century. Popular "plays" called congos, featuring the coronation of Negro royalty and accompanying music and dancing, became common in Brazil and were probably much like those reported in 1706: "Each district or parish had its own king and queen with a court, the coronation taking place on the feast of our Lady of the Rosary, the crown being placed on the head of the fortunate Negro by the parish priest. This was the pretext for sumptuous banquets and African dances at the sugar plantation to which the king belonged."[32]

For such festivities African immigrants were given permission to appear in African costumes and to celebrate with native songs and dances. Henry Koster described a typical appearance of black Brazilian royalty during the March festival of Our Lady of the Rosary in 1810:

> There appeared a number of male and female negroes, habited in cotton dresses of colours and of white, with flags flying and drums beating; and as they approached we discovered among them the king and queen, and the secretary of state. Each of the former wore upon their heads a crown, which was partly covered with gilt paper, and painted of various colours. The king was dressed in an old-fashioned suit of divers tints, green, red, and yellow; coat, waistcoat, and breeches; his scepter was in his hand, which was of wood, and finely gilt. . . . As the king belonged to Amparo, the eating drinking, and dancing were to be at that place.[33]

North America also was influenced by African-American royal festivals; the traditional Pinkster festivities in New York, for example, had by the 1750s become an essentially black "Saturnalia" under the rule of African royalty.[34] Significantly, the Albany Pinkster celebrations, such as that of 1803, were watched by what was described as an interracial "motley group of thousands" and featured quêting (trick-or-treat begging) much like that found in the John Canoe celebrations elsewhere and in the Cowbellions' Mobile celebration in particular. When Albany's African-born king returned from Pinkster Hill, he and his attendants wandered the streets, "calling at one door after another, and demanding tribute, which demand he enforce[d] by . . . a horrid noise and frightful grimaces."[35]

In nearby Rhode Island during the same era, large biracial audiences watched local blacks celebrate the colony's election day with a royal parade and a celebration style of their own: "Every voice upon its highest key, in all the various languages of Africa, mixed with broken and ludicrous English, filled the air, accompanied with the music of the fiddle, tambourine, the banjo, drum, &c. The whole body moved in the train of the Governor-elect, to his master's house, where, on their arrival a treat was given by the gentlemen newly elected, which ended the ceremonies of the day."[36]

These North American examples were typical of the African-style holiday festivities found throughout the Caribbean basin. Consider an early-nineteenth-century example from Jamaica, where during public holidays the black slaves celebrated with characteristic style: "Each of the African tribes upon the different estates formed itself into a distinct party, composed of men, women, and children. Each party had its King or Queen, who was distinguished by a mask of the most harlequin-like apparel. They paraded or gambolled in their respective neighborhoods, dancing to the rude music, which was occasionally drowned by the most hideous yells from the whole party by way of chorus."[37]

Humor was always part of these celebrations. As James Phillippo explained, "when attracting the gaze of the multitudes at their annual carnivals by their grotesque appearance and ridiculous gambols, the blacks have been often known to indulge in the keenest satire and merriment at their own expense."[38] Timothy Flint had seen the same kind of holiday cutting-up in New Orleans in the 1820s where he noted that black slaves were given the liberty to "dance through the streets" as "merry Bachanaliars" whose antics "convulsed even the masters of the negroes with laughter."[39] This, of course, has strong similarities to the humor of Mardi Gras and the satiric behavior of the later famed black Zulu Krewes of New Orleans who, at one and the same time, parodied both racist stereotypes of Africa and the pretensions of the white Mardi Gras krewes.[40]

At least twenty years before the arrival of King Rex and his queen in New Orleans and Emperor Felix and his queen in Mobile, carnival in Trinidad was marked by a festive Saturnalia with "bands of music parading" to honor a black king and queen.[41] So, too, in early-nineteenth-century Saint Lucia the various Negro societies elected kings and queens to preside over their holiday dances.[42] And in British Guiana, it was said, "Parties of slaves go from different plantations to spend the mirthful hours with more particular friends or acquaintances. . . . Many crowds are met in every quarter, dressed in all the gaudy trappings they can collect, and with their hair cut, and fashioned into multitudes of whimsical shapes, representing various figures, wigs, crowns and the like."[43]

Other characters, like devils and carnival Indians, who would later be featured in New Orleans Mardi Gras festivities, had made prior appearances elsewhere in the Americas. In Cuba, for example, the numerous African secret societies traditionally paraded on the Day of Kings with their "little devils."[44] And when Leon Beauvallet observed the 1857 festivities in Havana, the black king was followed by a band of subjects, some clad in "outrageous garments" while others were disguised as Indians: "Patagonian Indians, as redskins, or as Apaches—others had painted their bodies with great splashes of yellow. For a headdress most of them wore splendid peacock feathers, plucked from the birds of the neighborhood and most of them had daubed their faces with whitening. Myriads of them passed through the streets until four o'clock, singing local songs to the accompaniment of rattles, tambourines, and tin pans."[45]

Thus it might be a syncretism of white and black traditions that led the Mistick Krewe of Comus to choose a devil theme for their first great New Orleans parade, which was "led by the festive Comus, high on his royal seat, and Satan, high on a hill . . . followed by devils large and small, devils with horns and devils with tails, and devils without!"[46] Formally, the devil theme was taken from Milton's *Paradise Lost*, but it may be more than coincidence that the devil-maskers and the whistles used by the captains of the Mobile and New Orleans krewes to direct members of the secret societies would also have been familiar to black holiday participants across the Americas.[47] Suggestively, a chronicler of the 1803 Pinkster celebration in Albany, New York, made a similar connection with Milton after watching the events there; the scenes of black festivity, he said, were such that not even "Milton, the biographer of devils, [could] describe."[48]

The crowns common to the carnival kings of Afro-America present another link between the royal parades in New Orleans and possible black precursors. In the early nineteenth century Monk Lewis described the typical John Canoe mask as a royal emblem, "fine as paint, paste-board, gilt paper, and looking glass could make it," topped with a glittering umbrella (symbolic of royal status in Africa) and a plume of feathers.[49] Similarly, in Havana in 1856, the black holiday king wore a red tunic with a "wonderful crown of gilded paper."[50]

In New Orleans the traveler Timothy Flint had seen the same institution in the 1820s where an African-American king wearing a gilt paper crown made a great show:

> Every year the Negroes have two or three holidays, which in New Orleans and the vicinity, are like the "Saturnalia" of the slaves in ancient Rome. The great Congo-dance is performed. Every thing is license and revelry. Some hundreds of Negroes, male and female, follow the king of the wake, who is conspicuous for his youth, size, the whiteness of his eyes, and the blackness of his visage. For a crown he has a series of oblong, gilt-paper boxes on his head, tapering upwards, like a pyramid. From the ends of these boxes, hang two huge tassels. . . . All the characters that follow him . . . have their own peculiar dress, and their own contortions. They dance, and their streamers fly, and the bells that they have hung about them tinkle.[51]

If they had a strong African-American essence, the New Orleans Mardi Gras and early Mobile Christmas and New Year celebrations would be only one more example of the general pattern of holiday celebrations in the New World during the era of slavery. Traditional European holidays established the occasions when masters would offer their slaves free time to gather and enjoy the festivities. But no matter what the whites were originally celebrating, or what the European customs had been, most New World festivities came to display forms heavily influenced by a general African-American pattern. The Feast of the Magi, Corpus Christi, Emperor of the Holy Ghost in Brazil; Day of Kings in Cuba; Corpus Christi in Martinique; Pinkster in New York; election day in New England; Christmas in Barbados, British Guiana, and Jamaica—in all of these and other holidays the blacks, directly or indirectly, soon came to dominate the streets with their satiric, musical parades and maskings—their own carnivals.

The mixed nature of the Mardi Gras heritage may even go much farther back, for as early as 1620 in Luanda, Angola, Jesuit missionaries sponsored a carnival celebration that featured dance troupes, satiric masqueraders, floats, kings, and the scattered tossing of small coins as alms to the poor. The Luanda carnival was European-African in design combining, as David Birmingham has noted, "a complete syncretism of pagan rituals from the Mediterranean pantheon, of Christian rituals from the Iberian church, and of Mbundu and Kongo rituals designed to foster fertility and prosperity."[52] In light of the form this festival took, it would be hardly surprising that the shaping force of the same European and African-style traditions should create a similar celebration 200 years later in New Orleans.

Another example of the coming together of European and African precedents is found in the competition of carnival "sets" of extravagantly dressed parade groups, each distinctively outfitted in their own identifying colors. In Jamaica set competition began with groups of black women called the "reds" and the "blues" who took to the streets in elaborate costumes to outdo one another in their magnificence while they danced and sang their way to nearby houses where they demanded to be honored with presents.[53] Although the competition between the red and blue sets has Mediterranean European origins,[54] it is equally important to understanding the New World incarnation to note that in the Americas these European pastorales were quickly taken over entirely by the blacks, who so Africanized them that whites would no longer participate.[55]

Black festivals honoring special holiday royalty came to be found throughout the Americas: in Antigua, Argentina, Barbados, Brazil, Connecticut, Cuba, Guadeloupe, Guiana, Haiti, Jamaica, Martinique, Massachusetts, Mexico, New Hampshire, New Orleans, New York, Panama, Paraguay, Peru, Rhode Island, Saint Croix, Saint Lucia, Tobago, Trinidad, and Venezuela.[56] And since such extremely similar festivals were found in Danish, Dutch, English, French, Portuguese, and Spanish colonial possessions, the African contribution is as obvious a source for the festive style as European culture is for the holiday occasion. Throughout the Americas, white observers noted how the parades, music, plays, costuming, and satiric content of these festivals had a strong African essence. But, in the end, the holidays were neither simply African nor European; they were in their mixed heritage plainly American.[57]

The Mardi Gras festival of New Orleans, like its counterparts elsewhere in the Americas, was produced by the cultural give-and-take of the New World. Even the most elitist aspects of the New Orleans Mardi Gras celebration—the Mardi Gras balls—were probably not immune to black influences. These balls seem to have had their origins in the Bal de Bouquet home dances popular among the white Creoles in 1830s New Orleans. "At the outset of the carnival season, a bachelor was elected as king. He then picked a lady to be his queen and share his power which he delegated by crowning her with a wreath of flowers. At the queen's house and in her name the ball was then given. After a few quadrilles were danced, the king conducted his queen from her throne to the center of the room where she chose and crowned the next king. . . . he in turn crowned a new queen."[58]

But these carnival masked balls common in early-nineteenth-century New Orleans were attended by blacks as well as whites. Moreover, the quadroon balls (where white males were introduced to mulatto females), which go back to at least 1805 in New Orleans, were the most popular carnival balls of all.[59]

Interestingly, the tradition of holding balls to introduce young black and mulatto women to potential white suitors can be traced back to the *folgars* of eighteenth-century Senegal where the *signares,* the great African trading ladies of Saint Louis and Goree, hosted mixed-race balls with European-style dancing to foster alliances between European traders and African women.[60] To assume that the carnival balls of New Orleans had to be only European in provenance and style, when European-African and African-American communities held similar balls that predated their New Orleans cousins, may once again presume too much.

Without a doubt, the celebration of Gulf Coast Mardi Gras began with a French holiday; but this European celebration never successfully adapted to American soil. Instead, the original French Mardi Gras and other European holiday activities were revitalized by being grafted to a hardier rootstock out of African-American culture (even if in this case it was, for the most part, an African-American style adopted by white Americans). When the holiday reached maturity, it produced a festival of American vintage whose palate shows its New World ancestry—a holiday created and celebrated by both the black and white heritages of Mobile and New Orleans.

Once the question about the origins of the Mobile/New Orleans Mardi Gras is shifted so that the African-American perspective becomes dominant, even if only for a moment, it is hard to again regain focus on the old European pattern that had earlier always seemed so stable. African-American history is important to Mardi Gras not because it was a black holiday but because without African-American history the essence of Mardi Gras simply cannot be understood correctly. It is that way with much of American history.

CHAPTER 7

The Mixed Bloodlines of the Early Ku Klux Klan

One aspect of the Reconstruction-era South that has not been analyzed by American historians is the strange similarity between the white-supremacist Ku Klux Klan in its formative years and the black secret enforcement societies common to the forest belt of West and Central Africa.[1] In fact, this is precisely the kind of question that would not come up unless Africa is taken seriously as having had the potential to influence the development of American culture. But once a comparative view is adopted, the unsettling correspondences raise unexpected questions. Could the surprising parallels between a secret organization that took up the defense of white America against the incursions of "Africanization" and similar covert organizations that protected the cultural mores of black Africa in the same era have been more than coincidental?

Clearly, there is much in African practices of the era that would seem familiar to southern historians. Like the earliest Klan, African secret societies were designed to regulate conduct and maintain law and order by the fear they inspired in the uninitiated. During public displays secret society members would suddenly appear in elaborate and fearsome full-body masks, their visitations forewarning of the supernatural retribution that would come to those who callously violated social norms. Someone so misguided as to continue willfully to disregard such cautions would receive a final warning during a nocturnal visit to his dwelling by spirits of the masked brotherhood, who might also physically threaten and abuse him. Any innocent townsperson out at night and unlucky enough to come accidentally on one of these dangerous maskers was also said to be in peril of his life.

In Africa, the anonymity of the societies' masks and the use of disguised voices and whistles to represent otherworldly speech accentuated the alien presence and authority of these frightening specters just as similar practices were designed to achieve the same effect for the Klan in America. In Africa, the visits of the secret brotherhoods were understood to be intrusions of sacred power into the human world by spirits whose essence was temporarily incarnated into the men within the fearsome masks. The Klan, of course, made similar claims. To symbolize both the potency of the spirits and the danger of their presence, African maskers were rumored to kill anyone who stumbled into their path, and they often left behind visible symbols of their passing such as lopped-off trees, in the same manner that Klansmen left behind their burning crosses.[2]

It could be, of course, that the similarities in masking traditions between the early Klan and its African counterparts were simply intriguing coincidences, products of the similar functions undertaken by both white and black secret organizations. After all, both institutions were designed to augment normal social controls, and the populations they meant to regulate—Africans and African-Americans—shared aspects of common cultural heritage. But the truth is probably more complex.

The Ku Klux Klan began in Pulaski, Tennessee, in the early summer of 1866 when, according to local historians, six young Confederate veterans desperate for amusement formed a social club. Pulaski traditions suggest that the veterans intended their new organization to be something like a college fraternity, with the central ceremony being a mock initiation, starting as if it were to be a serious ritual but ending as a form of humorous hazing. According to local tradition, the initiation ended in a ridiculous practice joke:

> At the conclusion . . . of the obligation the presiding officer, after a few appropriate remarks would ask, "What shall be done to the new brother whom we delight to honor?" Several suggestions were usually offered, but the agreement would be reached that he should be arrayed in royal apparel.
>
> Attendants were then ordered to bring forth the royal robe and put it on him; belt a sword about his waist; and place the royal crown on his head. Bear in mind gentle reader, that the candidate is still blind folded.

But as you are not, you may observe that the "royal robe" is a donkey's skin carefully tanned with the hair left on it; the sword-belt, is a surcingle, and the crown is a piece of stage property used in the presentation of "Midsummer Night's Dream," a donkey's head. Then as the attendants chanted:

"O'wad the powers some giftie gie us,
To see ourselves as others see us."

The hoodwink was removed, and the candidate was permitted to observe his full length reflection in the mirror. Instead of a prince in royal robes with a crown on his head, behold a jackass standing on his hind legs.[3]

As they remembered it in Pulaski, once the good-natured laughter was over, several of the attendants, ostensibly to prove their good will, suggested that the neophyte Klansman be given an important responsibility. But an argument followed as others hotly contended that the new brother was not yet dependable enough for a hazardous task. Finally a test was proposed to let the new man prove his worthiness. The group moved outside where the initiate was told to jump into what appeared to be an open cistern. Naturally, the new Klansman balked at this absurdly dangerous command, upon which the Cyclops ordered him pitched into the well; only too late to save his boasted bravery did the apprentice Klansman discover that the top of the cistern had been moved a few feet from the real well, and that this test, too, was part of the joke.[4]

This story is not necessarily improbable. The supposition that the Klan began in relatively innocent fraternal playfulness seems reflected in the mystic name of the organization—Ku Klux Klan—an alliterative take-off on the Greek letter organizations spreading across American colleges in that era. Moreover, the puffed-up titles the Klansmen gave themselves—Grand Cyclops, Grand Magi, Grand Turks, Grand Exchequers, Lictors, and so on—were also well suited to harmless farce.[5]

That the Klansmen soon adopted bizarre masquerades for their public appearances could be explained in the same way—and is in local histories. In order to be able to continue their initiation pranks the Klansmen needed new victims—thus the brotherhood's attendance at fairs and other social gatherings in exotic and mysterious regalia and their communication by grotesquely disguised voices or coded signals on small cane whistles. Such actions would certainly attract attention and by attracting attention would draw new recruits.[6]

As the Klansmen chose to remember it, it was only later, and after the fact, that they discovered the effect of their outfits on the area's black population. As local historians Mr. and Mrs. W. B. Romine explained,

> The change from a crowd of young men at play to the serious mission which caused the Ku Klux Klan to be known and feared everywhere, came about by accident. The men who organized the Klan and took part in those early initiations, never dreamed of the development and results, which came almost with the suddenness of an explosion.
>
> One night when the outside sentinel was standing at his post waiting for the approach of a brother with a candidate, a young negro man from a nearby farm came along, coming into town. He did not see the white robed figure standing by the roadside till directly opposite. When he did see the sentinel, he called out in fright: "Who's that?" On the spur of the moment, the sentinel in a deep, sepulchral voice responded, "I'm a ghost." Several people had been killed in the storm that struck that part of the town a few months before. And the combination of circumstances was too much for Ham's nerves, and his feet ran away with him.
>
> When the initiation of the evening was over, the sentinel told, simply as a joke, the story of his adventure with the young negro man. The members joined in a hearty laugh. Then the thought occurred to one man, and he suggested to others, the possibility of utilizing the new and mysterious organization, to restrain young negroes, who were beginning to run amuck at social conditions, by taking advantage of the negroes' superstitious fear of ghosts. It was agreed to give this man's theory a trial.[7]

According to local white traditions, a more formal testing of Klan regalia on Negro superstition then took place at a home on Third Street in Pulaski where three or four young black women and their "noisy . . . rough, profane, and vulgar" friends took special delight in "being offensive and aggressive" to whites.[8] Allen Trelease in his study of the Klan, *White Terror*, gives an example of the kind of thing that white Pulaskians were finding especially offensive in those days: "When a Negro saloonkeeper in Pulaski hung out a sign in front of his establishment bearing the name Equal Rights, it was hauled down the same day" by a gang of young white men from the countryside.[9] Would the strange Klan garb help put down such shocking black impudence?

Already, if we are to believe the tale, the Klan had decided to be not just any ghosts but the ghosts of the Confederate veterans of Shiloh. The proof would be in the performance.

> And to make it impressive and give the appearance of great numbers, they decided to conduct a horseback parade. Robes were prepared for the horses as well as men. And one evening about nine o'clock there was formed a procession of silent ghostlike men, each mounted on an equally ghostlike horse, all covered with long, white robes so that the blacks, bays and sorrels, all looked alike. The procession moved slow and silent. . . . The men rode two by two, and kept a good distance apart so as to form quite a long procession. . . . The leader silently reined up at the front gate [of the Negro family] and politely asked one of the young negroes in the yard for a drink of water. The negro brought a dipper of water which the horseman drank, said it was good, and asked if he might have some more. A second dipper was brought. Again the negro was thanked, and asked to bring the water bucket. The horseman had a rubber bag concealed under his robe, into which he emptied the contents of the bucket. But to the astonished negro it looked like he drank it. Then passing the empty bucket back to the negro with polite thanks, he remarked that was the best water he had tasted since Shiloh. . . . No reference was made to the boisterous conduct of the negroes. No threat nor admonition. The horseman silently returned to his place at the head of the procession and the procession silently moved on till it turned the corner, then vanished from sight. The men removed their own robes, and those of the horses, and the ghostlike procession had vanished into thin air. But the effect of that visit remained. Boisterous revelry ceased in that yard quite as suddenly as if there had been a funeral in the family. Visitors came no more at night, and soon the negroes found more congenial quarters in another locality.[10]

Probably this anecdote is at best a condensation of history. The trick is too complicated and the performance too well thought out to be a spur-of-the-moment test of the ghost theory. Clearly, however, something had convinced the early Klansmen that their black neighbors would be especially susceptible to maskers disguised as returned war dead. Pulaskian historian W. B. Romine suggested as much:

"Thoughtful men had been studying and praying over conditions as they were [that is, white supremacy had been threatened] but though they sought diligently, no ray of light penetrated the blackness of despair which surrounded them, till the thought came like the voice of inspiration to one of God's prophets, that there is power in organization and cooperation, and that the negro by nature has a superstitious fear of ghosts."[11]

Oddly enough, given the intent to portray ghostly figures, the first costumes of the Klan were not the traditional white sheets we have come to associate with both ghosts and Klansmen. Instead, in the early years individual Klansmen (officially called "Ghouls") appeared in a wide variety of outfits. Some of the young men wore "Spanish jackets"; wide trousers were common as were caps with feathers or horns protruding, and others wore exotic red robes and candy-striped hats; very few wore the simple Halloween-style sheets we might have expected from imitators of European-style ghosts.[12] Not until several years later were the costumes standardized around the stereotypically Klanish conical hats, full masks, and long gowns when, according to John C. Lester,

> each member was required to provide himself with the following outfit: a white mask for the face, with orifices for the eyes and nose; a tall, fantastic cardboard hat so constructed as to increase the wearer's apparent height; a gown, or robe, of sufficient length to cover the entire person. No particular color or material were prescribed. These were left to the individual's taste and fancy, and each selected what in his judgement would be most hideous and fantastic, with the aim of inspiring the greatest amount of curiosity in the novice. These robes, of different colors, often on the most flashy patterns of "Dolly Varden" calicos, added vastly to the grotesque appearance of the assembled Klan.
>
> Each member carried also a small whistle, with which, by means of a code of signals agreed upon, they held communications with one another. The only utility of this device was to awaken inquiry.[13]

That local blacks seemed frightened by the grotesque hooded figures does not prove the ghostly effectiveness of the disguises since surely the sensible attitude for any black to take in those days when faced with a gang of masked white men behaving in a strange and ominous manner was to exhibit extreme caution.[14] Because the Klan was involved in intimidating both white and black victims, masks were probably necessary for their illegal work. The odd thing about the early Klan is not that they wore masks but the peculiar nature of their disguises and associated behaviors. Since frightening local blacks apparently increased the Klansmen's fun as well as their effectiveness, Klan members may have begun exaggerating those qualities of their costuming that appeared to have the greatest effect on their black victims. Thus it is possible that the Klansmen built up their stereotypical regalia as part of a feedback mechanism of intimidation.

Clearly, the early Klansmen adopted a pattern of bizarre strategies specifically designed to frighten those African Americans "impudent" enough to exercise their freedom into believing the Klansmen were avenging ghosts. What makes this the more peculiar is that throughout the era of slavery unvarnished forms of violence—whippings, beatings, and outright murder—had effectively held slaves in check. Things had not changed so much that whites had to be particularly subtle to get their racist warnings across to the new freedmen. Nonetheless, the early Klan seems to have been acting on a new theory of intimidation, a point apparent in the testimony of Lorenzo Ezell describing an 1868 Klan visit to his mother's house in South Carolina: "First time dey come to my mamma's house at midnight and claim dey soldiers done come back from de dead. Dey all dress up in sheets and make up like spirit. Dey groan around and say dey been kilt wrongly and come back for justice. One man he look just like ordinary man, but he spring up about eighteen feet high all of a sudden. Another say he thirsty; he ain't have no water since he been kilt at Manassas Junction. He ask for water and he just kept pourin' it in. Us think he sure must be a spirit to drink dat much water."[15]

False pasteboard skulls were also among the bizarre equipment said to have been used to astonish and horrify local Negroes: "Another awe-inspiring performance was for one of the Ku Klux to wear his robe over the top of his head, surmounted with a false head (consisting generally of a large gourd with a mask attached) which could be removed in the negro's presence. 'Here, hold my head a minute,' the Klansman would say, thrusting the masked gourd at the negro, which never failed to reduce the victim to a state of quaking terror."[16]

Were southern blacks really deluded by such disguises? Not in the way that Klan traditions later interpreted it. A greater understanding of the issue requires reexamining how the Klan came to develop their curious and singular uniforms.

Neither the old slave patrols nor the white charivari bands of the region had ever adopted such bizarre costuming. During Reconstruction the home guards, white-leaguers, and red-shirt clubs all rode openly about the country brandishing weapons and using old-fashioned violence to intimidate blacks without finding it necessary to hide behind exotic costuming. An armed white mob in the southern night clearly did not need strange robes and conical hats or horns to intimidate a black citizenry that had been continually victimized by white violence.

One theory that was developed to explain the anomaly held that masters and overseers in slavery times had actually started the masking tradition by telling their bondspeople ghost stories and then disguising themselves in white sheets to frighten the slaves and keep them from wandering about at night. However, the evidence for this theory came from oral interviews with black residents of Washington, D.C., in 1964, and therefore cannot be taken as historically reliable tradition.[17] Moreover, beliefs in spirits and ghosts were at least equally as pervasive in Africa and Afro-America as among European-Americans, and therefore whites had no need to create such ideas, although the key to the Klan may well be in white intentions to exploit what they believed to be black "superstitions."

The Klan regalia was something new in the South's European-American masking traditions. The legends of the early Klan contend that originally Klan costumes were simply designed to be eye-catching and that only later and accidentally did Klansmen discover that local blacks were frightened by the ghostly appearance of the white robes.[18] Yet the physical evidence strongly suggests that most, if not all, the original robes were primarily red—a color almost invisible at night—and not at all ghostlike from either an African-American or a European-American perspective.

A picture of founding Pulaski Klansman J. R. Brunson in his original regalia shows him wearing a red body-length robe trimmed with a border of white stripes and featuring an irregular five-pointed star and crescent appliqué on the left breast. At the waist hung an odd

Abakuá masker of nineteenth-century Cuba, patterned after Leopard
Society masks, Nigerian Coast, West Africa

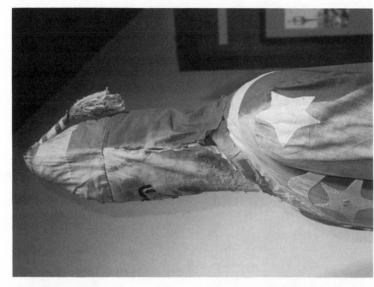

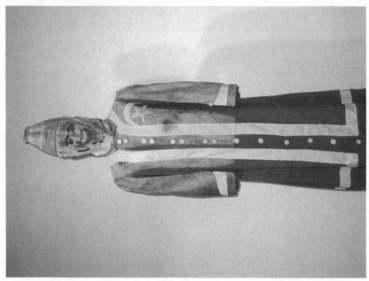

Original Klan robes. Courtesy United States Marshal Service

bag with vertically striped tassels tied to a button. Over his face the Klansman wore a full mask attached to a tall conical hat with wide red and white horizontal stripes topped by a narrow, curving candycane-striped projection of twisted cloth with a red and white tassel at the end.[19]

This robe has survived, and firsthand inspection reveals on the robe's arms at both shoulders five-pointed white appliqué stars which, like the white star and crescent on the chest, were cut freehand and not measured geometrically. At the center of the star on the breast of the robe is a small multicolored appliqué circle. The back of the face mask is red, and on the back of the robe the two white stripes run into a V shape between the shoulder blades with a white button attached for decoration below. On the front of the face mask (which is white in color) eyeholes were cut, and a red nose patch and black cloth eyebrows and beard were sewn on.[20]

Another surviving Pulaski robe was also red with white trim (in this case a diamondlike pattern on the fringes) with a full mask and a more narrowly white-striped red flannel conical hat with a strange diamond-shaped design at the front and a red tassel on the top.[21] Joseph Gill, who had been whipped by Klansmen in Madison County, Alabama, in 1868, told congressional investigators that the Klansmen wore "gowns . . . that came down to the toes, and some would be red and some black. . . . some of them had horns about as long as my finger, and made black."[22] Given European-American ghost beliefs, it is hard to imagine that any of these early Klansmen thought they looked like ghosts in general, much less like Confederate ghosts.

Moreover, had a white robe been the impetus for an accidental discovery that superstitious blacks mistook the robed Klansmen for ghosts, then both white and black traditions should have suggested that future robes of the ghostly nightriders be primarily white.[23] But they were not, at least not until several more years had passed. Nonetheless, the fear-of-ghosts tradition might explain why in the longer run, as the Klan expanded, European-Americans—many of whom knew little about African-American ways—began to drop the red gowns, the candy-striped hats, the flashy patchwork, the horns and feathers of the earliest costumes, so as to adopt the white robes their own folk traditions associated as ghostly.

Later, to give greater nobility to their otherwise ridiculous-looking regalia, the Klan rationalized that the white robes with red trim were chosen to symbolize the purity and dedication of the "Lost Cause" (although Confederate red and gray would have seemed a more appropriate color scheme).[24] But here again the color and patterns of the first robes and the way they were used do not support the Klan's later explanations.

Though it is possible that the anomalously red and strangely shaped early costumes were designed to catch the eye of potential white initiates before the accidental discovery of the impact of Klan robes on local blacks, we still might wonder who created or suggested the designs, why those particular patterns appealed to them, and who the seamstresses were who put these odd robes together for the young men. Local tradition says that the sister of one of the original Klansmen designed and made the first costume, which served as a pattern for the others, and family-made costumes remained the custom.[25]

But the seamstresses may not have all been white since the region's white women often used black servants to help them in their labors. Indeed, congressional testimony from 1871 shows that a black seamstress, Christina Page of Union, South Carolina, was hired by a white woman to help make "party costumes," which in actuality went to the local Klan. The South Carolina disguises featured a full body robe and triangular face masks made from folded handkerchiefs with the point facing up and reinforced to achieve a hornlike prominence; holes were cut for the eyes and mouth, and the colors varied.[26] Whatever the case in regard to the seamstresses, the early Klan costumes clearly adopted an aesthetic alien to local white traditions but very much at home with the region's African-American tastes, which emphasized highly contrasting bright colors, offbeat patterning, striping, and appliqué normally considered "flashy," "fantastic," "grotesque," and "hideous" in the eyes of Anglo-Americans.[27]

According to the testimony of G. Wiley Wells of Holly Springs, Marshall County, Mississippi, during the Senate investigation of the Klan in 1868, early Mississippi gowns were much like those of Tennessee except that the red gowns trimmed in white were giving way to white gowns trimmed in red.[28] The basic attributes of the design were still the same: "This disguise is decorated with white pieces sewed on to it in patterns representing the moon and stars, hearts crosses, &c. in different parts of the body. Here are various face-disguises—one red, two of them are white, with holes cut in them for eyes and mouth. This one, which is a terrible-looking one, is an officer disguise, and has a flap over the mouth so contrived that upon his blowing it makes a vibrating noise."[29]

A likely explanation for the red color so common in the early outlandish costuming is that the original Klansmen (or the women— white or black—who sewed their costumes) designed Klan regalia in full knowledge that red was the color of greatest supernatural significance in African-American tradition (although not the color of ghosts).[30] But if the Klan's choice of color had been intentional, then perhaps other aspects of the design might also have been chosen for their probable effect on black targets.

Indeed, if any of the original Klansmen had knowledge of the "devil-maskers" of the African secret societies of their era, several of which featured maskers with conical hats and red flannel terror masks trimmed with white appliqúe, or had seen or knew of their New World counterparts, such as the *ireme* characters of African societies of mid-nineteenth-century Cuba who were masked messengers of the fearsome leopard spirit dressed in red and white checked or striped patchwork body masks topped with pointed conical hats tasseled at their apex, then the striking similarity of appearance between the masking costumes of African and African-American secret societies and those of the early Klansmen of Tennessee would seem far less remarkable.[31] The *ireme* devil-maskers of the Leopard Society of Cuba (who even today in modern incarnations look remarkably Klanish) were considered by the local African Cubans to be "visible dead" who came to officiate over society rites; moreover, by the middle of the nineteenth century they were well enough known by white Cubans to be featured on cigar boxes such as those manufactured in Havana around 1870 (and perhaps earlier).[32]

Similar African-American traditions were found in Haiti, where the black peasantry feared leaving their homes at night because of the dangerous "Red Sect," a secret society whose members were said to have gathered after dark in cemeteries (a spot commonly chosen by early Klansmen as well) to invoke the god of death with human sacrifices. Robed in red and white gowns topped with hoods or conical straw hats, sometimes with tin horns protruding, the guards of the Sect Rouge were transformed into demons who roamed through the darkness looking for victims unfortunate enough to be abroad in the night.[33] Throughout the years, the secret societies of Haiti continued to function as tribunals and enforcers, much as their predecessors had in Africa.[34] An analogous society seems also to have been at work in Brazil, as Daniel Kidder reported in 1839: "There is a singular secret society among the negroes, in which the highest rank is assigned to the man who has taken the most lives. They are not so numerous as formerly, but from time to time harm the unoffending. These blacks style themselves *capoeiros,* and during a festa they will rush out at night and rip up any other black they chance to meet."[35]

It is surely possible that in their reading or during the war the Pulaskian Klansmen could have learned something of the dangerous secret societies of Africa and Afro-America with their devil-maskers and strange conical hats and bright red and white costumes. The red robes, the stripes and diamonds, the horns, the strange moon shapes, the feathers, all would better accord with white attempts to approximate African-style supernatural devil-maskers and evil spirits than they would with attempts to re-create the hallowed essence of Confederate war dead.

Many of the European travelers and slavers who visited the African coast, the West Indies, and Brazil commented on the secret societies. The slave trader Hugh Crow, for example, suggestively reported in 1830 that the Egbo Society of Old Calabar "seemed especially designed to keep" women, slaves, and the masses of the population in subjugation.[36] And the level of white familiarity with West African secret societies was high enough that, at least in the Niger Delta, European merchants wishing to improve their economic position were known to have joined such groups as the Egbo and Ekpe (leopard) societies.[37] Thus the Report of the Select Committee of Parliament on British Possessions on the West Coast noted in 1842 that "The master of a vessel belonging to Liverpool purchased what is called 'Egbo' [the right to join the society was typically purchased], that is making himself a partner in the exhibition of some disgusting mummeries which they have to their deities there. This man dressed up, and danced, and all that kind of thing, and went through all this just for the purpose of getting in a cargo of oil quickly."[38]

It does not seem too farfetched that the founders of the Klan could have heard how such secret societies in Africa operated and thought that here was a perfect mode of social control, letting African "superstitions" keep the black population of the South in its place. The hypothesis that the Klansmen designed their early costuming with the intention of frightening local freedmen is also strengthened by the likelihood that the strange bag tied to a button near the waist of the original Klansman's robe was a conspicuously displayed mojo "hand" or *nkisi* charm.[39]

Thus it is quite possible that from its inception the Klan intentionally adopted a masking tradition from African-American folk culture, after which it attempted to pattern its own practices. Fanny Kemble had heard such a rumor in 1876 when she wrote to a friend about the Klan's attempts to intimidate black voters:

> I heard a most curious story this evening upon the intimidation to which the negro voters had been subjected in some places in the South. Though very few of them are African born . . . they retain, nevertheless, the traditions of the African Obi [Obeah] worship in a great many curious forms of what they consider of evil omen, unlucky, uncanny. The white inhabitants of the southern states are well aware of these superstitious terrors of the blacks, and on the day of the election secured the absence of the negroes from the polls by sending grotesquely dressed-up men to tie various colored ribbons round the liberty-masts erected at the booths, where the voting-tickets were taken. These incomprehensible, mysterious signals were considered by all the negroes what they called *Obi,* and they were effectually scared from voting by them.[40]

Kemble's rumor makes it clear that at least some white southerners knew enough about long-standing African-American folk beliefs to consciously design their activities to mimic African-style masking and even to turn white liberty poles into black obeah sticks.[41]

Given such speculation about the likelihood of African-American influences on the choices of the early Klan, even the original initiation rite could be rethought. Tradition says that the intent of placing a donkey skin and donkey-head on the unsuspecting initiate was a joke out of the Shakespearean *Midsummer Night's Dream* tradition.[42] It could have been. But the wearing of animal skins and animal-head masks was also nearly universal in fierce displays of African hunting societies and in African-American masking traditions such as those commonly practiced by the John Canoers of North Carolina and by the horsehead and cowhead maskers of the West Indies. Consider the description of a parade of African-American maskers in 1820 Jamaica: "The performers were two gigantic men, dressed in calf-skins entire, head, four legs, and tail. The skin of the head was made to fit like a hood . . . a handkerchief, of some flaming pattern, tied round the waist. There were also two flute players in sheep skins, looking still more outlandish from the horns on the animals' heads being preserved."[43]

The effect on a proud white initiate of being discovered in such an outlandishly African-American-looking outfit would have been a double roll reversal of great ludic potential in the Reconstruction South. Moreover, Klansmen did occasionally appear disguised as "donkey devils," rushing about inside the skin of a donkey in an attempt to frighten black freedmen—an activity that surely cannot be construed as either Shakespearean or in honor of the late Confederate war veterans.[44]

Such actions suggest more than a passing white acquaintance with African and African-American masking traditions, which commonly featured animal skins and the concept of devil-maskers as well as false-headed masks like those used by the early Klan.[45] Nonetheless, speculation is not proof, and it remains possible, although to my way of thinking unlikely, that despite the strong and suggestive parallels between black and white maskers none of the Klan's costuming choices were more than coincidentally patterned in the African-American tradition and that the earliest robes were not originally intended to intimidate the region's black population. Even so, African-American culture would still have been a powerful formative influence on the Klan simply by shaping the black response to Klan regalia and thereby changing Klan behavior. As Fanny Kemble suggested, older blacks who saw or heard of the strange maskers likely connected them to folk traditions about dangerous night spirits and even older stories about the fearsome secret societies of Africa and the West Indies.

That Africans or African Americans respected members of the spiritual world who came among them, however, does not mean they were simply scared of ghosts, as tradition has it, or easily deluded by members of the secret societies.[46] Africans believed that when a man put on a society mask he was infused with its spirit; he was a known person outside the mask, but within it he was transformed into something quite different by the spirit.[47] As A. B. Ellis reported in 1894 of the Yoruba Egungun masker of the Nigerian region: "He is supposed to have returned from the land of the dead in order to ascertain what is going on in the land of the living, and his function is to carry away those persons who are troublesome to their neighbors. . . . Although it is very well known that Egungun is only a disguised man, yet it is popularly believed that to touch him, even by accident, causes death."[48]

Not only was it prohibited to touch a man in such a spirit mask; observers were also not even allowed to say that he was human, as Robert Campbell reported in 1859: "The *Agugu*, a fantastically attired individual, is frequently seen at Abbeokuta and other places interior. He represents the spirits of the departed, who are frequently consulted through him. No one is permitted to say he is a man, nor to touch him under penalty of death. If he touches any one, the party touched must die. . . . He is so dressed to leave no part of his body exposed, and speaks in a gutteral voice, assumed as a disguise."[49]

When first faced with masked Klansmen, older blacks in the American South probably responded in line with an African world view whose remnants seem to appear in the autobiography of civil rights worker Anne Moody. When Moody grew up in the Mississippi of the 1950s, the Emmet Till murder was explained by her mother in terms similar to this kind of African perspective: "When I asked her who killed the man and why, she said, 'An Evil Spirit killed him. You gotta be a good girl or it will kill you too.' So since I was seven, I had lived in fear of that 'Evil Spirit.' It took me eight years to learn what that spirit was."[50]

Southern blacks knew the maskers were violent and vicious white men in odd costumes, but they also understood the Klan represented a society of death, the highly dangerous reincarnated spiritual power of the old slaveholders of the Confederacy. Who would say, given Klan actions, that black observers were wrong? That was exactly what the Klansmen intended. In Mississippi, Klansmen carried and shook skeleton bones, and in that and similar ways the Klan attempted to induce "the belief among the negroes that they were spirits of those slain at Shiloh, and that they know every act that people performed." Others claimed, apparently in accord with the strange moon and star shapes on their costumes, that they came from the moon.[51] They were not simply attempting to be ghosts as white Americans usually described them; it seems more likely they were trying to imitate the exotic and fearsome spirits of black secret societies, at least as they understood them.

Clearly, the strange costuming and odd behaviors were not typical of traditional white regulators, who openly attempted to intimidate through noisy violence. John C. Lester and Daniel L. Wilson, original members of the Klan, claimed Klan riders, instead "swept noiselessly by in the darkness with gleaming death's heads, skeletons, and chains."[52] Nor do such bizarre activities seem likely to have been designed to honor the Confederate dead as later Klan traditions would have it. Plainly, the activities were intended to influence blacks whom Klansmen thought could be intimidated by the spiritual presence of otherworldly visitors.

What was remarkable was how similar the Klan costumes were to their African counterparts. The shape of the Klansman's hat, for example, may have been singular in the white South, but such shapes were common enough on the West Africa coast where maskers and rulers often wore conical hats, and executioners, dressed in a single full-body cloth, towered menacingly over their victims by virtue of the way the top of the cloth rose conically into a sugar-loaf shape two or three feet above their heads.[53]

Similarly, crosses that would appear as Christian symbols to white southerners had long been associated in African-American lore with African symbols of danger, death, and spiritual power.[54] During early 1867, when the Klan was still just a rumor for most of the region's blacks, it is likely that the old people were asked to interpret the significance of these strange figures, and the elders in turn may have thought back to what the Africans from the old country had said about the dangerous secret brotherhoods and their spirits of the night.

Looking at the question from a far different perspective, a recent study of southern history has suggested that Klan ritual behavior and costuming were derived from the European charivari.[55] Although there are strong continuities between charivari traditions of social coercion and public ridicule and the growing violence of later, more European-American Klan activities, the earliest Klan rituals were something far different, taking place in an eerie silence without any of the rowdy crowd behavior and rough cacophonous music that define white charivari customs.[56] It could also be noted that there are distant European (although few white American) parallels to Klan masking traditions—Merlin-like hats, festival wildmen, and bizarre holiday costuming—but once again the associated behaviors were not Klan-like, nor were they found in the Protestant South or institutionalized into secret society activities like those common in Africa and the Caribbean.[57]

There were two folk traditions deep within the southern blood: one from Europe but the other from Africa. The silent, ghostly, secret society maskers typical of the Klan's early years who communicated with whistles and dressed in outlandish red and white costumes, hooded with striped and tasseled conical hats, or who topped themselves with false heads, feathers, and horns and claimed to be spirits come back to control antisocial activity seem far more in tune with African and African-American masking traditions than with the raucous charivari bands of white America, however much European-American charivari rituals and mob violence came to dominate later Klan activities.[58]

Indeed, Klan tradition has always admitted that the Klan's choices of costumes and strategy were heavily influenced by their understanding of African-American beliefs and attitudes. Thus, whether by intention or by feedback, the Klan had become to a degree Africanized. African Americans were not responsible for what the Klan intended to be or for what it became; they were the innocent victims of its violence. But such was the pervasive power of African-American culture in the American South that even a racist organization designed to protect white civilization paradoxically had to become African-American to be effective.

CHAPTER 8

Mammy, Indeed!

The revealed wisdom of one generation is often a source of amused condescension for the next. So it has been with the idea of the American "melting pot"; once an article of national faith, the cultural melting pot has more recently been ridiculed as an elitist oversimplification that blinded us to the continued ethnicity of American life. But although the variety of America clearly is one of the distinguishing marks of our civilization, the vast majority of citizens have also shared much in the way of a common culture, a common culture that has been heavily influenced by its African and African-American roots, even though that influence seemed invisible to several generations of American historians. The shaping force of African culture has been especially strong in the southern United States, but recognition of this fact was long obscured by a kind of intellectual gerrymandering of southern studies into two relatively separate scholarly spheres: one white and called southern, the other black and labeled African-American. In reality, as we are more and more coming to understand, the division was artificial and misleading.

That African Americans joined with Scots-Irish and Anglo-Americans as primarily shapers of southern culture should not be surprising, considering how intermixed blacks were within the southern population. But since the mass of the African Americans were in bondage during the formative years of culture building, their political powerlessness and lack of economic autonomy seemed adequate reason for many observes to discount African-American contributions to the traditional lifestyle of southern whites. The truth, however, was otherwise; African Americans shaped the culture of the white South, just as European Americans influenced the traditions and values of black America.

One of the central ironies of racial slavery was that as masters exploited their bondsmen the lives of both intersected with inevitable results unintended by the dominant class. Edward Kimber, a British gentleman visiting Virginia in 1736, saw the aftermath clearly: "One thing [the whites] are very faulty in, with regard to their Children . . . is . . . that when young, they suffer them too much to prowl among the young Negroes, which insensibly causes them to imbibe their Manners and broken Speech." In 1820 the *Southern Evangelical Messenger* lamented that the interactions of master and man meant that far too often blacks were instructing whites. The slaves, the magazine reported, "are of necessity the constant attendants upon [white] children in their early years. From them they mostly learn to talk; from them their minds receive their first impressions; and from them a taint is often acquired which remains the whole of their succeeding lives."[1]

Though white masters and mistresses sometimes tried to control such unintended education, they were rarely successful. "Good man," complained South Carolina's Mary Chaplin to her husband in 1851, "the little Negroes are ruining the children, I couldn't tell you half the badness they learn from them." But Thomas Chaplin learned how difficult the problem was to correct when he removed the slave boy Jack from the main house, fearing Jack's influence on his son Ernest. Chaplin noted with resignation: "Next thing, Jack is mounted behind Ernest on a horse and sent off together to get plums."[2] White children on the farm or plantation simply could not be separated effectively from black role models. Thus far more of the early childhood education of the white master class was in the hands of black instructors than we might have supposed.

Southern Speech

The results of this system can best be seen in southern speech patterns. Since we learn speech without guile or pretense, our native way of talking mirrors the culture that suckled us. The irony of the slave South was that whites were learning to speak, and act, not so much like Western Englishmen as like African Americans. What Thomas L.

Nichols asserted about southern speech in 1864 also held for much of southern culture: "Southern speech is clipped, softened, and broadened by the Negro admixture. The child learns its language from its Negro nurse, servants, and playmates, and this not unpleasant patois is never quite eradicated."[3]

At that time, it was usual for most observers of the slave states to assume that the southern drawl was a corruption of standard English that had resulted from whites adopting an African-American style of speech. As the *Southern Presbyterian Review* complained: "Our children catch the very dialect of our servants, and lisp all their perversions of the English tongue, long before they learn to speak it correctly." As early as 1758 Le Page du Pratz had warned his countrymen in Louisiana, "never . . . suffer [black slaves] to come near your children, who . . . can learn nothing good from them, either as to morals, education, or language." Moreover, the effects of this cultural sharing were long lasting; as Charles Lyell put it in 1849, "The whites . . . often learn from the negroes to speak broken English, and, in spite of losing much time in unlearning ungrammatical phrases, well-educated persons retain some of them all their lives."[4]

This black-to-white acculturation in patterns of speech spread across southern culture so that by the end of the Civil War Sidney Andrews observed from South Carolina that "the language of the common people of the State is a curious mixture of English and African." Indeed, he contended, "the language of the lower classes of the whites is so much like that of the negroes that it is difficult to say where the English ends and the African begins." Actually, the adoption of black speech was always more pronounced among the region's white "aristocracy," as Mrs. Anne Royall explained: "But the children of both classes are good specimens of dialect, as the better sort in this country, particularly, consign their children to the care of Negroes. . . . Those who have black nurses . . . are at much pains and cost for teachers to unlearn them what they need never have learned, had they kept illiterate people from them at first. This is not the case with the poorer class of people, as the children are nursed by themselves, and speak their language."[5]

The end result of the South's system of informally and unintentionally educating the children of its elite under the tutelage of black nurses and in the company of black playmates was a man like Benjamin

Allston, master of the Turkey Hill plantation, South Carolina, whose language, it was reported, "was like a negro's, not only in pronunciation, but even in tone." This was normal for many of the richest and most powerful southern masters and reflects an upbringing like that described by Louis H. Blair when he noted in 1889 that "Most of us above thirty years of age had our mammy. . . . Up to the age of ten we saw as much, perhaps more, of the mammy than of the mother. . . . The mammy first taught us to lisp and to walk." On the plantations along the Carolina and Louisiana coasts many white planters in effect spoke two languages, being fluent throughout their lives in both black Gullah, or Creole and white English.[6]

That southern speech was a "Negro mode of talking" had been quickly recognized by foreigners like the English actress Fanny Kemble who was appalled at the degree to which southern white women took up their slaves' manner of speaking:

> The children of [slave] owners, brought up among [black bondsmen], acquire their Negro mode of talking—slavish speech surely it is—and it is distinctly perceptible in the utterances of all Southerners, particularly of the women, whose avocations, taking them less from home, are less favorable to their throwing off this ignoble trick of pronunciation than the more varied occupation . . . of men. The Yankee twang of the regular down-Easter is not more easily detected by any ear, nice in enunciation and accent, than the thick Negro speech of the Southerners: neither is lovely or melodious; but, though the Puritan snuffle is the harsher of the two, the slave slobber of the language is the more ignoble, in spite of the softer voices of the pretty southern women who utter it.[7]

When in 1839 Kemble began to raise her own daughter on a plantation in Georgia, she noted how this assimilation of black speech came about. Speaking of her daughter, she observed: "Apparently the Negro jargon has commended itself as euphonious to her infantile ears, and she is now treating me to the most ludicrous and accurate imitations of it every time she opens her mouth. Of course I shall not allow this, comical as it is, to become a habit. This is the way the Southern ladies acquire the thick and inelegant pronunciation which distinguishes their utterances from the Northern snuffle."[8]

Similarly, in Virginia, Maria Taylor Byrd complained of the upbringing of her six-year-old granddaughter: "I am greatly disturbed at the education of the little lady at Belvidere who's mamma ly's in bed till noon and her chief time is spent with servants and Negro children her play fellows, from whom she has learnt a dreadful collection of words, and is intolerably passionate."[9]

The situation was the same throughout the Americas, where most whites also considered the Africanization of European-American culture as an unfortunate contamination.[10] This explains why Edward Long bemoaned what he considered to be the inevitable influence of Jamaican blacks: "Another misfortune is the constant intercourse [of whites] from their birth with Negro domestics, whose drawling dissonant gibberish . . . they insensibly adopt. [They] learn it from their nurses in infancy, and meet with much difficulty, as they advance in years, to shake it entirely off, and express themselves with correctness." Lady Nugent seconded his views after visiting the same island, but she could have been speaking of all plantation America when she complained, "The Creole language is not confined to the negroes. Many of the ladies, who have not been educated in England, speak a sort of broken English, with an indolent drawing out of their words," which she noted as "very tiresome and disgusting." Josiah Quincy, Jr., agreed after his visit to the American South in 1773, noting that not only did the children adopt black ways—"a negroish kind of accent, pronunciation and dialect"—but "even many of the grown people, and especially the women, are vastly infected with the same disorder."[11]

This supposition that Africanization was tantamount to corruption blinded most whites to the improvements that Africans were bringing to the cultures of Euro-America. John Gabriel Stedman was unusual for his time in admitting the truth that African-American speech was making the local language both "wonderfully expressive" and more pleasing to the ear: "it is so sweet," he said, "so sonorous and soft, that the genteelest Europeans in Surinam speak little else." Since his time, many non-English-speaking Europeans have felt similarly attracted by the sensuous cadences of southern speech, for as Fanny Kemble put it so well: "indeed, the voices of all these [dark] people, men as well as women, are much pleasanter and more melodious than the voices of white people in general."[12]

When in later years white southerners, and white scholars for that matter, became more self-conscious about the idiosyncrasies of southern speech, they developed a theory that the southern tongue was simply a more archaic form of English and closer to its traditional roots than was standard American English; the pretense of white superiority simply would not allow an admission of the truth about how much black Americans have influenced the southern way of life.[13]

The Africanicity intermixed at the core of southern culture is also reflected in its most basic oral vocabulary. Southern English has contributed to standard American speech a number of interjections with African roots that have become commonplace as "Americanisms": "uh-huh," "unh-unh," "wow," and perhaps "OK." And if an African heritage does not seem unusual in terms from the black subculture like "funky" and "jazz," it seems more surprising that a quintessential American country greeting like "Howdy" had its African-American influences. The greeting "Howdy" came into general usage in the Caribbean and the American South by way of a reinforcing syncretism between the English question "How do ye?" or "How-d' ye-do?" and the African-American inquiry "How de massa?" and the common African-American greeting "Huddy" or "Hodi" (used by the Maroons in the backcountry of Dutch Surinam as early as 1779).[14]

It is also extremely likely that the African and African-American emphasis on public speaking and long-winded oratory helped shape the same predisposition for loquaciousness famous among southern politicians. As southern historian W. J. Cash explained:

> In the South there was the daily impact upon the white man of the example of the Negro, concerning whom nothing is so certain as his remarkable tendency to seize on lovely words, to roll them in his throat, to heap them in redundant profusion one upon another until meaning vanishes and there is nothing left but the sweet, canorous drunkenness of sound, nothing but the play of primitive rhythm upon the secret springs of emotion. Thus rhetoric flourished here [in the South] far beyond even its American average; it early became a passion—and not only a passion but a primary standard of judgment, the sine qua non of leadership. The greatest man would be the man who could best wield it.
>
> But to speak of the love of rhetoric, of oratory, is at once to suggest the love of politics. The two, in fact, were inseparable.[15]

Note how well Bryan Edwards's description of the speech patterns of eighteenth-century West Indian slaves also fits those of the proverbial Old Guard southern politico: "They are as fond of exhibiting set speeches, as orators by profession; but it requires a considerable share of patience to hear them throughout; for they commonly make a long preface before they come to the point." Or, as James Stewart put it, the blacks "no sooner begin to expatiate . . . than they become tedious, verbose, and circumlocutionary."[16]

The value blacks placed on "fancy talk" in both the United States and the Caribbean was carried from West Africa, as folklorist Newbell Niles Puckett recognized when he noted that "both in Africa and America the Negro seems to find a decided pleasure in altioquent speech." Richard Austin Freeman reported on this love of grand oratory among the Ashanti in 1898: "The art of oratory is . . . carried to a remarkable pitch of perfection. At the public palavers each linguist stands up in turn and pours forth a flood of speech, the readiness and exuberance of which strikes the stranger with amazement. . . . These oratorical displays appear to afford great enjoyment to the audience, for every African . . . is a born orator and connoisseur of oratory." As Alexander Alland explained from the Ivory Coast, West Africans maintained a deep respect for forensic skill: " 'He speaks well' is the highest compliment one West African can pay to another."[17]

But because the language of the black speakers of fancy talk seemed flowery and grand far beyond the often menial stations of the orators and was moreover often full of malapropisms, contemporary white observers often tended to disparage the African-American interest in oratory, as J. H. Ingraham did of the speech of Natchez slaves in their Sunday gatherings of 1835: "They converse with grave faces and in pompous language, selecting hard, high-sounding words, which are almost universally misapplied, and distorted, from their original sound as well as sense to a most ridiculous degree—astounding their groping auditors 'ob de field nigger class,' who cannot boast of such enviable accomplishments."[18]

Southern Manners

The white ethnocentrism that ridiculed black speech patterns also led the American South to overlook the way in which African culture influenced the development of the region's sense of manners and etiquette. It is doubtful that a continuation of British Cavalier ways or the Scots-Irish ethic of honor should alone account for the renowned tradition of southern politeness and grace found among the richer plantation owners, since the region's poorer whites, from whom many in the planter aristocracy arose, were so commonly stereotyped as vulgar and crude.

Instead, we should look once again to the slaves who raised the children of the southern upper class, the generations of black nurses called mammies who as Africans and scions of Africans were a people of manners, some being the only true nobility in antebellum America. The thousands of Africans, including many from aristocratic or royal families, who were taken in slavery to the Americas maintained their dignity, pride, and devotion to proper social etiquette even in bondage; it was these Africans who set the tone for generations of slave factotums to follow. Thus the daughter of Lucy, an enslaved African princess, was remembered rather typically by her family as "a born aristocrat" of "exquisite manners."[19]

The African cultural heritage was the shaping force behind what white observers claimed was the "nature" of their servants: "Negroes," said South Carolinian Elizabeth Allston Pringle, "are by nature aristocrats, and have the keenest appreciation and perception of what constitutes a gentleman." Susan Dabney Smedes of Mississippi, another planter's daughter, agreed; the blacks, she said, "are all aristocrats by nature," and "in no hands was the dignity of the family so safe as with the negro slaves."[20]

Thomas Wentworth Higginson, who commanded a Negro regiment during the Civil War, soon discovered that blacks preferred a similar dignity in their leaders. "An officer of polished manners can wind them round his finger," he reported, "while white soldiers seem rather to prefer a certain roughness. The demeanor of my men to each other is very courteous." This remarkable "courtesy of the men" and of local blacks resulted, he believed, "partly from natural good manners, partly from the habit of deference."[21] He does not seem to have considered that if black deference was partly conditional on a white man's style of leadership successful whites may have shaped their behavior, at least subconsciously, to win this respect.

Clearly, black condescension toward whites who displayed poor manners and crude ways was vital in separating southern "aristocrats" from "poor white trash," and whites of all classes knew it. Frederick Douglass illustrated this in explaining why his fellow bondsmen gave no respect to Captain Thomas Auld, who had gained his slaves only through marriage and lacked the natural disposition to command: "Slaves, too, readily distinguished between the birthright bearing of the original slaveholder, and the assumed attitudes of the accidental slaveholder; and while they could have no respect for either, they despised the latter more than the former."[22]

When northerners entered the South and failed to adjust to black ways, they found themselves, like Thomas Auld, unable to assert their potential power fully; thus Gustavus A. Ingraham on opening a small business in Atlanta in 1840 reported that the blacks "are . . . too sycophantic as a race but there are some exceptions and these are too proud to speak to a common white man like myself." Frances Butler Leigh who had grown up on a Georgia plantation had better insight into what was necessary; she reported that an aristocratic bearing was essential in commanding slaves. A white manager of a plantation had to be a gentleman, she said, to get the respect of the black workers; anything less would receive contempt.[23]

This was probably why Williamsburg blacks of 1783 pointed out to a visiting traveler the superiority of French over English manners: "Negro cooks, women waiters, and chambermaids made their courtesies with a great deal of native grace and simple elegance and were dressed neatly and cleanly. They yet recall and speak with evident delight of the politeness and gallantry of the French officers."[24]

The black bondspeople felt free to judge because they knew themselves to be a people of manners. As Fanny Kemble reported, the better class of blacks displayed an ingrained aristocracy, showing toward their erstwhile white masters "a rather courtly and affable condescension," which she attributed to "the natural turn for good manners" that she believed was "a distinctive peculiarity of Negroes."[25] By using the term "natural" the white observers were really referring to a cultural predisposition to good manners that the slaves had brought with them from Africa and which was beyond the ken of most European Americans.[26] For example, whereas Europeans in tropical Africa were disturbed by what they felt to be the public nakedness of the locals, Pieter de Marees noted that Africans, for their part, were offended by the public flatulence of their European visitors: The Africans, he reported, "are very careful not to let a Fart, if any bodie be by them; they wonder at our Netherlanders, that use it so commonly, for they cannot abide that a man should Fart before them, esteeming it to be a great shame and contempt done unto them." Given such sensitivities, we can only speculate what African slaves would have thought of activities like the gaseous mock duel contested by two Williamsburg belles and described by Anne Blair in a letter to her sister in 1768.[27]

In the early nineteenth century, southern novelist John Pendleton Kennedy described the superior quality of black manners as an anachronism, noting, "the older negroes here have—with some spice of comic mixture in it—that formal, grave and ostentatious style of manners, which belonged to the gentlemen of former days; they are profuse of bows and compliments, and very aristocratic in their way." And travelers like Lady Emmeline Stuart-Wortley, also commented on the "Chesterfieldian manners" that marked the American slave elite.[28]

But good manners were not some atavistic survival of European etiquette peculiarly attaching itself to black slaves; instead, good manners were something out of the African-American heritage which the blacks could teach many whites, as Mary Gay noted in referring to a boorish schoolteacher: "I hope he might learn in time from the negroes in return for some book learning, as they are singularly gentle and courteous in their manners." Even a modern epitome of the southern planter mentality like William Alexander Percy agreed: "It is incredible, I insist, that two such dissimilar races should live side by side with so little friction, in such comparative peace and amity. This result is due solely to good manners. The Southern Negro has the most beautiful manners in the world, and the Southern white, learning from him, I suspect, is a close second."[29]

Too often the fine manners of house servants and other proud blacks have been treated as some kind of servile obsequiousness or shameful big-house pretension. But such manners had little to do with European Americans; they were required in common black society across the Americas even when no whites were present. As Mrs. A. C. Carmichael noted from the West Indies, "the punctilio observed by negroes toward each other, is past belief of those who never witnessed it," or, as Richard Ligon sarcastically explained of class distinctions in 1657, every black "knows his better, and gives him precedence, as cows do one another, in passing through a narrow gate." Even more suggestively, the so-called obsequiousness of black slaves declined with assimilation rather than increasing—an observation recorded by William Francis Allen in describing the South Carolina Gullah: "In their manners they are very respectful and often obsequious; less obsequious, Mr. P[hilbrick] says, than formerly."[30] Therefore, a reasonable hypothesis is that the fine manners of Afro-America had far more to do with African mores than with pretensions or imitations of "whiteness."

When black slaves adopted a posture of great deference toward their masters they were not necessarily responding to the threat of physical violence. The Africans among them, at least, were aware of the proper way to greet chiefs and other great men. This was a matter of knowing correct form, not shameful loss of face. Thus Philip Fithian described how one of Robert Carter's slaves brought a complaint to his master in 1774 in an African-style posture: "An old Negro Man came with a complaint to Mr Carter. . . . The humble posture in which the old Fellow placed himself before he began moved me. . . . He sat himself down on the Floor clasp'd his Hands together, and with his face directly to Mr Carter, and then began his Narration."[31] More Americanized slaves were usually much less respectful, at least to whites.

When in 1835 J. S. Buckingham observed black slaves at their Sunday liberty in Richmond, Virginia, he remarked on their disconcertingly superior airs: "From the bowings, curtseying and greetings in the highway one might almost imagine one's self to be at Hayti and think that the coloured people had got possession of the town and held sway, while the whites were living among them by sufferance." Charlotte Forten observed similar behavior among the isolated (and therefore very African) Gullah peoples of the Sea Islands of Georgia more than a generation later:

> These people are exceedingly polite in their manner towards each other, each new arrival bowing, scraping his feet and shaking hands with the others, while there are constant greetings such as "Huddy? How's yer lady?" ("Howd'ye do? How's your wife?"). The hand-shaking is performed with the greatest possible solemnity. There is never the faintest shadow of a smile on anybody's face during this performance. The

children, too are taught to be very polite to their elders, and it is the rarest thing to hear a disrespectful word from a child to his parent, or to any grown person. They have really what the New-Englanders call "beautiful manners."[32]

Black observers agreed. Frederick Douglass, who grew up in Maryland, explained that a rigid code of manners was a necessary part of plantation life taught to all blacks by their elders:

These mechanics were called "uncles" by all the younger slaves, not because they really sustained that relationship to any, but according to plantation etiquette, as a mark of respect, due from the younger to the older slaves. . . . There is not to be found among any people a more rigid enforcement of the law of respect to elders, than they maintain. I set this down as partly constitutional with my race and partly conventional. There is no better material in the world for making a gentleman than is furnished in the African. He shows to others, and exacts for himself, all the tokens of respect which he is compelled to manifest toward his master. A young slave must approach the company of the older with hat in hand and woe betide [the youngster], if he fails to acknowledge a favor, of any sort, with the accustomed "tank ee," etc. So uniformly are good manners enforced among slaves, that I can easily detect a "bogus" fugitive by his manners.[33]

Of course, among the slave-owning elite, white children too had to toe this line of manners set by the black servants, for as a northern visitor to South Carolina noted, "In infancy the same nurse gives food and rest to her own child and to her master's; in childhood the same eye watches and the same hand alternately caresses and corrects them." White novelist William Faulkner recalled that he was taught to be "respectful to age" by his black nursemaid, who herself had been born a slave in 1840. And even into her adulthood Elizabeth Allston Pringle, an important planter's daughter, recalled one of these early lessons in manners; when she and her friends began to sing in a carriage as it rode through Charleston, the head coachman, Aleck Parker, reprimanded her stiffly: "Miss Betsy, if unna kyant behave unna self, I'll tek yu straight home! Dis ain't no conduk fu de Gubner karridge!"[34] People in the big house were polite not because house servants were mimicking their masters but because just the reverse was true; white "aristocrats" were taking their fine sense of manners from their slaves.

West and Central African cultures were cultures of shame and honor that placed particular emphasis on the formality of greetings, respect for elders and relatives, personal pride, and general good manners.[35] Consider the etiquette of the Akus described by Robert Campbell in 1859: "There is not a more affable people found any where than are the Akus. Not even Frenchmen are more scrupulous in their attention to politeness than they. Two persons, even utter strangers, hardly ever pass each other without exchanging salutations, and the greatest attention is paid to the relative social position of each in their salutations.... The young always prostrate to the aged.... They never suffer any thing to interfere with the observation of these courtesies."[36]

These values were passed on to both the white and the black children raised on the slave plantations. Thus a crucial factor in making the white southern gentleman essentially different from his Yankee kinsman was the African cultural heritage the southern planter had absorbed from infancy.

This shaping hand of "African" culture has never really been a secret among white southerners, even if the larger implications are rarely drawn out; W. J. Cash, for example, in his study of the southern mind undertaken in 1941, frankly considered the connection:

> And in this society in which the infant son of the planter was commonly suckled by a black nanny, in which gray old black men were his most loved story-tellers, in which black stalwarts were among the chiefest heroes and mentors of his boyhood, and in which his usual, often practically his only, companions until he was past the age of puberty were the black boys (and girls) of the plantation—in this society in which by far the greater number of white boys of whatever degree were more or less shaped by such companionship, and in which nearly the whole body of whites, young and old, had constantly before their eyes the example, had constantly in their ears the accent, of the Negro, the relationship between the two groups was, by the second generation at least, nothing less than organic. Negro entered into white man as profoundly as white man entered into Negro—subtly influencing every gesture, every word, every emotion and idea, every attitude.[37]

The culture of the South rested on honor and shame to the same degree that of the Yankee North depended on conscience and guilt. It is not coincidental that the African cultures from which the slaves were taken were also based on shame and honor, for the African heritage was a major contribution to the shaping of southern distinctiveness.[38]

Though southern whites were obliged to feel that slaves as a class lacked honor, that was not their opinion of the old family servants who had been closest to them. J. G. Clinkscales, for example, admitted that he learned less about manhood from his own father than from black "Unc' Essick"—"One of the best and truest and noblest men I ever knew—white or black"—and William Faulkner likewise remembered his "Mammie" as "brave, courageous, generous, gentle, and honest . . . much more brave and honest and generous than me."[39] The southern code of honor was far more a product of African-American attitudes than the social stratifications of slavery.

Like the southern aristocracy, Africans were outer-directed, placing an unusually high regard on public opinion and fearing public humiliation as the ultimate shame. It is likely that this traditional African emphasis on inducing feelings of shame rather than guilt to control behavior influenced the early upbringing that black servants gave their masters' children. The slaves, after all, were not puritanical in their Christianity, nor did they have ultimate physical power over their charges. Shame more than sin or physical punishment would have had to have been their hickory stick.

Annie Laurie Broidrick of Vicksburg, Mississippi, had an indelible memory of how her black nurse, "Mammy Harriet," corrected her behavior. When Annie wished to go into the kitchen, Mammy forbade it: "She never allowed us to go into the kitchen. That was considered extremely low taste; and she would say with an emphatic shake of her old, turbaned head, 'Nobody but niggers go in thar. Sit in de parlor wid'er book in yo'r hand like little white ladies.'" And when Annie disobeyed her own mother, Mammy likewise reproved: "But, honey, why does yer make y'r ma so mad acting like sich po'r white trash?"[40] That is, why are you acting as ignorant as a white who hasn't had the good fortune to have been educated by a black mentor?

Ironically, given their humble station, it was the black women of the big house who seemed to have been the ultimate authorities on proper behavior. After a young white woman, Minerva Cain, had grievously offended her sister, her mother rebuked her: "I should not offer my services to walk out with you . . . any more, and indeed I do not expect *your old nurse* will be anxious to go with you again. She said she was very sorry you behaved as you did. If you do not treat your brothers and sisters well you will never be respected by any one, either old or young, black or white."[41] And as Mammy saw it, improper behavior was not sinful; it was worse. It was shameful.

So much of the southern code of honor would have made perfect sense to Africans: autocratic rule, the need for revenge, the value of hospitality and gregariousness, the prestige given to eloquent oration, and the respect for ancestors. All these values were far more common in West Africa than in nearby New England. And though it is true that all cultures value certain codes of honor and that similarities between cultures do not necessarily imply connections, when the codes of southern whites seem closer to those of Africa than to those held by nearby northern whites we should at least consider that the parallels might not be coincidence. At the minimum we could say that African codes of honor reinforced, if they did not shape, the codes of behavior growing up among the southern whites.

Southern Cooking

Clearly this is also the case with southern cuisine. Cooking was another such area of southern life heavily influenced by African and African-American ways. The black women who served as the big-house cooks brought with them their African tastes for foods little appreciated in Europe but whose use now characterizes much of southern foodways: okra, black-eyed peas, collard greens, yams, sorghum, eggplant, benniseed (sesame), and watermelon. The most distinctive of southern soups, for example, are marked by their African choice of ingredients: peanut, eggplant, and gumbo.[42] Historically, purveyors of American foodstuffs symbolically recognized the black expertise in southern cooking by picturing the characters of Uncle Ben and Aunt Jemima so prominently on their products for many years.

It was far more likely a black cook who first decided to fry spicy chicken chopped into pieces than it was one of Kentucky Colonel Harland Sanders's kinsmen. Europeans traditionally favored roasting, but Africans who lacked large ovens used a common pot. Therefore, from colonial times whites sawed their meats to be prepared roasting-style in a manner quite different from the blacks who traditionally cut theirs to fit into stews, a difference that much annoyed Fanny Kemble when she moved south: "Such is the barbarous ignorance of the [black] cook . . . that I defy the most expert anatomist to pronounce on any piece (joint they cannot be called) of mutton brought to our table. . . . Remonstrances and expositions have produced no result whatever, however, but an increase of eccentricity in the chunks of sheeps' flesh placed on the table; the squares, diamonds, cubes, and rhumboids of mutton."[43]

If, however, Kemble did not care for black butchering techniques, she agreed with most southern whites about the excellence of black cooking. "Cooking," she said, "was a natural gift with them, as with Frenchmen."[44] The Georgian R. Q. Mallard agreed, noting, "if there is any one thing for which the African female intellect has a natural genius, it is for cooking." Thomas Jefferson consciously blended the French and African-American traditions by training members of his own domestic staff in France and bringing them back to the White House to introduce French (or was it African-French?) cuisine to the American political elite.[45]

So much that marks southern cooking—the pots of greens, the rice and black-eyed peas, the hush puppies, the use of okra, the heavy seasonings of Cajun cooking, the jambalayas, gumbos, pepper pots, and hoecakes—was created under the influence of African and African-American foodways.[46] Even if we rarely think of those most basic American Fourth of July picnic favorites—corn on the cob and fried chicken—as being as African-American as the accompanying watermelon, they are.

The taste for roasting ears of corn came originally from the foodways of the American Indians, and some southern whites may have adopted the custom directly. But most Europeans looked down on eating the kernels off the cob as animalistic. Africans, on the other hand, took to roasting corn after its arrival in Africa and later carried their taste for roasting ears to the West Indies and back to the southern United States, reinforcing the original Indian preference for eating corn directly on the cob.[47] Peanuts were another food originally of native American origin that came into southern foodways by way of Africa and led to the development of a variety of southern favorites, such as the peanut brittle long sold by the black "maumas" of Charleston as groundnut cakes. The southern custom of eating black-eyed peas and collard greens at the New Year to bring wealth or good luck is another cultural blending of foodways and perhaps folkways, in this case between Africa and Europe.[48]

Southern Religion

Like southern cuisine, the southern religious spirit in southern Protestantism and its more recent Pentecostal and evangelical offshoots was similarly infused and blended with an African-American style and essence. The dry preaching styles brought from Great Britain had to be emotionalized and made more melodious to appeal to illiterate slaves with their African notions of grand oratory and participatory religion. Such religious interactions between white preachers and black congregations clearly had a reinforcing if not developmental effect on the revivalist preaching of the Great Awakening of the 1740s, during which the evangelists noted with surprise the remarkable effects their new sermon styles had on blacks, young people, and women.[49]

The style of the preaching was especially important to the black listeners because African Americans, like West Africans, valued musicality and fluidity of speech as among a man's greatest personal assets. Black congregations, the Reverend George Wilson Bridges reported from Jamaica, would "scarcely give any attention to a religious speaker who [possessed] a harsh or discordant voice." This meant that white preachers who wished to receive an electrifying chorus of black responses had to emphasize tone, rhythm, and gesture in their preaching. As W. P. Harrison, a nineteenth-century church scholar, explained, "There was a peculiar unction that descended upon the preacher in the presence of these sable children of Africa. While they were not good judges of rhetoric, they were excellent judges of good preaching, and by their prayers and that peculiar magnetism which many have felt and none can explain the power of the Holy Ghost seemed often present in the preacher and hearer."[50]

When the itinerant preacher Simon Peter Richardson remarked to a Florida physician in the late 1840s on how well the Negroes in his Key West congregation sang, the doctor replied, "Yes, and how well you preach when you preach to them: Why not preach that way to the whites?" Richardson eventually became intrigued by this approach. He noticed the remarkable emotional power of a Saint Marys, Georgia, meeting among whites where he had separated the men and women and sent them to the woods to pray. The men came back "shouting" and singing where "they rounded to under the stand and continued the excitement." He likewise found the women "in rings," seated on the grass "singing" and "shouting." So great was the excitement that he "could not control the meeting, and several times tried to close it."[51]

Religious shuffling circular dances called "ring shouts" that would slowly increase in intensity into a form of near mass hysteria were the common pattern of black worship in the coastal sea islands; these "shouts" were an African-American reconciliation of African religious possession with Christian theology.[52] Richardson was at first disturbed by the practice among whites, but when he considered the increased conversions, he began to encourage shouting. He reasoned that whites could be more quickly ignited by spiritual fire if they were encouraged to shout like the blacks. To speed up the process he decided to preach first to the Negroes and "have them shout, then bring them up to the white church," consciously attempting to evangelize whites into a more emotional form of African-American Christianity.[53]

Black ministers faced the same preaching requirements, a situation that led A.M.E. Bishop Daniel Alexander Payne to complain about the excesses of less literate (and more African) preachers: "And what is more deplorable, some of our most popular and powerful preachers labor systematically to perpetuate this fanaticism. Such preachers never rest till they create an excitement that consists in shouting, jumping and dancing."[54]

White churchgoers, like white preachers, were soon moved by the more emotional and interactive nature of worship they witnessed among the blacks. The missionary George W. Moore caught this process in action when he reported from nineteenth-century South Carolina: "I have often seen Mrs. Baring [the mistress of Baring plantation], when the Negroes were singing, catch the motion of their bodies and do just as they did." In 1819 John F. Watson, commenting on the religious services of blacks—many of whom were recently arrived in Philadelphia from the South—complained that African-

Methodist shout and ring-dance practices, all-night songfests, and tunes "sung in the merry chorus-manner of the southern harvest field" had "already visibly affected the religious manners of some whites" at camp meetings.[55]

Frederick Law Olmstead discovered for himself how such imitations came about when he visited a black church in New Orleans: "Sometimes the outcries and responses were not confined to ejaculations . . . , but shouts, and groans, terrific shrieks, and indescribable expressions of ecstasy—of pleasure or agony—and even stamping, jumping, and clapping of hands were added. . . . I was once surprised to find my own muscles all stretched, as if ready for a struggle—my face glowing, and my feet stamping—having been infected unconsciously."[56]

Firsthand descriptions of this process of whites assimilating black ways are rare, but an interesting account of a Georgia camp meeting implies a great deal about how black folk religion began to shape the practice of white Protestantism in the South. In 1807 Jesse Lee, a Georgia evangelist, watched the religious enthusiasm of his meeting increase as the day became later and more blacks joined the congregation: "The first day of the meeting, we had a gentle and comfortable moving of the spirit of the Lord among us; and at night it was much more powerful than before, and the meeting was kept up all night without intermission. However, before day the white people retired, and the meeting was continued by the black people." Black enthusiasm had aroused the white preachers, and when the sun rose the white worshipers, too, returned with a new invigoration: "The next day at ten o'clock the meeting was remarkably lively, and many souls were deeply wrought upon; and at the close of the sermon there was a general cry for mercy, and before night there were a good many persons who professed to get converted. That night the meeting continued all night, both by the white and black people, and many souls were converted before day."[57]

Slowly, the same kind of shaping took place throughout the South as whites and blacks worshiped together. Thus, when the black parishioners pulled out of the Methodist churches of Charleston in 1818, a white contemporary lamented with his own emphasis: "the galleries, hitherto crowded, were almost deserted and it was a vacancy that could be *felt*. The absence of their responses and hearty songs were really felt to be a loss to those so long accustomed to hear them."[58]

Black congregations believed in responding verbally and emotionally to the "Good News," and eventually similar responses came to characterize nearly the whole range of southern Protestantism. European possession patterns of swooning trances, visions, and disability were joined by more active African ones featuring convulsive dancelike motions and even literal possession by the spirit. African beliefs about death and dying, funerals, mourning, and grave decorations also found their way into southern attitudes. Over time southern white burials became more emotional and often included such African-American customs as second funerals and grave gifts.[59] Today much of southern evangelical Protestantism moves to the strains of Gospel music and preachers shouting the Good News, punctuated with answering cries of "Amen" and "Yes, Lord." This essential oneness of southern Christianity, black and white, was produced as much by white assimilation of African-American style as by black assimilation of European doctrine and faith.[60]

In regard to those concepts of African-American folk religion that are often called superstitions, there is no doubt many of these beliefs too were passed along from black to white. As the ex-slave Ezra Adams reflected, "De white chillun has been nursed by colored women and they has told them stories 'bout hants and sich lak. So de white chillun has growed up believin' some of dat stuff 'till they natchally pass it on from generation to generation." Edward Pollard, for example, recalled learning "superstitions" from the slaves of his youth, noting that he still remembered a slave woman telling him that a little bird was the soul of a child who was killed and eaten by his parents.[61]

Georgia planter Howell Cobb warned his countrymen against this "social evil of no small magnitude," this "imbibing by [white] children of the superstitions, fears, and habits of the negroes, with whom they are necessarily, to some extent, reared." But it was not only the children who were affected. Edward Long reported that in Jamaica the white women were "narrowed" by spending too much time with "the tricks, superstitions, diversions, and profligate discourses of black servants." And many whites throughout the Americas repaired to black "doctors" for charms to improve their love lives or to injure an enemy.

George Washington Cable explained how it worked in New Orleans: "And it is not only the colored man that holds to these practices and fears. Many a white Creole gives them full credence. What wonder, when African Creoles were the nurses of so nearly all of them? Many shrewd men and women, generally colored persons, drive a trade in these charms and in oracular directions for their use or evasion; many a Creole—white as well as other tints— . . . will pay a Voodoo '*monteure*' to 'make a work,' i.e., to weave a spell."[62]

It seems likely that the South's regional interest in patent medicines was in part a result of the long African-American tradition in herbal cures and root work, both of which passed into white southern life as well as remaining active in black communities.[63]

Whether the custom of poor southern whites jumping the broomstick during informal wedding ceremonies was also related to local African-American culture or earlier British customs is unclear. In the United States, broomstick weddings were found only in the southern region where plantation masters often oversaw slave ceremonies which featured a bride and groom jumping over a broomstick.[64] If the tradition illustrates the disrespect with which some whites viewed black marriages, we should also note that it is not unlikely that the custom was also influenced by the attitudes of African slaves, who understood the nuptial significance of the broomstick in ways of their own.

In Africa brooms had a variety of sacred associations with different deities, and the southern custom as the African slaves may have originally understood it probably was related to an Americanization of the ceremonial use of the *ileeshin* (sacred broom) of Nana Bukuu, a goddess known from Nigeria to Ghana. This broom, which contained the power of fertility, was believed to be able to kill any male it touched and seems to have been used to promote fertility in Catholic rites in Brazil as well as the American South.[65] In Haiti at the end of the eighteenth century, M. L. E. Moreau de Saint-Méry reported that what irritated an African-born black man the most was to see a broom touch some portion of his body, for afterward "he remains convinced that this shortens his life." A Virginia slave, recalling her mother's recollections of such a broomstick wedding, remembered the important role of women in the ceremony. After giving his permission for the slaves to marry, the master sent the two young people to Aunt Lucy, who assembled the quarter's slaves in a circle, read a few Bible verses, and then had the couple lock arms and jump over the broomstick.[66]

Patterns of Work

If the sacred world of religion was a zone of cultural convergence, so too was the secular world of work. Throughout the South and the West Indies, the African predisposition toward the use of the hoe agriculture so familiar to black field hands from the old country shaped the local systems of farming, making the imposition of plows extremely slow despite the clear European-American preference for plowed fields. The effect of this African preference for the traditional hoe was captured in Fanny Kemble's frustration over her slave Jack's inefficiency in digging up a new flower bed for her: "I think I could have managed a spade with infinitely more efficiency, or rather less incapacity, than he displayed. Upon my expressing my amazement at his performance, he said the people here never used spades, but performed all their agricultural operations with the hoe. Their soil must be very light and their agriculture very superficial I should think."[67]

The explanation for the choice of the hoe as the chief tool was, of course, not simply in the soil (although that was part of it since hoes protect tropical soils from too rapid a rate of oxidation) but in the preferences of the African Americans who tended it.

African familiarity with rice agriculture helped create the first successful money crop for the white planters of South Carolina. Whites respected African knowledge about rice. As Beauchamp Plantagenet reported in 1648 from Virginia, where a non-African-style rice was grown, "Climate is very proper for [producing rice] as our Negroes affirme, which in their Country is most of their food." Africans knew how to clear swamps for rice fields and how to make the necessary drains from hollowed-out tree trunks; just as in Africa, Carolina rice production made use of slash-and-burn clearing, hoes rather than plows, and the African-style mortar and pestle to husk the grain. Africans may have also contributed to the open-range cattle keeping used in the Southeast, although similar patterns were brought from Somersetshire, England, and later from Spanish America. African skills in canoe making, hunting, and fishing also survived along the coast from Virginia to Louisiana and merged with Native American and European techniques to enrich the local industry. Even today the white men and boys of the Atchafalaya Basin of Louisiana speak a special *français nègre* language on their hunting and fishing expeditions that reflects the earlier African-American expertise.[68]

In much the same way African and African-American workers who built a large part of the housing in the early South blended their own traditional patterns with similar British ones to influence the southern innovations of radically lightened frames, roof coverings as structural elements, dogtrot-style joining of buildings, separation of kitchens from the main house, cabins built on a twelve-foot standard, "shotgun" houses, and broad, open front porches.[69]

Sometimes the whites themselves began taking over the African work patterns of their slaves; George Washington, for example, complained about his English overseer, a Mr. Bloxham, who, when he found it difficult to teach the blacks the English methods of farm labor, instead "slided into theirs." Mrs. Carmichael complained about the same thing on her visit to the West Indies: "I hardly ever saw a negro who could be coaxed not to do his work in his own way; and I would ask any lady resident in the West Indies, if she ever could even prevail upon her washerwoman—her own slave—not to starch every article of her wardrobe, to a degree that in England would render many things unfit for use. Even the pocket handkerchief—all are condemned to wear it in 'negro fashion.'" It is likely that Nicholas Bryor Massenburg assigned the task of basket making on his plantation to men rather than women because his African workers preferred it that way.[70]

We can see the same mechanism in operation in the naming of work horses noted by the Reverend I. E. Lowery from South Carolina: "It will be noticed that the word 'old' precedes the names of these horses. This does not signify that they were naturally old, but it was simply a designation given to them by the slaves, and the white folks accepted it and so styled the horses also."[71]

Those "old" horses lead to some interesting thoughts on the origins of southern "good ole boys," white men who are the archetypes of "cracker" or "redneck" culture; the term "ole" was out of the black tradition and seems, like the usage "ole Massa," to be an adaptation of black honorifics. In this case, as in so many others, southern whites so completely incorporated a style they copied from the blacks that we forget its African-American heritage.

The same adaptation and misunderstanding of African-American honorific patterns explain the tendency of southern whites prior to the civil rights movement to refer to older blacks generically as Aunty and Uncle instead of by their given names. White southerners were familiar with the African-American etiquette for greeting described by Monk Lewis: "among Negroes it is almost tantamount to an affront to address by the name, without affixing some term of relationship such as 'grannie,' 'uncle,' or 'cousin'" to honor the one addressed.[72] Although the custom of whites using such terms toward blacks eventually came by the late twentieth century to be considered paternalistic and demeaning, when African-American elders originally taught a sense of manners to southern children of both races the use of "Aunty" and "Uncle" was intended to give honor and to acknowledge connection.

Probably the southern penchant for honorific titles such as "Colonel" and the regional custom of addressing adults honorifically with "mister" or "Miz" attached to their first names owe much to the same source.[73] To understand the truth of the southern heritage we not only must understand that African-American traditions were sometimes twisted away from their original meanings but must also see where the customs (like our modern term "Ms") came from and what they originally meant. Otherwise, we are in danger of forgetting how African-American much of our culture is in its origins and of misunderstanding what it all means.

Masters often adopted strategies of gang labor in order to adjust to the working styles of African slaves who preferred to organize many of their tasks around labor groups, using friendly competitions and satiric work songs much as they had in Africa.[74] We can see how the outward and nominal control of the masters was counterbalanced by the choices of slaves when we examine the functioning of similar work gangs in southern prisons. In the early years, gang labor became a southern regionalism because blacks chose to work in groups as they had in Africa, not simply because whites preferred the economies of gang labor; so too black prisoners enlivened their labor with work songs because they wished to make their labor easier and more sociable, not because whites intended to ease their "hard time."[75] In these instances, as in many others, whites adapted to African-American ways because the inefficiency costs of resisting black labor preferences were too high.

Frederick Douglass had noted the black predisposition to sing while at work, and he suggested that "the natural disposition of the negro to make a noise in the world may account for the almost constant singing among them when they work." Natural, of course, equates with African in such contexts, and the African-based preference soon came to be accepted as both normal and desirable by the whites too—for as Douglass noted, "slaves were expected to sing as well as to work. A silent slave was not liked, by masters or by overseers." An insight into how this came to be can be found in Daniel Kidder's report that an attempt was once made in Brazil to quiet the streets by forbidding the songs of the black laborers, but "as a consequence," he noted, the blacks "performed little or no work; so the restriction was in a short time taken off." In fact, in the antebellum South slaves were sometimes paid to serve as song leaders to speed up work gangs.[76]

A cultural blending or syncretism of customs took place most easily when both blacks and whites saw a tradition as natural and useful to their own ends. One of the best times of the year for both races was the "southern Christmas" when masters in the big houses released slaves from work and distributed "Christmas gif'" in answer to the happy cries of expectant bondsmen who serenaded their proud owners in return. Slaveholders used these occasions to reinforce their own image of themselves as lords of the manor and beloved father figures.[77]

But the traditional southern Christmas was not just a darker version of old English customs replacing white peasants with black slaves. Nor was it precisely what the masters intended it to be. The black performers who offered songs of praise for "ole Massa" in exchange from drams of whiskey or other treats may have been paralleling aspects of British tradition, but they were also maintaining a traditional African holiday pattern—a form of "extorting" performance, praising or spoofing a great man to win a reward. Similar African patterns appeared whenever New World blacks had a holiday and were especially common in the South and Caribbean during regional John Canoe festivals.

The Musical Arts

Not only was the music of the black South recognized by white over-seers as part of the necessary work and holiday routines, it soon became a model for white patterns of performance as well. On stage such copy-ing at first had been banned as inimical to white supremacy. In 1810 the British traveler John Lambert noted that blacks were not allowed on the Charleston stage; instead, African characters were played by whites who never blackened their faces or dressed as African Americans: "This I afterwards learned," he said, "was occasioned by motives of policy, lest the negroes in Charleston should conceive, from being represented on the stage, and having their colour, dress, manners, and customs imitated by the white people, that they were very important personages."[78] But the power of culture is stronger than the power of law; whites simply could not resist a certain "blackness" they felt within themselves.

A generation later, J. Kennard commented in *Knickerbocker Magazine* on the manner in which the musical culture of the slaves was conquering that of their so-called masters:

> Who are the true rulers? The Negro poets to be sure. Do they not set the fashion, and give laws to the public taste? Let one of them in the swamps of Carolina, compose a new song, and it no sooner reaches the ear of a white amateur, than it is written down, amended (that is almost spoilt), printed and then put upon a course of rapid dissemination, to cease only with the utmost bounds of Anglo-Saxondom, perhaps with the world. Meanwhile, the poor author digs away with his hoe, utterly ignorant of his greatness.[79]

Kennard was describing the origins of the blackface minstrelsy, the most popular entertainment form of the nineteenth century. Blackface minstrelsy was a clear example of white performers taking over black southern music and black style of performance.

How this took place can be seen in the history of early minstrel performers. For example, E. P. Christy, leader of the most famous early minstrel troupe, had supervised a New Orleans ropewalk worked by slaves whose singing fascinated him, and he regularly visited Congo Square where he studied the "queer words and simple but expressive melodies" of the black musicians. Even later, when he began his career in Buffalo, he continued to trade "down-home talk," probably about his music, with One-Legged Harrison, a local black singer. Similarly, Thomas D. Rice, the originator of the famous Jim Crow characterization, took his act directly from an old black man he had seen dance in 1828. Both Rice and pioneering minstrel George Nichols also borrowed material from Old Corn Meal, a New Orleans street vendor. Much like Rice, J. W. McAndrews of Buckley's New Orleans Serenaders not only learned his most famous song and routine from a black street merchant but even bought the street musician's whole outfit—clothes, cart, and donkey—and he kept the character he thereby created, "The Watermelon Man," as part of his act for the next forty years.[80]

Billy Whitlock of the original Virginia Minstrels remembered that when he was not performing he would "steal off to some negro hut to hear the darkies sing and see them dance, taking a jug of whisky to make things merrier." Banjoist Ben Cotton, who worked Mississippi riverboats, recalled sitting with blacks in front of their cabins: "We would start the banjo twanging, and their voices would ring out in the quiet night air in their weird melodies. They did not quite understand me. I was the first white man they had seen who sang as they did; but we were brothers for the time being and were perfectly happy." When asked about a particularly beautiful tune he had just performed, Eugene Stratton, a minstrel known for his character "Whistling Coon," explained: "You see that young man over there? . . . He was a slave, and the song you have just heard was one they used to sing upon their plantation. He hummed it over to me and I have set it to music."[81]

The most important minstrelsy instruments, the banjo, tambourine, and bones, were brought to the United States from Africa. Although Europeans had already borrowed the tambourine, the banjo and bones were played almost exclusively by blacks until the 1830s when white players in the South such as the famous minstrel Joel Walker Sweeny began to take them up. Sweeny seems to have learned the banjo from slaves on his family's plantation. Then, through the teaching and playing of Sweeny and other blackface performers on the minstrelsy stage and in medicine shows, the music soon spread to mountain whites.[82]

Unfortunately, white artists in the minstrelsy and medicine shows reshaped the African-American performance style to the extent that today most Americans would find their shows offensive. Minstrels pandered the folk style of plantation slaves into a popular art form that kept much of the sound and humor of black music but demeaned and prostituted the source. The upbeat melodies remained, but the biting satire directed against whites was reversed. Performance styles were given farcical exaggeration. The minstrelsy had become a way for whites to imitate and enjoy African-American musical traditions without acknowledging African-American artistic excellence in a way that would have endangered institutions of racial oppression and exploitation that were built on myths of black inferiority.

There is a direct line between the blackface minstrelsy tradition and the white "soul music" of the South that has been characterized as American country music. Early country artists were commonly southern-born-and-bred white musicians who had begun their professional careers as imitation Negroes playing in blackface for small-time medicine or minstrel shows. Uncle Dave Macon ("The King of the Hillbillies"), Jimmie Rodgers ("The Father of Country Music"), Roy Acuff ("The King of Country Music"), Lasses White, Honey Wilds, Clarence Tom Ashley, John Carson, Hobart Smith, Dock Walsh, Bradley Kincaid, Bob Wills, and Gene Autry are prime examples of early white country artists who learned their trade while imitating and exaggerating black musical styles.[83]

But the connection between the music of the African-American South and country music is stronger than the minstrelsy experience of many of its early musicians. Early country performers never hid a more important debt to the region's black folk artists, even if the American public never fully understood the extent of the borrowing. Among the better-known white country artists who credited black musicians for teaching them to play or sing, or helping them perfect their skills, were an all-star list: Uncle Dave Macon, Dr. Humphrey Bate, Jimmie Rodgers, Hank Williams, Red Foley, Maybelle Carter, Moon Mullican ("The King of Hillbilly Piano Players"), the McGee Brothers, Bill Monroe ("The Father of Bluegrass Music"), Ike Everly, Dock Boggs, Jess Young, Riley Puckett, and Hobart Smith.[84]

Consider, for example, the "Father of Country Music," Jimmie Rodgers. So influential was Jimmie Rodgers in the developing field of country music that Ernest Tubb estimated in 1962 that 75 percent of his country contemporaries were directly or indirectly pulled into becoming entertainers by listening to Rodgers in person or on recordings. But who influenced Rodgers? It is more than coincidental that the performer of "Mule Skinner Blues," with its line "Hey little waterboy, bring that water around," worked on the Mobile and Ohio Railroad as a waterboy for black construction gangs; it was during this period that Rodgers formed his musical style, often sitting in with black "pickers" on Tenth Street in Meridian, Mississippi, and it was here that he gathered materials that he would later incorporate into his songs.

Not only was Rodgers's style of playing the guitar essentially African American, but his wife Carrie said black musicians also both taught him to play the banjo and guitar and gave him a repertoire of "darky songs" including "moaning chants and crooning lullabies." She also explained that his "peculiar caressing slurring" of words like "go" and "snow" was copied from his black mentors.

When Rodgers began his professional career as a blackface entertainer in a traveling show, he put his knowledge of African-American folk music to good use. According to Kentucky singer Cliff Carlisle who caught his act, "Jimmie reminded me more of a coloured person, or a negro, or whatever you want to call them . . . than anybody I ever saw." Later, Rodgers's famous blue yodel became distinctive among white performers because of its close association with the African-American falsetto blue note. Frederick Olmstead had first noted "Negro jodling" or what he called "the Carolina yell" among black railroad workers on his visit south in 1853. And Robert Ferris Thompson has traced African-American blues yodeling back to Kongo music and also noted its close connection in black culture with the lonesome train whistles of the southern night.[85]

Country great Hank Williams was also profoundly influenced in his youth by black street singers, especially one from Greenville, Alabama, named Rufe Payne or "Tee-tot," who taught him much of what he knew about playing guitar and capturing an audience. Hank put it more simply: "All the musical training I ever had was from him." In much the same fashion Moon Mullican, the famous "hillbilly" piano player, received his only music lessons when he was just a boy from Joe Jones, a black farmhand in Polk County, Texas; Harmonica player Dr.

Humphrey Bate learned most of his repertoire in his boyhood from an old Negro slave. And likewise Sam and Kirk McGee developed their celebrated finger-style guitar playing under the guidance of two black section workers named Stewart who taught them while taking breaks at the general store outside Nashville owned by Sam and Kirk's father.[86]

Black string music, blues, and spirituals were part of the southern air. As Red Foley recalled, "I would walk one hundred yards up the road and listen in at the Negro church and later I could hear them from the front porch . . . and then an old Negro would walk by carrying his guitar in a burlap sack . . . and I gradually learned the spirituals and the blues."[87]

White boys were often drawn into the music by hearing black men play traditional Anglo-American and African-American tunes. Mountaineer folk singer Hobart Smith, for example, recalled seeing his first guitar about the time of World War I when a black construction gang laid rails into Saltville, Virginia. Whites who already loved to play often sharpened their skills by sitting alongside more experienced black musicians just as bluegrass artist Bill Monroe did during his formative years playing with black fiddler Arnold Schultz and a variety of black laborers around western Kentucky. Banjoist Dock Boggs recalled, "there was a colored string band playing for a dance in Norton [his native town in Virginia], I stuck my head in at the door and I liked the way the banjo-player played, so I said to myself, I am going to learn to play that way."[88]

Another way black music entered the white country repertoire can be seen in the history of the Carter family singers. A. P. Carter hired Leslie Riddles, a gifted black singer and guitarist from Kingsport, Tennessee, to visit Appalachian black mining communities and listen to and learn the country tunes played by the black miners during their Saturday evening gatherings. Carter would then copy down the lyrics and tunes, and the Carter family would record the compositions as their own. Leslie Riddles also heavily shaped the guitar styling of both Maybelle and Sara Carter with African-American influences such as picking out melodies on the bass strings while strumming chords.[89]

Similarly, many of the songs recorded by Uncle Dave Macon were learned before 1900 from black musicians in McMinnville, Tennessee, where Macon grew up and later from black workers along the

Mississippi River levee. Blind guitarist Riley Puckett was unusual in specifically crediting his sources when on one of his records he introduced a tune called "Darkey's Wail" done in bottleneck style by saying, "I'm going to play for you this time a little piece which an old Southern darkey I heard play, coming down Decatur Street the other day, called 'His Good Gal Done Throwed Him Down.'"[90]

The indirect musical influences of black on white were even greater. The country banjo is, of course, an African-derived instrument. And much in the way of country guitar playing—so-called nigger pickin' in the Merle Travis style, the flat-top style of Sam McGee, or the bottleneck manner of Riley Puckett—stems directly from earlier African-American styles. Sam McGee, for example, remembered the black street musicians of his youth, whose playing influences were so strong, he recalled, that they "would just ring in my head." But he was also specifically influenced by black banjoist and guitarist Jim Sapp. The blues connections are also an integral part of country music. Indeed, Nashville's Grand Ole Opry even got its name following a moving rendition of "Pan American Blues" by early Opry artist Deford Bailey, a black harmonica player.[91]

In much the same way that country music was influenced by a strong African-American heritage, American fiddle playing and square dance calling were shaped by the African and African-American musical preferences of the innumerable black musicians who played the fiddle for most early American social gatherings, white or black. Frontier humor caught this black contribution in a tale of competition between black Cato and a musically inclined French fur trader:

> The Frenchman stole a march on the dusky musician . . . and announced to the whites that he had a violin. This was as cheering news as if a runner had come bearing tidings that Clark had captured Vincennes. This joy was short-lived because the Latin violinist could not play "Virginia" music. He only knew how to play the polite minuet, the branle, and the pavan. These were strange dance tunes to the Americans, whose taste for music was more vigorous. . . .
>
> Cato's moment had come. He had watched the unsatisfactory proceedings of the evening with grim delight. When his competitor had sacked his violin, Cato waltzed onto the floor with his battered fiddle under his chin, and blasted out a rip-roaring "toe smasher" from Old

Virginny. In a moment melancholic frontiersmen were swinging their gals through reels that were more uproarious than the mighty falls themselves.[92]

The adoption of black-influenced musical beats and looser and more pelvic dancing styles had a long history in the American South. As early as the middle of the eighteenth century, traveler Andrew Burnaby noted that Virginia whites were dancing "a jig they learned from the Negroes" (probably under the direction of a black fiddler), and a few years later Nicholas Cresswell reported witnessing a jig danced by whites "to some Negro tune." Even worse, in his eyes, was that others came, he said, and "cuts them out." This was patterned on the way that challenging black dancers entered and left their dancing circles; but for the visiting Cresswell it was "more like a Bacchanalian dance than one in polite company." In the same way, Robert Cantwell has argued that the style known in country music as "breakdown" developed out of European-style reels influenced by "the African practice of annealing rhythms to melodies." "Generally speaking," he explains, "the reel became a breakdown when the accent shifts from the third to the second and fourth beats."[93] At first, most of the musicians involved in the process were African Americans, but now the country breakdown is considered a mainstay of white folk music.

In the middle of the Civil War, Mary Chesnut confided to her diary that the honorable Senator Semmes from Louisiana entertained a house party by dancing a hoedown: "a Negro corn-shucking, heel-and-toe fling with a grapevine twist and all." Under the influence of a little liquor, the black man hidden within the white southerner was quick to come out, and over the years the one became part of the other. This imitation of black ways was a common pattern throughout the wider Americas; thus, as early as 1698 Père Labat noticed that the Creoles of Saint Domingue had been Africanized in regard to their dancing: "[The calenda] has . . . become so popular with the Spanish Creoles of America, and so much in vogue among them, that it now forms the chief of their amusements, and even into their devotions. They dance it even in their churches and in their processions, and the nuns seldom fail to dance it Christmas night."[94]

The apotheosis of the process came when the Tupelo-born Elvis

Presley began to imitate the rhythm-and-blues black music he loved; and in "covering" black tunes with toned-down white versions, Presley and other performers created rock and roll—a music whose name is based on a sexual metaphor out of black speech—a music that went on to capture America and the world.[95] This assimilation of African-American ways has always been hard for many whites to admit or accept. But as we reflect back over the past it is crucial that we not forget that although the white South, and the nation as a whole, cruelly exploited and oppressed its black population whites were not impervious to the powerful countercurrents of African-American culture.

Even during the cruel Jim Crow years of the late nineteenth and early twentieth centuries black baton-twirling performances at southern sporting events and other festivities were coming to influence the beginning of white cheerleading. Among the adoptions taken up by white twirlers was the *pose Kongo* of Central Africa and Haiti where the twirler stands left hand on hip and right hand twirling or over the heart.[96] In the same way, male drum majors took up a gravity-defying, knees-up, spine-back, cakewalking entrance onto the field. And in recent years, white cheerleaders have dispensed almost altogether with the traditional European-American cheering stance whose rigidity is reminiscent of Yale men and military drill and have begun to emphasize, instead, the swirling, provocative pelvic movements commonly associated with African-American dance.

Conclusion

Much of what made the southern way of life distinctive, and of which southern whites remain most proud—their hospitality and manners, their code of honor and aristocratic style, their gregariousness, their shaded front porches, their cooking, music, speech, and while we are at it, probably even their baton twirling, loose body posture, and rebel yell[97]—is at least partly of African-American descent.

The black cultural heritage of southern whites can be symbolized in "Dixie," the nominal national anthem of the Confederacy. The song was composed by white entertainer Dan Emmett in imitation of African-American music and was used as a "walk-around" for blackface minstrel shows; not even the word "Dixie" in the song's name is fully white, for the term derives from an African-American pronunciation of the word "Dixon," as in the Mason–Dixon Line.[98] Whether whites or blacks now wish to acknowledge it, the cultures of Afro-America and Euro-America blended; this was especially true in the South where the melting pot really worked far better than most southerners or modern social theorists have been willing to admit.

Throughout this book I have argued that to see America clearly we must expand our perspectives; we must develop a more holographic image of American culture to replace the shadowbox outline of majority history set against a darker background of minority concerns. Unfortunately, the continuing redivision of scholarly work into ethnic specialties may lead us back down the familiar path to separatism, a road we should realize is like the ones in old Hollywood sets that wind their way back into a beautiful sunset and smack into the flat backdrop of a world that never was. We have much to learn from one another; and although many of us do not like to admit it, what we have learned together has always been our greatest strength.

NOTES

CHAPTER I *Why God's Black Children Suffer*

1. Some of the material in this section of Chapter 1 first appeared in William D. Piersen, "White Cannibals, Black Martyrs: Fear, Depression, and Religious Faith as Causes of Suicide among New Slaves," *Journal of Negro History* 62, no. 2 (April 1977), 147–59. In addition to the many examples cited herein, see Bryan Edwards, *The History, Civil and Commercial, of the British Colonies in the West Indies*, 3 vols. (London, 1793–1801), 2:127 n., who offers an Ashanti example. Similar beliefs were held by Ali Eisami, a recaptive from Nigeria taken to Sierra Leone; see Phillip D. Curtin, ed., *Africa Remembered* (Madison, 1968), 215. For such beliefs in Angola, see G. A. Cavazzi, *Istorica descrizione de' tre Congo, Matamba, et Angola . . .* (Bologna, 1687), 164; John Atkins, *A Voyage to Guinea, Brazil, and the West Indies* (London, 1735), 175; and the testimony of James Frazier, in *Abridgement of the Evidence Taken before a Committee of the Whole House . . . to Consider the Slave-Trade* (hereafter cited as *Evidence of the House*), 4 vols. (London, 1789–91), 2:34.

2. Crowther is quoted in Curtin, *Africa Remembered*, 307–8. Moreover, the natural psychological depression of enslavement was intensified by a physiological depression engendered by starvation or by the dehydration often caused by dysentery; see Kenneth F. Kiple, *The Caribbean Slave* (Cambridge, 1984), 63.

3. Mungo Park, *Travels in the Interior Districts of Africa* (London, 1799), 360.

4. *Biography of Mahommah G. Baquaqua, a Native of Zoogoo, in the Interior of Africa . . . Written and Revised from His Own Words, by Samuel Moore . . .* (Detroit, 1854), as quoted in Robert Edgar Conrad, ed., *Children of God's Fire* (Princeton, 1983), 26.

5. Olaudah Equiano, *Equiano's Travels: The Interesting Narrative of the Life of Olaudah Equiano or Gustavus Vassa the African*, abridged and ed. Paul

Edwards (1789; rpt. ed., Crawley, Sussex, 1967), 25–26, 31. Likewise, on such Ibo beliefs in the late seventeenth century, see John Barbot, "A Description of the Coasts of North and South Guinea, and of Etheopia Inferior, Vulgarly Angola," in Awnsham Churchill and John Churchill, eds., *A Collection of Voyages and Travels,* 6 vols. (London, 1746), 5:327; and at the end of the eighteenth century, see Hugh Crow, *Memoirs of the Late Captain H. Crow of Liverpool . . .* (1830, rpt. ed., London, 1850), 199–200.

6. *Report of the Select Committee of the House of Lords, Appointed to Consider the Best Means which Great Britain Can Adopt for the Final Extinction of the African Slave Trade: Session 1849* (London, 1849), 163. Similarly, see the testimony of Olaudah Equiano: "I have seen some of these poor African prisoners most severely cut for attempting [to jump overboard], and hourly whipped for not eating"; *Equiano's Travels,* 27. White slavers took brutal action because they feared the consequences of doing nothing, such as when two boatloads of new slaves bound for South Carolina were said to have purposely starved themselves in 1807 out of fear that they were to be eaten; see Charles W. Elliot, *Winfield Scott* (New York, 1937), 17. For a general discussion of forced feeding aboard the slavers, see Daniel P. Mannix and Malcolm Cowley, *Black Cargoes* (New York, 1962), 119.

7. *Report of the Select Committee: Session 1849,* 163.

8. Testimony of John Barnes, *Evidence of the House,* 1:19; William Snelgrave, *A New Account of Some Parts of Guinea and the Slave Trade* (1734; rpt. ed., London, 1971), 163; William Bosman, *A New and Accurate Description of the Coast of Guinea* (1705; rpt. ed., London, 1967), 489; and Ottobah Cugoano, *Thoughts and Sentiments on the Evil of Slavery* (1787; rpt. ed., London, 1969), 9.

9. Francis Moore, *Travels into the Inland Parts of Africa* (London, 1738), in *The World Displayed; or, A Curious Collection of Voyages and Travels* (Dublin, 1779), 17:103.

10. See, for example, Reay Tannahill, *Flesh and Blood* (New York, 1975); Eli Sagan, *Human Aggression, Cannibalism, and Cultural Form* (New York, 1974). And, as W. Arens reminds us, "I soon became aware that the cannibal epithet at one time or another has been applied by someone to every human group"; *The Man-Eating Myth* (New York, 1979), 13 and passim.

11. Thomas Winterbottom, *An Account of the Native African in the Neighborhood of Sierra Leone,* 2 vols. (1803; rpt. ed., London, 1969), 1:166–67. At the same time, Winterbottom also notes that no cannibalism existed in the area of the Sierra Leone coast; "nor," he said, "is there any tradition among the natives which can prove it ever was the custom." Snelgrave, *New Account of Guinea,* 41–42, contended that the people of Ardra and Whidaw were especially frightened by what they believed to be Dahomean cannibalism. Robert

Norris, *Memoirs of the Reign of Bossa Ahadee, King of Dahomey . . . and a Short Account of the African Slave Trade* (1789; rpt. ed., London, 1968), x, 70, says the Dahomeans were not cannibals (although "they scruple not to eat a devoted victim at the public festivals") but that they falsely reproached their neighbors the Toree as such. Crow, *Memoirs of the Late Captain*, 200, relates that the Ibos regarded the Ibibios, whom he calls Quaws, as man-eaters, perhaps in part because they sharpened their teeth. This ornamental affectation was not uncommon in West and Central Africa and may have originally been designed for its terrifying effect on foreigners. In any case, it surely achieved that effect with certain foreign observers. When Richard Burton asked the Fán people (reputed cannibals) north of the Gabon River if they ate their sick and dead, he reports, "the people shouted with laughter"; Richard F. Burton, *Two Trips to Gorilla Land and the Cataracts of the Congo*, 2 vols. (London, 1876), 1:213. Arens points out that most accusations of African cannibalism were almost always secondhand and should not be taken as factual; see *Man-Eating Myth*, 83–96.

12. Mrs. A. C. Carmichael, *Domestic Manners and Social Conditions of the . . . West Indies*, 2 vols. (London, 1833), 1:314–15; and, for another example of this rumor at the Laurel Hill estate, Trinidad, see ibid., 2:171. An Ibo woman captured as an adolescent said her mother was eaten by her captors in an interior war and testified she was forced to eat her own mother's heart, ibid., 1:304. For some comparative evidence from the Ashanti and from Dahomey on the ritual of eating war captives' hearts, see T. Edward Bowdich, *Mission from Cape Coast Castle to Ashantee* (1819; rpt. ed., London, 1966), 300; John Beecham, *Ashantee and the Gold Coast* (1841; rpt. ed., New York, 1970), 211; and Norris, *Memoirs of Bossa Ahadee*, 35. In Africa local people, too, often accused foreign nations of cannibalism; as the slaver Robert Norris reported in 1789, "from the concurrent and credible testimony of those who have been at Bonny, it is well known that a Bonny man kills and eats an Audony man; and an Audony man treats a Bonny man in the same way"; *Memoirs of Bossa Ahadee*, x.

13. James M. Phillippo, *Jamaica: Its Past and Present State* (Philadelphia, 1843), 92; Edwards, *History of the West Indies*, 2:90; and John G. Stedman, *Narrative of a Five Years' Expedition against the Revolted Negroes of Surinam in Guiana on the Wild Coast of South America from the Years 1772 to 1777*, 2 vols. (1796; rpt. ed., Barre, MA, 1971), 2:367.

14. Such a speculation was first suggested by William Bosman, *New Description of Guinea*, 489.

15. Tom Havisson, *Savage Civilization* (New York, 1937), 192.

16. On the mythology of Carib cannibalism, see Richard B. Moore, "Carib 'Cannibalism': A Study in Anthropological Stereotyping," *Caribbean*

Studies 13 (Oct. 1973), 117–35. For an example of such sailors' tales at work aboard a slaver, see George Howe, "The Last Slave Ship," _Scribner's Magazine_ 8 (July 1890), 116.

17. Testimony of John Fountain, _Evidence of the House_, 1:53.

18. The widespread use of fears of alien cannibalism to keep order among new slaves is illustrated in the testimony of a girl recently purchased from the Central Sudan in the early twentieth century who reported that when her new masters camped near some nomadic Arabs they told her to keep out of their camp because those Arabs "had tails and ate human beings." See Appendix 69, Arkell Papers, Library, School of Oriental and African Studies, University of London, as quoted in Jay Spaulding, "The Business of Slavery in the Central Anglo-Egyptian Sudan, 1910–1930," _African Economic History_ 17 (1988), 37. The relatively weak Niger Delta peoples were able to keep thousands of slaves in subjugation by threatening to send recalcitrant servants to the Aro Oracle, who was believed to eat slaves. Actually, the Aros sent such victims into the Atlantic slave trade, and Basil Davidson, _The African Slave Trade_ (Boston, 1961), 212, speculates that the belief in the Oracle's cannibalism may have been transferred to belief in European cannibalism by the Igbo, who understood that the Oracle did not actually eat slaves.

19. Bowdich, _Mission to Ashantee_, 410.

20. David Livingstone, _Missionary Travels and Researches in South Africa_ (New York, 1858), 502.

21. Richard F. Burton, _A Mission to Gelele, King of Dahome_ (1864; rpt. ed., New York, 1966), 305. The rumors that white men were cannibals continued well past the European partition of Africa; see George Shepperson, "Comment," in Stanley L. Engerman and Eugene D. Genovese, eds., _Race and Slavery in the Western Hemisphere: Quantitative Studies_ (Princeton, 1975), 105; and Davidson, _African Slave Trade_, 98.

22. _The History of the Lives and Bloody Exploits of the Most Noted Pirates: Their Trials and Executions_ (New York, 1926), 159–60.

23. Wright is quoted in Curtin, _Africa Remembered_, 331.

24. Crowther is quoted in ibid., 313.

25. Louis M. J. O. de Grandpré, _Voyage à la Côte Occidentale d'Afrique, fait dans les années 1786 et 1787_, 2 vols. (Paris, 1801), 1:xi; and J. H. Bernardin de Saint-Pierre, _Voyage à l'Ile-de-France_, in _Oeuvres complètes de Jacques-Henri Bernardin de Saint-Pierre_, 12 vols. (Paris, 1818), 2:154.

26. Dr. Francisco Damiao Cosme, in Louis de Pina, ed., "Tractdo das queixas endemicas, a mais fataes nesta Conquista (Luanda, 1770)," _Studia_ 20–22 (1967), 264, as noted with other citations in Joseph C. Miller, _Way of Death_ (Madison, 1988), 4–5.

27. John Newton, _Thoughts upon the African Slave Trade_ (London, 1788),

103. For examples of captains who tried to assuage the fears of their cargo, see Crow, *Memoirs of the Late Captain,* 199–200, and Snelgrave, *New Account of Guinea,* 162–63.

28. Testimony of Thomas King, *Evidence of the House,* 1:254.

29. Equiano, *Equiano's Travels,* 31.

30. Ibid., 36.

31. James Pope-Hennessy, *Sins of the Fathers* (New York, 1967), 105–6.

32. Edwin P. Hoyt, *The Amistad Affair* (New York, 1970), 37; for a similar case, see Atkins, *Voyage to Guinea,* 175.

33. Edwards, *History of the West Indies,* 2:150–51. Such a scramble sale led some thirty new slaves to jump overboard in Kingston, Jamaica, according to Alexander Falconbridge, *An Account of the Slave Trade on the Coast of Africa* (London, 1788), 34–35. Similarly, see Equiano, *Equiano's Travels,* 32.

34. Le Page du Pratz, *The History of Louisiana* (1758; rpt. ed., New Orleans, 1949), 357–58; and M. L. E. Moreau de Saint-Méry, *Description . . . de la partie française de l'Ile Saint-Domingue,* 2 vols. (1797; rpt. ed., Paris, 1958), 1:39. Most of these tales of Africans or new slaves mistaking wine for blood come from French authors, which seems to imply that the French community involved in the Atlantic slave trade commonly knew of the African belief in white cannibalism.

35. Thomas Weston, *History of the Town of Middleboro, Massachusetts* (Boston, 1906), 101–2.

36. Arens, *Man-Eating Myth,* 12–13.

37. On the curse of Cain and Ham in folk tradition, see Lawrence W. Levine, *Black Culture and Black Consciousness* (Oxford, 1977), 84; for later racial theories, see Philip D. Curtin, *The Image of Africa,* 2 vols. (Madison, 1964), 1:227–58, 2:363–87. During his visit to Kumasi on the Gold Coast of West Africa in 1817, Thomas Edward Bowdich heard the curse-of-Ham explanation from a foreign-born Moslem, or "Moor," and then later used the story himself to justify white superiority when another Moor said "he thought God intended to change the power of white men, and give it to the blacks and Moors." Nonetheless, this biblically based story was probably not commonly known by the adherents of the local faiths of the West and Central African coastal regions. See Bowdich, *Mission to Ashantee,* 273, 413.

38. Phillis Wheatley Peters, *Poems of Phillis Wheatley* (Chapel Hill, 1966), 48. Similarly, see Jupiter Hammon, *An Address to the Negroes in the State of New York* (New York, 1787), 19; and "The African Servant's Prayer," quoted in Lindley Murray, ed., *Narratives of Colored Americans* (New York, 1877), 100–101.

39. *Memoir of Mrs. Chloe Spear, a Native of Africa, Who Was Enslaved in Childhood, and Died in Boston, January 3, 1815 . . . Aged 65 Years* (Boston, 1832),

51. The same sentiments appear in Samuel Wilson's letter of 18 May 1818 to Richard Allen regarding the need to immigrate to Sierra Leone: "Do you not know that the land where you are is not your own? Your fathers were carried into that to increase strangers' treasure, but God has turned it all to good, that you might bring the gospel into your country." Wilson is quoted in Miles Mark Fisher, *Negro Slave Songs in the United States* (1953; rpt. ed., New York, 1990), 43.

40. For the black versions of the Cain and Ham curses, see Levine, *Black Culture*, 85.

41. Theophile Conneau, *Adventures of an African Slaver* (1854; rpt. ed., New York, 1928), 153.

42. M. L. E. Moreau de Saint-Méry, *A Civilization that Perished: The Last Years of White Colonial Rule in Haiti,* ed. and trans. Ivor D. Spencer (1797; English-language ed., New York, 1985), 66.

43. This tale is retold in Eduardo Galeano, *Memory of Fire,* 3 vols. (1982; English-language ed., New York, 1985), 1:279.

44. Bosman, *New Description of Guinea,* 146–47; the Bosman version was later cited by J. H. Bernardin de Saint-Pierre, *Etudes de la Nature* (Paris, 1784), who added nothing new.

45. Bowdich, *Mission to Ashantee,* 261–62.

46. Brodie Cruickshank, *Eighteen Years on the Gold Coast of Guinea,* 2 vols. (1853; rpt. ed., London, 1966), 2:164–65. Beecham's account is simply a retelling of Bowdich's version, not a new version of the tale; see Beecham, *Ashantee and the Gold Coast,* 172–73. It is not clear whether Richard Burton was speaking from firsthand experience or from his reading when he said of the Gold Coast: "There is the usual African tradition. . . . God, say the people, made two men, one white, and the other black. To these he presented for choice a calabash full of writing materials, and another full of gold—it is needless to say how the selection was made, and what the results were"; Burton, *Two Trips to Gorilla Land,* 1:172.

47. Pieter de Marees, *Description and Historical Account of the Gold Kingdom of Guinea,* trans. and ed. Albert van Dantzig and Adam Jones (1602; rpt. ed., Oxford, 1987), 72–73.

48. Snelgrave, *New Account of Guinea,* 48.

49. Crow, *Memoirs of the Late Captain,* 129, 137. Similarly, see the comment of King Sai Tootoo Quamina of the Ashanti, who told T. E. Bowdich, "the Englishmen knew more than Dutchmen or Danes—that black men knew nothing"; Bowdich, *Mission to Ashantee,* 46. And see Thomas Phillips, "A Journal of a Voyage Made in the Hannibal of London, 1693–1694," in Churchill and Churchill, *Voyages and Travels,* 6:242.

50. Richard Price, *Alabi's World* (Baltimore, 1990), chap. 2.

51. *Periodical Accounts Relating to the Missions of the Church of the United Brethren Established among the Heathen* (London, 1790–1834), 3:425–26, as quoted in Price, *Alabi's World,* 297. See also Richard Price and Sally Price, *Two Evenings in Saramaka* (Chicago, 1990).

52. Phillippo, *Jamaica,* 188–89.

53. See, for example, William Loren Katz, *Black Indians: A Hidden Heritage* (New York, 1986). On the considerable African influence on Native American folklore from the Southeast region, see Alan Dundes, "African Tales among the North American Indians," in his *Mother Wit from the Laughing Barrel* (1973; rpt. ed., Jackson, MS, 1990), 114–25.

54. Thomas L. McKenney and James Hall, *History of the Indian Tribes of North America,* 2 vols. (Philadelphia, 1838), 2:38–39. In 1824 James Pierce was told a similar story by the chief of Sanfalasco, a Seminole town in northern peninsular Florida: "The chief informed us that according to Indian traditions, the world was created by the Great Spirit: that he formed three men, an Indian, a white and a black man; the Indian was the most perfect: They were called into his presence, and directed to select their employments; the Indian chose a bow and arrow, the white man a book, and the Negro a spade." Pierce is quoted in William C. Sturtevant, "Seminole Myths of the Origin of the Races," *Ethnohistory* 10 (1963), 80–86. On this tale, see also William G. McLoughlin, "A Note on African Sources of American Indian Racial Myths," *Journal of American Folklore* 89, no. 353 (1976), 331–35.

55. Henry C. Davis, "Negro Folk-Lore in South Carolina," *Journal of American Folklore* 27, no. 105 (1914), 244. A suspiciously similar tale lacking proper source notes is found in Stith Thompson, ed., *The Frank C. Brown Collection of North Carolina Folklore,* 5 vols. (Durham, 1952), 1:633.

56. Zora Neale Hurston, *Mules and Men* (1935; rpt. ed., Bloomington, IN, 1978), 81.

57. Gates Thomas, "South Texas Negro Work Songs," *Publications of the Texas Folklore Society* 5 (1926), 172; Thomas W. Talley, *Negro Folk Rhymes* (New York, 1922), 57. See also the discussion and citations in Levine, *Black Culture,* 249–50.

58. Thomas, "South Texas Negro Work Songs," 165; Levine, *Black Culture,* 250, cites a number of twentieth-century versions of this "nigger learns to steal" refrain. For the Asheville example, see Lawrence Gellert, "Negro Songs of Protest," in Nancy Cunard, ed., *Negro An Anthology* (New York, 1984), 229; and see also the song "Good Old Turnip Greens," quoted in Tony Russell, *Blacks, Whites, and Blues* (New York, 1970), 56.

59. Edward C. L. Adams, "Education," *Nigger to Nigger* (1928), reprinted in Edward C. L. Adams, *Tales of the Congaree* (1927; rpt. ed., Chapel Hill, 1987), 161. Since Adams was white and not above literary embellishment

of his tales, his work must be treated with some caution; nonetheless, he is considered generally reliable, and the ideas he captures here are part of an ongoing folk tradition.

60. Hurston, *Mules and Men*, 80.

61. Richard M. Dorson, *American Negro Folktales* (1956; rpt. ed., Greenwich, CT, 1967), 173.

62. Daryl Cumber Dance, *Shuckin' and Jivin'* (Bloomington, IN, 1978), 9.

63. Dorson, *American Negro Folktales*, 173; similarly, see J. Mason Brewer, *The Word on the Brazos* (1958; rpt. ed., Austin, 1976), 86–87. In the Texas version, the Jewish character is replaced by the black man's boss, "Mistuh Hawkins," as would be more fitting for the rural Brazos environment, but the basic point remains the same: The black man can't keep his wealth in a tricky white world.

64. Alex Haley, *The Autobiography of Malcolm X* (New York, 1966), 192–93.

65. Dance, *Shuckin' and Jivin'*, 154.

66. Mary A. Livermore, *The Story of My Life* (Hartford, 1897), 306–7.

67. "The Long Look," 2–3 (n.d.), Penn School Papers, vol. 1, Southern Historical Collections, as quoted in Margaret Washington Creel, *"A Peculiar People": Slave Religion and Community-Culture among the Gullahs* (New York, 1988), 260. A favorite black folk song of the early twentieth century also reflected this attitude: "White man go tuh meetin'. / Can't get up a smile; / Nigger go tuh meetin', / Boys, yuh hyeuh him shout a mile." On such black attitudes toward superior black spirituality, see Levine, *Black Culture*, 184–85.

68. Riis, *A Hundred Years: The Story of the Presbyterian Training College, Akropong*, 16.

69. Livingstone, *Missionary Travels in South Africa*, 26–27. Similarly, in the early 1700s an African-born slave told Boston's Benjamin Colman that God had taught Africans the technique of variolation for smallpox because he had already given the whites so much more knowledge and skill; Benjamin Colman, *Some Observations on the New Method of Receiving the Small Pox by Ingrafting or Inoculation* (Boston, 1721), 16.

70. It wasn't really "medicine" that kept the societies of East Africa food-sufficient before colonialism as much as it was traditional patterns of exchange relations and sharing, but the truth is that the hunger that came with the era of the white men did weaken traditional African cultures and could not be corrected once Western value systems were accepted; see James Giblin, "Famine and Social Change during the Transition to Colonial Rule in Northeastern Tanzania," *African Economic History* 15 (1986), 85–105.

71. John S. Mbiti, *African Religions and Philosophies* (New York, 1970),

65; and for similar beliefs, see Ray Huffman, *Nuer Customs and Folk-Lore* (1931; rpt. ed., New York, 1970), ix, 1.

72. Francis Mading Deng, *Africans of Two Worlds* (New Haven, 1978), 70–71.

73. Ibid., 71.

74. Ibid., 73.

75. E. J. Alagoa, "The Slave Trade in Niger Delta Oral Tradition and History," in Paul E. Lovejoy, ed., *Africans in Bondage* (Madison, 1986), 130.

76. J. C. Cotton, "Calabar Stories," *Journal of the African Society* 18 (Jan. 1906), 193–94.

77. Deng, *Africans of Two Worlds*, 76–77.

78. Veronika Gorog-Karady, "Parental Preference and Racial Inequality: An Ideological Theme in African Oral Literature," in Bernth Lindfors, ed., *Forms of Folklore in Africa* (Austin, 1977), 104–34; see also her "L'origine de l'inégalité des races; Etude de trente-sept contes africains," *Cahiers d'Etudes Africaines* 8, no. 30 (1968), 310–17.

79. R. Finnegan, *Limba Stories and Story-Telling* (Oxford, 1967), 261–63, as quoted in Gorog-Karady, "Parental Preference," 120–22.

80. Dugmore Boetie, *Familiarity Is the Kingdom of the Lost* (Greenwich, CT, 1970), 142.

81. This tale is taken from Thérèse Georgel, *Contes et légendes des Antilles* (Paris, 1963), as quoted in Michel Giraud and Jean-Luc Jamard, "Travail et servitude dans l'imaginarie antilleis: Une littérature orale en question," *L'Homme* 25, no. 4 (Oct.–Dec. 1985):83 and translated by me.

CHAPTER 2 *"Das How Dey Ketch Um"*

1. Esteban Montejo, *The Autobiography of a Runaway Slave*, ed. Miguel Barnet (New York, 1973), 16.

2. George P. Rawick, ed., *The American Slave: A Composite Autobiography*, 31 vols. (Westport, CT, 1972–77), 13, pt. 3:331.

3. Zora Neale Hurston, *Dust Tracks on a Road* (1942; rpt. ed., Urbana, IL, 1970), 200.

4. Daryl Cumber Dance, *Shuckin' and Jivin'* (Bloomington, IN, 1978), 10.

5. Richard Jones is quoted in B. A. Botkin, *Lay My Burden Down* (1945; rpt. ed., Chicago, 1958), 57.

6. Savannah Unit, Georgia Writers' Project, Work Projects Administration, *Drums and Shadows* (1940; rpt. ed., Athens, 1986), 121.

7. Crasson is quoted in Belinda Hurmence, ed., *My Folks Don't Want Me to Talk about Slavery: Twenty-one Oral Histories of Former North Carolina Slaves* (Winston-Salem, 1984), 17.

8. Robert W. Harms, *River of Wealth, River of Sorrow* (New Haven, 1981), 37.

9. Johann Wilhelm Müller, *Die afrikanische auf der quineischen Gold Cust gelegene Landschafft Fetu* (Hamburg, 1673), 151–58, as discussed in John Thornton, "Precolonial African Industry and the Atlantic Trade, 1500–1800," *African Economic History* 19 (1990–91), 18–19.

10. Henry M. Stanley, *In Darkest Africa*, 2 vols. (New York, 1890), 1:159, 1:108.

11. Rawick, *The American Slave*, 17:336.

12. Edward C. L. Adams, *Nigger to Nigger* (1928), reprinted in Edward C. L. Adams, *Tales of the Congaree* (1927; rpt. ed., Chapel Hill, 1987), 277.

13. Rawick, *The American Slave*, 2, pt. 1:122.

14. Savannah Unit, GWP, *Drums and Shadows*, 70.

15. Ibid., 175–76.

16. Ibid., 145. The legends about flying back to Africa were related to early African-American beliefs in the translation of souls back to Africa; suicides who hung themselves were said to have flown back home; see William D. Piersen, "White Cannibals, Black Martyrs: Fear, Depression, and Religious Faith as Causes of Suicide among New Slaves," *Journal of Negro History* 62, no. 2 (April 1977), 152–53.

17. Savannah Unit, GWP, *Drums and Shadows*, 164. Similarly, see the testimony of Floyd White of Saint Simons, who learned about the process of enslavement from the Ibo-born Tom Floyd: "I heah lot ub em tell how dey git obuh yuh. Dey trap em on a boat wid a red flag"; ibid., 184.

18. Harms, *River of Wealth*, 38.

19. Quoted in A. M. H. Christensen, *Afro-American Folk Lore: Told Round Cabin Fires on the Sea Islands of South Carolina* (1892; rpt. ed., New York, 1969), 4–5. Similarly, Chaney Mack, interviewed by WPA workers in the 1930s, recalled his African-born father telling him how he and his brother were hired to help load a slave ship and then were tricked into staying aboard until it was too late, but in Mack's story no red cloth was required; see James Mellon, ed., *Bullwhip Days: The Slaves Remember* (New York, 1988), 49–50.

20. James Habersham to the Countess of Huntington, Savannah, 19 April 1775, Georgia Historical Society, Savannah, *Collections*, 6:242–43. Comparatively, see William D. Piersen, *Black Yankees: The Development of an Afro-American Subculture in Eighteenth-Century New England* (Amherst, 1988), 30–31.

21. W. E. B. Du Bois, *The Souls of Black Folk* (1903; rpt. ed., New York, 1970), 72–73.

22. Solomon Northup, *Twelve Years a Slave: Narrative of Solomon Northup* (1853 ed.), in Gilbert Osofsky, ed., *Puttin' On Ole Massa* (New York,

1969), 343. And, indeed, the historian Charles Joyner found red "to be the color mentioned most commonly" in sources describing the colors of slave clothing in South Carolina; see Charles Joyner, *Down by the Riverside* (Urbana, IL, 1984), 109.

23. On the supernatural use of red in the American South, see Newbell Niles Puckett, *Folk Beliefs of the Southern Negro* (Chapel Hill, 1926), 220–21. For comparative African-American and African examples, see Martha Warren Beckwith, *Black Roadways* (Chapel Hill, 1929), 108; Victor Tuner, *The Forest of Symbols* (Ithaca, 1967), 74; Robert Brain, *Art and Society in Africa* (Hong Kong, 1980), passim; and Robert Ferris Thompson, *Flash of the Spirit* (New York, 1984), 6, 131, who notes red cloth used in "danger *minkisi*" (charms) by the Bakongo in Central Africa.

24. Frederick Douglass, *Narrative of the Life of Frederick Douglass, an American Slave* (1845; rpt. ed., New York, 1982), 84.

25. See, for example, P. E. H. Hair, "The Enslavement of Koelle's Informants," *Journal of Negro History* 6 (1965), 193–203; Paul E. Lovejoy, *Transformations in Slavery: A History of Slavery in Africa* (Cambridge, 1983), 3–4, 83–87; and Colin A. Palmer, *Human Cargoes* (Urbana, IL, 1981), 23–28. Alexander Falconbridge, who made several slaving voyages to the African coast, argued that contrary to European beliefs most Africans were indeed originally kidnapped, but the victims were then sold to a series of African merchants who passed them along to the European traders of the coast; see *An Account of the Slave Trade on the Coast of Africa* (London, 1788), 14.

26. Nicholas Owen, *Journal of a Slave Trader* (London, 1930), 37–38. In 1701, when a trader carried off a slave from Joal without paying, the local ruler took over the Royal African Company factory and confiscated the goods, which he refused to return even after the company had replaced the slave; J. M. Grey, *History of the Gambia* (London, 1966), 130.

27. Ladman is quoted in Palmer, *Human Cargoes*, 26.

28. Newton is quoted in James Pope-Hennessy, *Sins of the Fathers* (New York, 1967), 175. Englishmen were stolen openly from London streets by naval impressment gangs, and both men and women from Great Britain and Ireland were often kidnapped (or trepanned) for bond service in America. As the Maryland maidservant lamented in Ebenezer Cook's poem "Sotweed Factor," "In better times e'er to this Land / I was unhappily trepann'd." On such kidnapping of white labor, see Richard B. Morris, *Government and Labor in Early America* (New York, 1946), 338–44. On the African side, Olaudah Equiano agreed with Newton about the man-stealing of interior African traders: "This practice of kidnaping induces me to think, that notwithstanding all our strictness, their principal business among us was to trepan our people. I remember too they carried great sacks along with them, which not long after I

had opportunity of fatally seeing applied to that infamous purpose"; Olaudah Equiano, *Equiano's Travels*, abridged and ed. Paul Edwards (1789; rpt. ed., Crawley, Sussex, 1967), 7.

29. Hagar Merriman, *The Autobiography of Aunt Hagar Merriman of New Haven, Connecticut* (New Haven, 1861), 3. Gold was found on Madagascar and was commonly made into jewelry, although exploiting the gold resources was a royal monopoly; see Gwen Campbell, "Gold Mining and the French Takeover of Madagascar, 1883–1914," *African Economic History* 17 (1988), 99–100. For another New England theft tale, see the autobiography of Mrs. Nancy Prince, *A Narrative of the Life and Travels of Mrs. Nancy Prince* (Boston, 1850), 5–6, who notes: "My mother was the daughter of Tobias Wornton, who was stolen from Africa, when a lad," and "My stepfather was stolen from Africa."

30. Savannah Unit, GWP, *Drums and Shadows*, 76.

31. Ibid., 163–64; her Ibo grandfather Calina was also stolen, and a recollection of his story has already been quoted.

32. Lindley Murray, ed., *Narratives of Colored Americans* (1877; rpt. ed., Freeport, NY, 1971), 64–65.

33. Equiano, *Equiano's Travels*, 16.

34. J. B. Moreton, *West India Customs and Manners* (London, 1793), 153.

35. *Anti-Slavery Reporter*, 1 Oct. 1850, 161, as quoted in Sterling Stuckey, *Slave Culture* (New York, 1987), 177. For other examples of this tune, see Dena J. Epstein, *Sinful Tunes and Spirituals* (Urbana, IL, 1977), 177.

36. Quoted in Hans Nathan, *Dan Emmett and the Rise of Early Negro Minstrelsy* (1962; rpt. ed., Norman, OK, 1977), 33. The word "buckra" is from the Efik *mbaraka*, meaning "he who governs," and in slavery times came to mean a white man.

37. Phillis Wheatley's poems are quoted in Sidney Kaplan and Emma Nogrady Kaplan, *The Black Presence in the Era of the American Revolution* (Amherst, 1989), 171–72, 179.

38. Jedediah Dwelley and John F. Simmons, *History of the Town of Hanover, Massachusetts* (Hanover, 1910), 185.

39. For the North American slave taken originally to Jamaica, see Murray, *Narratives of Colored Americans*, 90. The Jinny Cole tale and other examples are cited in Piersen, *Black Yankees*, 106. An alternative version appeared in the personal history of Caesar, a slave of Port Royal Island, South Carolina, of whom it was said in 1863 that he "had left children in Africa when stolen away"; Edward L. Pierce, "The Freedmen at Port Royal," *Atlantic Monthly* 21 (Sept. 1863), 301.

40. Murray, *Narratives of Colored Americans*, 100–1.

41. Jeremiah Asher, *Autobiography* (Philadelphia, 1862), 2–4.

42. Alex Haley, *Roots* (New York, 1976), 126; similarly, see 18, 24, 47–49. Haley's characters explain the man-stealing in terms of the white man's cannibalism.

43. From the historian's perspective, Kunta Kinte is probably an entirely fictional character; see Donald R. Wright, "Uprooting Kunta Kinte: On the Perils of Relying on Encyclopedic Informants," *History in Africa* 8 (1981), 205–17. But, as in the case of the legends, his story was accepted as morally true nonetheless. For a general discussion of the Senegambia's role in the slave trading era, see Philip D. Curtin, *Economic Change in Precolonial Africa* (Madison, WI, 1975).

CHAPTER 3 *A Resistance Too Civilized to Notice*

1. Some of the arguments and examples in this chapter were first published in *Research in African Literatures* 7, no. 2 (1977), 166–80, and republished in Daniel J. Crowley, ed., *African Folklore in the New World* (Austin, 1977), 20–34.

2. Richard F. Burton, *Wanderings in West Africa from Liverpool to Fernando Po*, 2 vols. (London, 1863), 2:169.

3. R. S. Rattray, *Ashanti*, 2 vols. (1923; rpt. ed., Oxford, 1969), 1:153.

4. Leroy Vail and Landeg White, "Forms of Resistance: Songs and Perceptions of Power in Colonial Mozambique," *American Historical Review* 88, no. 4 (Oct. 1983), 888.

5. Ibid., 887–88.

6. Hugh Tracey, *Chopi Musicians: Their Music, Poetry, and Instruments* (New York, 1948), 3.

7. Melville J. Herskovits, *The New World Negro* (Bloomington, IN, 1969), 138.

8. Rattray, *Ashanti*, 1:151–71.

9. Ibid.

10. William Bosman, *A New and Accurate Description of the Coast of Guinea* (1705; rpt. ed., London, 1967), 158. See also John Barbot, "A Description of the Coasts of North and South Guinea, and of Etheopia Inferior, Vulgarly Angola," in Awnsham Churchill and John Churchill, eds., *A Collection of Voyages and Travels*, 6 vols. (London, 1746), 5:317.

11. John Atkins, *A Voyage to Guinea, Brazil, and the West Indies* (1735; rpt. ed., London, 1970), 53.

12. Brodie Cruickshank, *Eighteen Years on the Gold Coast of Guinea*, 2 vols. (London, 1853), 2:265–66.

13. Thomas Winterbottom, *An Account of the Native African in the Neighborhood of Sierra Leone*, 2 vols. (1803; rpt. ed., London, 1969), 1:112. A similar

description can be found in Horatio Bridge, *Journal of an African Cruiser* (New York, 1853), 16–17.

14. Winterbottom, *Account of the Native African*, 1:112.

15. Kenneth Little, *The Mende of Sierra Leone* (New York, 1967), 246–51; Oludare Olajubu, "Iwi Egungun Chants: An Introduction," in Bernth Lindfors, ed., *Forms of Folklore in Africa* (Austin, 1977), 159; and Phoebe Ottenberg, "The Afikpo Ibo of Nigeria," in James L. Gibbs, Jr., ed., *Peoples and Cultures of Africa* (New York, 1966), 14–15, 34.

16. Little, *The Mende*, 251; and M. G. Smith, "The Social Functions and Meaning of Huasa Praise-Singing," in Elliot P. Skinner, ed., *Peoples and Cultures of Africa* (Garden City, NY, 1973), 561.

17. Alan P. Merriam, "Song Texts of the Bashi," *Zaire* 8 (1954), 41; similarly, see the examples provided from the Tiv area of northern Nigeria in Elenore Smith Bowen, *Return to Laughter* (New York, 1964), 64.

18. James Pope-Hennessy, *Sins of the Fathers* (New York, 1969), 167.

19. T. Edward Bowdich, *Mission from Cape Coast Castle to Ashantee* (1819; rpt. ed., London, 1966), 59, 292. Similarly, for a more modern example, see Bowen, *Return to Laughter*, 291–92.

20. Cruickshank, *Eighteen Years on the Gold Coast*, 2:266.

21. Alfred B. Ellis, *The Tshi-Speaking Peoples of the Gold Coast of West Africa* (London, 1887), 328.

22. Hugh Clapperton, *Journal of a Second Expedition into the Interior of Africa* (1829; rpt. ed., London, 1966), 55. There continue to be Egungun maskers who specialize in lampooning the white man; see Olajubu, "Iwi Egungun Chants," 156. The tradition probably began with satirical take-offs of other African peoples such as are still practiced by the Egungun; see Margaret Thompson Drewal and Henry John Drewal, "More Powerful than Each Other: An Egbado Classification of Egungun," *African Arts* 11, no. 3 (April 1978), 35–36.

23. René Caillié, *Journal d'un voyage à Temboctou et à Jenne dans l'Afrique Centrale* (Paris, 1830), as quoted in Christopher Hibbert, *Africa Explored: Europeans in the Dark Continent, 1769–1889* (New York, 1984), 169.

24. Richard F. Burton, *A Mission to Gelele, King of Dahome* (1864; rpt. ed., New York, 1966), 130. See also his *Wanderings in West Africa*, 2:291: "Africans are uncommonly keen in perceiving and in caricaturing any ridicule."

25. Herskovits, *New World Negro*, 139.

26. Bryan Edwards, *The History, Civil and Commercial, of the British Colonies in the West Indies*, 3 vols. (London, 1793–1801), 2:103.

27. James M. Phillippo, *Jamaica: Its Past and Present State* (Philadelphia, 1843), 75.

28. Richard R. Madden, *A Twelvemonth's Residence in the West Indies during the Transition from Slavery to Apprenticeship,* 2 vols. (Philadelphia, 1835), 1:107, 2:passim.

29. Clement Caines, *The History of the General Council and General Assembly of the Leeward Islands . . .* (Saint Christopher, 1804), 110–11. The custom of "singing" someone, or being "put on the banjo" as it was sometimes called, seems closely related to the African-American custom of blacks "talking to themselves" loudly in public about personal grievances. "The negro is very fond of talking to himself or herself, or at least of publishing in the streets his private opinions on his own private affairs for the benefit of the public at large . . . to 'put it to you' whether he has been fairly dealt with. The women are particularly prone to this"; Charles William Day, *Five Years' Residence in the West Indies,* 2 vols. (London, 1852), 1:23. See also "Sketches in the West Indies," *Dublin University Magazine* 56 (Nov. 1860), 613; Rev. J. S. Scoles, *Sketches of African and Indian Life in British Guinana* (Demerara, 1885), 48; and the *Virginia Gazette,* 7 March 1777, runaway advertisement for an African woman described as "remarkable for talking to herself," in Lathan A. Windley, comp., *Runaway Slave Advertisements,* 3 vols. (Westport, CT, 1983), 1:180.

30. Robert Renny, *An History of Jamaica* (London, 1807), 241.

31. Ernst von Bibra, *Reise in Sudamerika* (Mannheim, 1854), 109–10.

32. Matthew G. Lewis, *Journal of a West India Proprietor, 1815–1817* (London, 1834), 322.

33. Jean Baptiste Dutertre, *Historie générale des Antilles habitées par les François,* 2 vols. (Paris, 1671), 2:497. It was the same for black work songs in Jamaica in the early twentieth century; see Walter Jekyll, *Jamaican Song and Story* (1907; rpt. ed., New York, 1966), 188.

34. Jean Baptiste Labat, *Nouveau voyage aux îles de l'Amérique* (La Haye, 1724), 57–58.

35. Lafcadio Hearn, *Two Years in the French West Indies* (1890; rpt. ed., Boston, 1922), 250–51. Melville Herskovits has also commented on the satire in Brazilian carnival songs; see *New World Negro,* 22.

36. J. G. F. Wurdemann, *Notes on Cuba* (Boston, 1844), 84. Satire was also connected to the calenda dance in the French West Indies; see M. L. E. Moreau de Saint-Méry, *Description . . . de la partie française de l'Ile Saint-Domingue,* 2 vols. (1797; rpt. ed., Paris, 1958), 1:44.

37. Edward Long, *The History of Jamaica,* 2 vols. (London, 1774), 2:423.

38. William Seabrook, *The Magic Island* (New York, 1929), 225–26. For an example of a white judge in New Orleans who was lampooned for the kind of dance he hosted, see George Washington Cable, "The Dance in Place Congo," in Bruce Jackson, ed., *The Negro and His Folklore* (Austin, 1967), 207.

39. Melville J. Herskovits, *Life in a Haitian Valley* (New York, 1937), 26; and Stanley J. Stein, *Vassouras: A Brazilian Coffee County, 1850–1900* (Cambridge, MA, 1957), 206–7.

40. Quoted in V. S. Naipaul, *The Loss of El Dorado* (New York, 1984), 293–94, 297.

41. Mrs. A. C. Carmichael, *Domestic Manners and Social Conditions of the . . . West Indies*, 2 vols. (London, 1833), 2:301; or see Lewis, *Journal*, 288, for the insurrectionary song of the "King of the Eboes."

42. *South Carolina Gazette*, 17 Sept. 1772, as quoted in Peter H. Wood, *Black Majority* (New York, 1974), 342.

43. Quoted in Marshall Stearns and Jean Stearns, *Jazz Dance* (New York, 1968), 22.

44. Peter Marsden, *An Account of the Island of Jamaica* (Newcastle, 1788), as quoted in Roger D. Abrahams and John F. Szwed, eds., *After Africa: Extracts from British Travel Accounts and Journals* (New Haven, 1983), 230.

45. James Stewart, *A View of the Past and Present State of the Island of Jamaica* (London, 1808), 266, as quoted in John W. Nunley and Judith Bettelheim, *Caribbean Festival Arts* (Seattle, 1988), 45.

46. Quoted in Rudi Blesh and Harriet Janis, *They All Played Ragtime* (New York, 1971), 96.

47. James R. Newhall, *History of Lynn, Essex County, Massachusetts* (Lynn, 1883), 49; see also William D. Piersen, *Black Yankees: The Development of an Afro-American Subculture in Eighteenth-Century New England* (Amherst, 1988), 137–38. Compare this to the similar report from Jamaica of Cynric R. Williams, *A Tour through the Island of Jamaica* (London, 1826), as quoted in Abrahams and Szwed, *After Africa*, 250: "The slaves sang satirical philippics against their master, communicating a little free advice now and then; but they never lost sight of decorum."

48. William Cullen Bryant, *The Life and Works of William Cullen Bryant*, ed. Parke Godwin, 6 vols. (New York, 1884), 6:26; and Harold Courlander, *The Drum and the Hoe* (Berkeley, 1960), 136.

49. Day, *Five Years' Residence*, 2:314.

50. Phillippo, *Jamaica*, 80.

51. Lyle Saxon, *Gumbo Ya-Ya* (Cambridge, 1945), 430.

52. Michael Scott, *Tom Cringle's Log* (1829–33; rpt. ed., London, 1969), 241–45, as quoted in Abrahams and Szwed, *After Africa*, 238. Roger Buckley notes that it was customary throughout the West Indies for European men to be nursed by mulatto women, who also often served as their mistresses; see Roger Norman Buckley, ed., *The Haitian Journal of Lieutenant Howard, York Hussars, 1796–1798* (Knoxville, 1985), 181.

53. Day, *Five Years' Residence*, 2:121–22. Another variant of this genre is

probably represented in the poem "Buddy Quow" (recorded in a Gullah-Jamaican dialect around the turn of the nineteenth century) in which Buddy's woman, Quasheba, gives birth to a mulatto child. See Donald R. Kloe, "Buddy Quow: An Anonymous Poem in Gullah-Jamaican Dialect Written circa 1800," *Southern Folklore Quarterly* 38, no. 2 (June 1974), 82–85, 87–88.

54. Nicholas Cresswell, *The Journal of Nicholas Cresswell* (New York, 1924), 18–19.

55. William Faux, *Memorial Days in America, Being a Journal of a Tour* (London, 1823), 195.

56. George Washington Cable, "Creole Slave Songs," in Jackson, *The Negro and His Folklore*, 239; similarly, see Trelawny Wentworth, *The West India Sketch Book*, 2 vols. (London, 1834), 2:240, 242; C. Schlichthorst, *O Rio de Janeiro como e, 1824–1826*, as quoted in Mary C. Karasch, *Slave Life in Rio de Janeiro, 1808–1850* (Princeton, 1987), 239; or Winterbottom, *Account of the Native African*, 1:112. Several good examples of satiric boat songs are noted in Dena J. Epstein, *Sinful Tunes and Spirituals* (Urbana, IL, 1977), 168–69.

57. John Lambert, *Travels through Canada, and the United States of North America, in the Years 1806, 1807, & 1808*, 2 vols. (London, 1816), 2:254.

58. See, for example, Kenneth M. Stampp, *The Peculiar Institution* (New York, 1963), 386; Lewis, *Journal*, 56; and for a similar Haitian example, see Courlander, *Drum and Hoe*, 107.

59. Harriet A. Jacobs, *Incidents in the Life of a Slave Girl* (Boston, 1861), 180–81.

60. Quoted in Norman R. Yetman, ed., *Life under the "Peculiar Institution"* (New York, 1970), 267.

61. James S. Lamar, *Recollections of Pioneer Days in Georgia* (n.p., 1928), as quoted in Roger D. Abrahams, *Singing the Master* (New York, 1992), 210.

62. Mary Ross Banks, *Bright Days on the Old Plantation* (Boston, 1882), 131.

63. Booker T. Washington, *The Story of the Negro*, 2 vols. (1904; rpt. ed., New York, 1940), 1:160.

64. Winterbottom, *Account of the Native African*, 1:112; and Melville J. Herskovits, *Trinidad Village* (New York, 1964), 278.

65. Frances Anne Kemble, *Journal of a Residence on a Georgia Plantation in 1838–1839* (1863; rpt. ed., New York, 1961), 141.

66. Frederick Douglass, *The Life and Times of Frederick Douglass* (Hartford, 1881), 181; similarly, see Saxon, *Gumbo Ya-Ya*, 450. On this topic in general, see Roger D. Abrahams, "Afro-American Worksongs on Land and Sea," in Roger D. Abrahams, Kenneth S. Goldstein, and Wayland Hand, eds., *By Land and Sea: Studies in the Folklore of Work and Leisure Honoring Horace P. Beck on His Sixty-fifth Birthday* (Hatboro, PA, 1985), 1–9.

67. Quoted in Yetman, *Life under the "Peculiar Institution,"* 113. The song appears to have been a well-known black folk song; other versions are noted in ibid., 149, and in James Mellon, ed., *Bullwhip Days: The Slaves Remember* (New York, 1988), 340.

68. Thomas Wentworth Higginson, *Army Life in a Black Regiment* (1869; rpt. ed., New York, 1984), 212, 238; the noisy complaints of the black troops eventually led Higginson to take an active part in calling for the repeal of the unjust pay differential between white and black soldiers.

CHAPTER 4   *The Aristocratic Heritage of Black America*

1. For an analysis of the ways in which Africans came to be slaves, see Paul E. Lovejoy, *Transformations in Slavery: A History of Slavery in Africa* (Cambridge, 1983), 66–87.

2. This estimation of the percentage of African Americans with royal or aristocratic blood is a very rough guess. Roland Oliver, *The African Experience* (New York, 1991), 146–48, estimates that about 2 percent of the typical population of an African state were associated with the court. Given the very large number of African royal states and the effects of polygyny, it does not seem farfetched that at least 2 percent of the slaves taken to America were also royals or aristocrats. With the black population doubling every thirty years or so, those carrying some blue blood in their veins would have been quadrupling in the same time frame, as royals married nonroyals, doubling the number of children with some royal ancestry with each doubling of the population.

3. In discussing the general topic of continued African consciousness, Herbert G. Gutman, *The Black Family in Slavery and Freedom, 1750–1925* (New York, 1976), 329–30, notes the familial connections of the African slaves behind the *Amistad* mutiny. Among them was Fakinna: "His father, Baw-nge [was] chief or king."

4. Ironically, most studies of the images of blacks in the United States have overlooked this important perception; see, for example, Jessie Carney Smith, ed., *Images of Blacks in American Culture* (New York, 1988), passim, where only Arlene Clift-Pellow recognizes this image, and even then it is only in reference to Bras Coupe, a character in a George Washington Cable novel; ibid., 150.

5. T. Edward Bowdich, *Mission from Cape Coast Castle to Ashantee* (1819; rpt. ed., London, 1966), 437. Melville J. Herskovits, *Myth of the Negro Past* (1941; rpt. ed., Boston, 1958), 66. Oliver, *African Experience*, 147–48, points out how small in size most precolonial African states were—numbering only four or five thousand citizens—and how relatively large the courts were—some one to two hundred people, many of whom were royals or aristocrats.

6. Thus it had been that Baquaqua was tricked into drinking too much and then shanghaied into bondage, eventually to be taken to Brazil. See *Biography of Mahommah G. Baquaqua, a Native of Zoogoo, in the Interior of Africa . . . Written and Revised from His Own Words, by Samuel Moore . . .* (Detroit, 1854), 34, as quoted in Robert Edgar Conrad, ed., *Children of God's Fire* (Princeton, 1983), 23–24. Similarly, see Robert Norris, *Memoirs of the Reign of Bossa Ahadee, King of Dahomy . . . and a Short Account of the African Slave Trade* (1789; rpt. ed., London, 1968), 10. See also, for example, the examination of Robert Heatley, 19 April 1788, in the Board of Trade Papers, Public Records Office, London, as quoted in Terry Alford, *Prince among Slaves* (New York, 1977), 23; Norris, *Memoirs of Bossa Ahadee,* 160; and Herskovits, *Myth of the Negro Past,* 106–7.

7. John G. Stedman, *Narrative of a Five Years' Expedition against the Revolted Negroes of Surinam in Guinana on the Wild Coast of South America from the Years 1772 to 1777,* 2 vols. (1796; rpt. ed., Barre, MA, 1971), 2:369.

8. Alonzo Lewis and James R. Newhall, *The History of Lynn* (Boston, 1865), 344; Laura E. Wilkes, "Missing Pages in American History," *The Negro Soldier* (Westport, CT, 1970), 32; J. H. Temple, *History of Framingham, Massachusetts* (Framingham, 1887), 237; Thomas F. Waters, *Ipswich in the Massachusetts Bay Colony,* 2 vols. (Ipswich, 1917), 2:219; George Sheldon, *A History of Deerfield, Massachusetts, 1636–1886,* 2 vols. (Deerfield, 1896), 2:896–97; Caroline Hazard, *College Tom* (Boston, 1893), 45; Alice Morse Earle, *In Old Narragansett: Romance and Realities* (New York, 1898), 81; Venture Smith, *Narrative of the Life of Venture Smith* (New London, 1798), 5; Esther B. Carpenter, *South County Studies* (Boston, 1924), 222–23; Charles W. Brewster, *Rambles about Portsmouth* (Portsmouth, 1859), 152; Theron W. Crissley, *History of Norfolk* (Everett, MA, 1900), 372; Orville H. Platt, "Negro Governors," in New Haven Colony Historical Society, *Proceedings* 6 (1900), 331.

9. Harriet Beecher Stowe, *Oldtown Folks* (1869; rpt. ed., New York, 1900), 52–53.

10. John Josselyn, *An Account of Two Voyages to New England Made during the Years 1638, 1663* (1674; rpt. ed., Boston, 1865), 26.

11. John R. Beard, *The Life of Toussaint L'Ouverture* (London, 1853), 24; or C. R. James, *The Black Jacobins* (New York, 1963), 19.

12. Michael Craton, *Testing the Chains: Resistance to Slavery in the British West Indies* (Ithaca, 1982), 54; similarly, see Alford, *Prince among Slaves,* 73.

13. Leslie B. Rout, Jr., *The African Experience in Spanish America* (Cambridge, 1976), 18. At other times the election of black kings was seen as threatening, such as during the *festa dos negros* in Colares near Lisbon in 1563; see A. C. De C. M. Saunders, *A Social History of Black Slaves and Freedmen in Portugal, 1441–1555* (Cambridge, 1982), 106.

14. See, for example, Gilberto Freyre, *The Masters and the Slaves* (London, 1956), 373; J. G. F. Wurdemann, *Notes on Cuba* (Boston, 1844), 114; Hugh Crow, *Memoirs of the Late Captain H. Crow of Liverpool . . .* (London, 1830), 297–99; Hubert S. Aimes, "African Institutions in America," *Journal of American Folklore* 18 (1905), 23–24; and William Dillon Piersen, "Afro-American Culture in Eighteenth-Century New England: A Comparative Examination" (Ph.D. dissertation, Indiana University, 1975), 245–46.

15. See, for example, Mungo Park, *Travels in the Interior Districts of Africa* (London, 1799), 287–98; and Douglas Grant, *The Fortunate Slave* (New York, 1968), 81. Hugh Jones, *The Present State of Virginia* (1724; rpt. ed., New York, 1865), 38; or, similarly, see Henry Koster, *Travels in Brazil*, 2 vols. (London, 1817), 2:252. Richard S. Dunn, *Sugar and Slaves* (New York, 1973), 232. S. W. Koelle, *African Native Literature* (Graz, 1963), 21; or, similarly, the testimony of Bartu, freed from the slave ship *Amistad*, as noted in Mary Cable, *Black Odyssey* (New York, 1977), 162. "The Capture and Travels of Ayuba Suleiman Ibrahima," in Philip D. Curtin, ed., *Africa Remembered* (Madison, 1968), 41. For a discussion of an ex-slave named Uncle Moreau (Omar Ibn Said), also a Fulbe and also reported to be a prince—but more likely simply the son of a very wealthy nobleman—see John W. Blassingame, ed., *Slave Testimony* (Baton Rouge, 1977), 470–74.

16. Testimony of Dr. Harrison, in *Abridgement of the Evidence Taken before a Committee of the Whole House . . . to Consider the Slave-Trade*, 4 vols. (London, 1789–91), 4:50; similarly, see the testimony of Dr. Thomas Trotter and Sir George Young, ibid., 3:81, 212. Wylie Sypher, *Guinea's Captive Kings: British Anti-slavery Literature of the XVIIIth Century* (New York, 1969), 143–44, contends that tales of noble slaves who committed suicide rather than accept the humiliation of punishment were legendary and became a set piece in antislavery literature, appearing in the poetry of Hannah More, Samuel Jackson Pratt, and even Johann Gottfried von Herder. See also James Ramsay, *An Essay on the Treatment and Conversion of African Slaves in the British Sugar Colonies* (London, 1784), 248.

17. Stedman, *Narrative of a Five Years' Expedition*, 2:369.

18. Fredericka Bremer, *The Homes of the New World*, 3 vols. (1856; rpt. ed., New York, 1868), 2:338–39. Stedman, *Narrative of a Five Years' Expedition*, 2:369. James Smith, *The Winter of 1840 in St. Croix, with an Excursion to Tortola and St. Thomas* (New York, 1840), 20–21.

19. Bremer, *Homes of the New World*, 3:142. M. L. E. Moreau de Saint-Méry, *Description . . . de la partie française de l'Ile Saint-Domingue*, 2 vols. (1797; rpt. ed., Paris, 1958), 1:30; similarly, see Alford, *Prince among Slaves*, 61. Donald Pierson, *Negroes in Brazil* (Chicago, 1942), 75; comparatively, see the

description of Uncle Dinkie in William Wells Brown, *My Southern Home* (Boston, 1880), 86.

20. Abd Rahman Ibrahima was a Fulbe prince taken into slavery to Natchez, Mississippi, in 1788; his story has been fully explored in Terry Alford's biography of him, *Prince among Slaves;* the Marschalk quotation is from ibid., 88. J. G. Flugel, "Pages from a Journal of a Voyage down the Mississippi to New Orleans in 1817," ed. Felix Flugel, *Louisiana Historical Quarterly* 7 (July 1924), 432. Elizabeth W. Allston Pringle, *Chronicles of Chicora Wood* (New York, 1922), 53–54. Similarly, J. G. Stedman reported the prince he interviewed in Surinam to have been "a remarkable goodlooking new negro"; see his *Narrative of a Five Years' Expedition*, 2:369.

21. William F. Gray, *From Virginia to Texas, 1835* (1909; rpt. ed., Houston, 1965), 159. Headmen on the Caribbean plantations often kept from two to four wives; see Bryan Edwards, *The History, Civil and Commercial, of the British Colonies in the West Indies*, 3 vols. (London, 1793–1801), 2:176; and Mrs. A. C. Carmichael, *Domestic Manners and Social Conditions of the West Indies*, 2 vols. (London, 1833), 1:182, 298.

22. Jose Honorio Rodrigues, *Brazil and Africa* (Berkeley, 1965), 43. Akawsaw Granwasa (James Albert) contends he kept his gold jewelry until it was taken from him by the captain of his slave ship; see James Albert, *A Narrative of the Most Remarkable Particulars in the Life of James Albert, Akawsaw Granwasa, as Dictated by Himself* (Catskill, NY, 1810), 25. Slaving captains handed out cheap confiscated jewelry after arriving in the Americas to lift the spirits of their slave cargo so as to improve their selling price; see Stedman, *Narrative of a Five Years' Expedition*, 1:114. At sales in Brazil, for example, newly arrived slave women often wore head kerchiefs and "some little ornaments of native seeds or shells"; see Robert Walsh, *Notices of Brazil in 1828 and 1829*, 2 vols. (London, 1830), 2:32.

23. Narrative of Ann Parker, in George P. Rawick, ed., *The American Slave: A Composite Autobiography*, 31 vols. (Westport, CT, 1972–77), 15, pt. 2:157.

24. Thomas Ewbank, *Life in Brazil* (New York, 1856), 439; similarly, see James C. Fletcher and Daniel P. Kidder, *Brazil and the Brazilians* (Boston, 1866), 135.

25. Sheldon, *History of Deerfield*, 2:897. Rawick, *The American Slave*, 15, pt. 2:156. Testimony of Robert Boucher Nicholls, *Evidence of the House*, 3:132; see also Alford, *Prince among Slaves*, 73. Charles Ball, *Fifty Years in Chains* (1858; rpt. ed., New York, 1969), 15.

26. Gray, *From Virginia to Texas*, 159; the date was 1835.

27. Pierre Verger, ed., *Les Afro-Américains*, Mémoires de l'Institut Français d'Afrique Noire, no. 27 (Dakar, 1953), 157–60.

28. Arthur Ramos, *The Negro in Brazil* (Washington, DC, 1939), 68–69.

29. Piersen, "Afro-American Culture," 211–309. Thomas R. Hazard, *Recollections of Olden Times* (Newport, 1879), 22; and Earle, *In Old Narragansett*, 81.

30. Eben D. Bassett to Orville H. Platt, as quoted in Platt, "Negro Governors," 331.

31. Lewis and Newhall, *History of Lynn*, 344; similarly, many of the Negro kings of Brazil were native African royalty; see, for example, Roger Bastide, *African Civilizations in the New World* (New York, 1971), 92.

32. Joel Munsell, ed., *Collections on the History of Albany from Its Discovery to the Present Time*, 4 vols. (Albany, 1865–71), 2:325. Walsh, *Notices of Brazil*, 2:185.

33. Robert Tallant, *Voodoo in New Orleans* (New York, 1946), 33; similarly see Cudjo, a tattooed African prince described in J. Marion Sims, *The Story of My Life* (New York, 1884), 70.

34. Olaudah Equiano, *Equiano's Travels*, abridged and ed. Paul Edwards (1789; rpt. ed., Crawley, Sussex, 1967), 2. Edwards, *History of the West Indies*, 2:127, 152, describes Esther, an Ibo woman, who had marks on her chest which she said proved her free birth and native stature.

35. Savannah Unit, Georgia Writers' Project, Work Projects Administration, *Drums and Shadows* (1940; rpt. ed., Athens, 1986), 188; similarly, ibid., 70. J. B. Cobb, *Mississippi Scenes* (Philadelphia, 1851), 173, 176.

36. Thomas Thistlewood, *Journals*, as quoted in Craton, *Testing the Chains*, 40. Julia Floyd Smith, *Slavery and Plantation Growth in Antebellum Florida, 1821–1860* (Gainesville, 1973), 33, 112–13.

37. Henry William Ravenel, "Recollections of Southern Plantation Life," *Yale Review* 25, no. 4 (June 1936), 750; similarly, Pringle, *Chronicles of Chicora Wood*, 54. Fanny Saltar, "Fanny Saltar's Reminiscences," *Pennsylvania Magazine of History and Biography* 40 (1916), 189.

38. Georges Balandier, *Daily Life in the Kingdom of the Kongo* (New York, 1969), 68. A. J. R. Russell-Wood, "Colonial Brazil," in David W. Cohen and Jack P. Greene, eds., *Neither Slave nor Free* (Baltimore, 1972), 126.

39. Ralph H. Vigil, "Negro Slaves and Rebels in the Spanish Possessions, 1503–1558," *The Historian* 33, no. 4 (Aug. 1971), 652.

40. According to palenque legend, Bioho's daughter, Princess Orika, was said to have had a fatal love affair with Francisco de Campos, a Spanish soldier sent to fight the rebels, whom she tried to rescue at the cost of both their lives; Aquiles Escalante, "El Palenque de San Basilio una comunidad negra en Colombia" (Barranquilla, 1954), as cited in Lavinia Costa Raymond, *Influence of African Culture upon South America* (Chicago, 1989), 109–10.

41. Rout, *African Experience in Spanish America,* 119.

42. David M. Davidson, "Negro Slave Control and Resistance in Colonial Mexico, 1519–1650," *Hispanic American Review* 46, no. 3 (May 1966), 247–48. The Veracruz rebellion of 1537 was also under an elected black king; see Gerald Cardoso, *Negro Slavery in the Sugar Plantations of Veracruz and Pernambuco, 1550–1680* (Washington, D.C., 1983), 52.

43. See, for example, Edison Carneiro, *O Quilombo dos Palmares* (Rio de Janeiro, 1966).

44. Albert Lamego, "O Carunkango," as cited in Cleveland Donald, Jr., "Slavery and Abolition in Campos, Brazil, 1830–1888" (Ph.D. dissertation, Cornell University, 1973), 130–31.

45. Captain Thomas Southy, *Chronological History of the West Indies,* 2 vols. (London, 1827), 2:338; similarly, see Edwards, *History of the West Indies,* 2:75. *A Genuine Narrative of the Intended Conspiracy of the Negroes at Antigua* (London, 1737), as quoted in Craton, *Testing the Chains,* 120, contends Tackey was not "as was commonly thought of Royal blood" but was "of considerable Family in his own Country."

46. Colonial Office Papers, quoted in Craton, *Testing the Chains,* 358 n.

47. Ramos, *The Negro in Brazil,* 37; Luiza Mahin was also the mother of abolitionist, politician, and journalist Luiz Gama—pen-named "Afro." Similarly, note the role of Cubah, the "Queen of Kingston," who sat in state "under a canopy, with a robe on her shoulders, and a crown upon her head." Cubah was a leader of the 1760 Jamaican slave revolt; see Craton, *Testing the Chains,* 132. Many other revolts were led by black "kings," but whether they were of royal African birth is uncertain; see, for example, the Bahia revolts of 1822, 1826, and the Salvador revolt of 1826, discussed in Howard Melvin Prince, "Slave Rebellions in Bahia, 1807–1835" (Ph.D. dissertation, Columbia University, 1972), 128, 129, 136.

48. Thomas E. Campbell, *Colonial Caroline: A History of Caroline County, Virginia* (Richmond, 1954), 71–72.

49. Le Page du Pratz, *The History of Louisiana* (1758; rpt. ed., New Orleans, 1949), 72; for greater detail, see Gwendolyn Midlo Hall, *Africans in Colonial Louisiana* (Baton Rouge, 1992), 107–10.

50. Frederick P. Bowser, *The African Slave in Colonial Peru, 1524–1650* (Stanford, 1974), 181.

51. Sypher, *Guinea's Captive Kings,* 99, 108–9; and David Brion Davis, *The Problem of Slavery in Western Culture* (Ithaca, 1966), 474–75. James Habersham to Willet Taylor, Savannah, 2 April 1764, Georgia Historical Society, Savannah, *Collections,* 6:22–23.

52. Behn is quoted in Sypher, *Guinea's Captive Kings,* 108. Oroonoko

was the subject of an illustration by Johann Heinrich Füssli sometime in the 1760s; see Hugh Honour, ed., *The Image of the Black in Western Art,* 4 vols. (Cambridge, 1989), 4, pt. 1:85.

53. See both Sypher, *Guinea's Captive Kings,* and Curtin, *Africa Remembered,* 5–6, for an introduction into the *romans africains,* as they were called in France. The same theme appeared in the abolitionist slave narratives; see the probably fictional *Life and Adventures of Zamba, an African Negro King: and His Experiences of Slavery in South Carolina, Written by Himself,* ed. Peter Nielson (London, 1847). The stereotype seems to have had influence in the United States, for when the black soldier Robert Sutton proved extremely brave during the Civil War, his white officers speculated that "he must be the descendent of some Nubian king"; see Charlotte L. Forten, *The Journal of Charlotte L. Forten* (New York, 1953), 165. For more modern examples from American literature, see Elizabeth Yates, *Amos Fortune, Free Man* (New York, 1950); Reynolds Price, "The Warrior Princess Ozimba," from his *Names and Faces of Heroes* (1963); Frank Yerby, *The Man from Dahomey* (London, 1971); and in children's literature, Scott O'Dell, *My Name Is Not Angelica* (Boston, 1989). Today the stereotype has been nearly forgotten by the man in the street, as is indicated in the rap lyrics of the Jungle Brothers, "Acknowledge Your Own History": "My forefather was a king; / He wore fat gold chains . . . ruby rings. / Nobody believes this to be true— / Maybe it's because my eyes ain't blue."

54. Victor Marie Hugo, *Bug-Jargal* (1826; rpt. ed., New York, 1896), 27.

55. [William Collins], *The Slave Trade: A Poem Written in the Year 1788* (London, 1793), as quoted in Honour, *Image of the Black,* 4, pt. 1:70.

56. Mrs. Bowdich, "The Booroom Slave," in Frederick Shoberl, ed., *Forget Me Not: A Christmas and New Year's Present for MDCCCXXVIII* (London, [1828]), 37–77.

57. Saunders, *Social History of Slaves and Freedmen,* 168.

58. Honour, *Image of the Black,* 4, pt. 1:74–75. Similarly, see the old English print *The African Prince,* in J. A. Rogers, *Sex and Race,* 3 vols. (1944; rpt. ed., Saint Petersburg, 1972), 3:73.

59. Curtin, *Africa Remembered,* 17–59.

60. This tale is recounted in Lindley Murray, ed., *Narratives of Colored Americans* (New York, 1877), 212–13.

61. Jean Baptiste Labat, *Voyages du Père Labat aux îles de l'Amérique* (1722; rpt. ed., Paris, 1956), 184–85. See also Curtin, *Africa Remembered,* 5. William Bosman, *A New and Accurate Description of the Coast of Guinea* (1705), in John R. Pinkerton, comp., *A General Collection of Voyages,* 17 vols. (London, 1812), 16:516.

62. William Snelgrave, *A New Account of Some Parts of Guinea and the Slave Trade* (1734; rpt. ed., London, 1971), 71–72.

63. Richard F. Burton, *Wanderings in West Africa from Liverpool to Fernando Po*, 2 vols. (London, 1863), 1:272–73 n.

64. Dr. Johnson is quoted in James Pope-Hennessy, *Sins of the Fathers* (New York, 1967), 20–21; see also Davis, *Problem of Slavery*, 477.

65. Brewster, *Rambles about Portsmouth*, 152; and Sidney Kaplan and Emma Nogrady Kaplan, *The Black Presence in the Era of the American Revolution* (Amherst, 1989), 50, who quote the pioneer black historian William C. Nell to the effect that Whipple was the son of "comparatively wealthy parents." Similarly, John Quamine, the son of a prosperous Fantee trader, was sent for an education for Anomabu on the Gold Coast in 1754 with a dishonest Rhode Island slaver who sold him in Newport; Ezra Stiles, *Literary Diary of Ezra Stiles*, ed. F. B. Dexter, 3 vols. (New York, 1901), 1:366.

66. Quoted in Crow, *Memoirs of the Late Captain*, 300.

67. Grandy King George is quoted in Pope-Hennessy, *Sins of the Fathers*, 218–19; similarly, see ibid., 202. Something similar probably happened to Gullah Joe, a chief's son; see Edward C. L. Adams, *Nigger to Nigger* (1928), reprinted in Edward C. L. Adams, *Tales of the Congaree* (1927; rpt. ed., Chapel Hill, 1987), 277–78.

68. Albert, *Narrative of Remarkable Particulars* (Catskill, NY, 1810, and other editions).

69. Richard R. Madden, *A Twelvemonth's Residence in the West Indies during the Transition from Slavery to Apprenticeship*, 2 vols. (Philadelphia, 1835), 2:108–10; see also 1:102 for a reference to black doctor Benjamin Cockran (Gorah Condran) whose "father was one of the lords in the Carsoe nation." Not all Europeans were so empathetic. Lieutenant Thomas Phipps Howard, who served with the British expedition to revolutionary Haiti, saw the loss of station of African princes as not so unusual: "As to the Vicicitudes of Fortune, sometimes experienced perhaps by their Chieftains & great Men, I will ask: is Africk alone the Country wherein that happens? or cannot France within these five Years shew Examples infinitely more numerous & cruel than any the Africain can complain of?" See Roger Norman Buckley, ed., *The Haitian Journal of Lieutenant Howard, York Hussars, 1796–1798* (Knoxville, 1985), 109.

70. The legendary Bras Coupe, known as the Brigand of the Swamp, was said to have been originally a slave of General William de Buys. At that time he was named Squier and was a famed Bamboula dancer. Later he became a runaway and the leader of a racially mixed robber band. Legends grew up among the blacks that he was invulnerable to wounds and a great herbalist. He was killed in 1837 near the Bayou Saint John. See Herbert Asbury, *The French Quarter* (1936; rpt. ed., Garden City, NY, 1938), 244–47.

71. George W. Cable, *The Grandissimes* (1880; rpt. ed., New York, 1903), 219–52. Cable's knowledge of African-American lore comes to the fore in his use of the voodoo curse and the belief that death brought a return to Africa. For example, fear of a voodoo oath like the one Bras Coupe put upon his master led the Ashanti to incapacitate their victims: "When a person is selected for execution, he is suddenly thrown down, and his mouth is at once skewered up with a knife to hinder him from swearing the death of any person or persons whom he might be disposed to mark out for destruction"; see John Beecham, *Ashantee and the Gold Coast* (1841; rpt. ed., New York, 1970), 222. On the translation back to Africa after death, see William D. Piersen, "White Cannibals, Black Martyrs: Fear, Depression, and Religious Faith as Causes of Suicide among New Slaves," *Journal of Negro History* 62, no. 2 (April 1977), 151–55.

72. *Gazette of the United States* (Philadelphia), 19 Aug. 1789.

73. Louise Davis, "Daddy Ben Was Hanged Three Times to Save His Master's Life," *The Tennessean* (Nashville), Nov. 1977, 74.

74. Crow, *Memoirs of the Late Captain*, 297–99.

75. Curtin, *Africa Remembered*, 17; Alford, *Prince among Slaves*, passim; Frank A. Rollin, *Martin R. Delany* (Boston, 1869), 15–17; and William J. Simmons, *Men of Mark* (Cleveland, 1887), 805.

76. Brantz Mayer, ed., *Captain Canot; or, Twenty Years of an African Slaver* (New York, 1854), 397–98. Similarly, Bowdich reports that two young sons of African rulers, who were taken to Europe to be educated, stayed in France for eight years before they returned home, where they "professed to be very anxious to return to [France], depicting the native habits not only as uncongenial, but disgusting to them"; Bowdich, *Mission to Ashantee*, 425.

77. Earle, *In Old Narragansett*, 7. In Dahomey, the Portuguese mulatto, Da Souza, traveled to Brazil to look for the deported mother of King Glele; see Herskovits, *Myth of the Negro Past*, 106.

78. Carpenter, *South County Studies*, 222–26. For other examples of folklore from African princesses, see Georgia Bryan Conrad, "Reminiscences of a Southern Woman," *Southern Workman* 30 (March 1901), 168; and Charles Seton Henry Hardee, "Reminiscences of Charles Seton Henry Hardee," *Georgia Historical Quarterly* 5 (June 1928), 159.

79. Crasson is quoted in Belinda Hurmence, ed., *My Folks Don't Want Me to Talk about Slavery: Twenty-one Oral Histories of Former North Carolina Slaves* (Winston-Salem, 1984), 19.

80. Rawick, *The American Slave*, 2, pt. 1:316. Cobb, *Mississippi Scenes*, 179; Nell S. Grayden, *Tales of Edisto* (Columbia, SC, 1955), 95. For modern examples, see E. Franklin Frazier, *The Negro Family in the United States* (Chicago, 1966), 9–13.

81. Silvio A. Bedini, *The Life of Benjamin Banneker* (New York, 1972), 17.

82. Victor Ullman, *Martin R. Delany* (Boston, 1971), 4.

83. Carter G. Woodson, *The History of the Negro Church* (Washington, DC, 1945), 155; Simmons, *Men of Mark*, 530; and for Peters, see Kaplan and Kaplan, *Black Presence in the Revolution*, 85–89.

84. W. M. Brewer, "Henry Highland Garnet," *Journal of Negro History* 13, no. 1 (Jan. 1928), 37. Robert Russa Moton, *Finding a Way Out* (Garden City, NY, 1921), 3–4.

85. Jeanne-Marie Miller, "Aldridge, Ira Frederick," in Rayford W. Logan and Michael R. Winston, eds., *Dictionary of American Negro Biography* (New York, 1982), 8–9.

86. Simmons, *Men of Mark*, 1132, 805, and (rpt. ed., New York, 1968), 323; Mungo M. Ponton, *The Life and Times of Henry M. Turner* (Atlanta, 1917), 33; Logan and Winston, *Dictionary of American Negro Biography*, 16, 609. Similarly, see John L. Jones, *History of the Jones Family* (Greenfield, OH [1930]), 9.

87. Ella Sheppard Moore, *Negro Womanhood: Its Past* (Boston, n.d.), 1.

88. William Seabrook, *The Magic Island* (1929; rpt. ed., New York, 1968), 143.

89. Logan and Winston, *Dictionary of American Negro Biography*, 545.

90. Willard B. Gatewood, *Aristocrats of Color* (Bloomington, IN, 1990), 19.

91. Logan and Winston, *Dictionary of American Negro Biography*, 674.

92. E. Franklin Frazier, *The Free Negro Family* (Nashville, 1932), 12.

93. Ibid., 13–14.

94. J. C. Furnas, *Goodbye to Uncle Tom* (New York, 1956), 373 n. Gatewood, *Aristocrats of Color*, 172.

95. Kathryn L. Morgan, "Caddy Buffers: Legends of a Middle-Class Negro Family in Philadelphia," *Keystone Folklore Quarterly* 11 (1966), 67–88, as quoted in Alan Dundes, ed., *Mother Wit from the Laughing Barrel* (1973; rpt. ed., Jackson, MS, 1990), 603.

96. Mary McLeod Bethune, "Faith that Moved a Dung Heap," *Who, the Magazine about People* 1, no. 3 (June 1941), 31–35, 54.

CHAPTER 5 *"Duh Root Doctuh Wuz All We Needed"*

1. Daniel J. Boorstin, *The Americans: The Colonial Experience* (New York, 1958), 209–27.

2. Joyce Leeson, "Traditional Medicine: Still Plenty to Offer," *Africa Report*, Oct. 1970, 25; John S. Mbiti, *African Religions and Philosophies* (New York, 1970), 217–24; Basil Davidson, *The African Genius* (Boston, 1969), 150–59; and Richard Ralston, "Medicine, Modernization, and Biculturalism in

Southern Africa" (Paper presented at the Third International Congress of Africanists, Addis Ababa, 1973), 10.

3. James L. Smith, *Autobiography of James L. Smith* (Norwich, CT, 1881), 56; similarly, see the case of the murder of the African woman Maladon described in B. W. Higman, *Slave Populations of the British Caribbean, 1807–1834* (Baltimore, 1984), 271–72.

4. Frederick Douglass, *The Life and Times of Federick Douglass* (1881; rpt. ed., Secaucus, NJ, 1983), 31.

5. Hugh Crow, *Memoirs of the Late Captain H. Crow of Liverpool . . .* (London, 1830), 227; for an American example of such an Ibo surgeon, see Savannah Unit, Georgia Writers' Project, Work Projects Administration, *Drums and Shadows* (1940; rpt. ed., Athens, 1986), 183.

6. Crow, *Memoirs of the Late Captain*, 226–27. The use of a sacrificial fowl (usually white to symbolize communication with the ancestors) was common in both African and African-American healing ceremonies; for example, George Brandon, "Sacrificial Practices in Santeria, an African-Cuban Religion in the United States," in Joseph E. Holloway, ed., *Africanisms in American Culture* (Bloomington, IN, 1990), 142.

7. Theophile Conneau, *Adventures of an African Slaver* (1854; rpt. ed., New York, 1928), 100; *Memoirs of Osifejunde of Ijebu, Nigeria*, as quoted in Philip D. Curtin, ed., *Africa Remembered* (Madison, 1968), 260–61; Jean Cuvelier, *Relations sur le Congo du père Laurent de Lucques* (1700; rpt. ed., Brussels, 1953), 131; and Phillippo Pigafetta and Oduaro Lopes, *A Report of the Kingdom of Congo . . .* (London, 1597), 32–33, 183–84; see also the comments of Dr. Hans Sloane, *A Voyage to the Islands of Madera, Barbados, Nieves, S. Christopher, and Jamaica*, 2 vols. (London, 1707), as noted in Richard S. Dunn, *Sugar and Slaves* (Chapel Hill, 1972), 309.

8. Cotton Mather, *The Angel of Bethesda*, 134, as quoted in George L. Kittredge, "Some Lost Works of Cotton Mather," Massachusetts Historical Society, *Proceedings* 45 (Feb. 1912), 431. For a wider discussion of this issue, see William D. Piersen, *Black Yankees: The Development of an Afro-American Subculture in Eighteenth-Century New England* (Amherst, 1988), 99.

9. "Colden's Letter," *American Museum* 3 (Jan. 1784), 58.

10. James Stewart, *A View of the Past and Present State of the Island of Jamaica* (1808; rpt. ed., Edinburgh, 1823), 303–4. Dr. David Mason, "A Descriptive Account of Framboesia or Yaws," *Edinburgh Medical and Surgical Journal* 35 (1831), 52–66, as quoted in Higman, *Slave Populations of the Caribbean*, 271, explained: "mothers inoculate their infants about the period of weaning, that they may be indulged in nursing them until their recovery; and many, from an African opinion and custom in that country, that children should undergo the disease at an early period of life."

11. Bryan Edwards, *The History, Civil and Commercial, of the British Colonies in the West Indies*, 3 vols. (London, 1793–1801), 2:81 n. R. S. Rattray, *The Tribes of the Ashanti Hinterland*, 2 vols. (Oxford, 1932), 1:55, 2:514. On Park's report, see Ernest Rhys, ed., *The Travels of Mungo Park* (London, 1923), 118, as quoted in Richard B. Sheridan, "The Guinea Surgeons on the Middle Passage: The Provision of Medical Services in the British Slave Trade," *International Journal of African Historical Studies* 14, no. 4 (1981), 608. Nonetheless, slavers did not seem to be aware of any greater resistance to smallpox by certain slaves; see Sheridan, "Guinea Surgeons," 601–25.

12. There is an excellent discussion of this issue in Higman, *Slave Populations of the Caribbean*, 295–98; similarly, see Mary C. Karasch, *Slave Life in Rio de Janeiro, 1808–1850* (Princeton, 1987), 138.

13. J. H. Russell, *The Free Negro in Virginia* (Baltimore, 1913), 53 n.; and Todd L. Savitt, *Medicine and Slavery* (Urbana, IL, 1978), 76. Similarly, see the *South Carolina Gazette*, 9 May 1750, as quoted in Peter H. Wood, *Black Majority* (New York, 1974), 289.

14. J. G. Stedman, *Narrative of a Five Years' Expedition against the Revolted Negroes of Surinam in Guinana on the Wild Coast of South America from the Years 1772 to 1777*, 2 vols. (1796; rpt. ed., Barre, MA, 1971), 2:409–10.

15. Le Page du Pratz, *The History of Louisiana* (1758; rpt. ed., New Orleans, 1949), 360.

16. On the history of quinine, see Henry Hobhouse, *Seeds of Change* (New York, 1985), 3–40.

17. Frederick P. Bowser, *The African Slave in Colonial Peru, 1524–1650* (Stanford, 1974), 142.

18. Richard R. Madden, *A Twelvemonth's Residence in the West Indies during the Transition from Slavery to Apprenticeship*, 2 vols. (Philadelphia, 1835), 1:99–102.

19. William Hillary, *Observations on the Changes in the Air and the Concomitant Epidemical Diseases in the Island of Barbados* (London, 1766), 341; George Pinckard, *Notes on the West Indies*, 3 vols. (London, 1806), 1:389. See also Karl Watson, "The Civilized Island: Barbados, a Social History, 1750–1816" (Ph.D. dissertation, University of Florida, 1979), 235; and W. Higman, *Slave Population and Economy in Jamaica, 1807–1834* (New York, 1977), 41.

20. Stanley J. Stein, *Vassouras: A Brazilian Coffee County, 1850–1890* (1957; rpt. ed., New York, 1970), 185; For a southern example of the treatment of snakebite by "an old woman, who doctored among the slaves," see Harriet A. Jacobs, *Incidents in the Life of a Slave Girl: Written by Herself*, ed. Jean Fagan Yellin (1861; rpt. ed., Cambridge, MA, 1987), 98–99.

21. *South Carolina Gazette*, 14 May 1750. Nearly a century later Dr. Francis P. Porcher of Charleston reported to the American Medical Associa-

tion in 1849 that the plants *Agave virginica* and *Veronica angustifolia* were "used by the negroes in South Carolina as a remedy for the bite of serpents." Porcher is quoted in Tom W. Shick, "Healing and Race in the South Carolina Low Country," in Paul E. Lovejoy, ed., *Africans in Bondage* (Madison, 1986), 111.

22. Thomas Ewbank, *Life in Brazil* (New York, 1856), 282.

23. Marie Tyler-McGraw and Gregg D. Kimball, *In Bondage and Freedom: Antebellum Black Life in Richmond, Virginia, 1790–1860* (Richmond, 1988).

24. Karasch, *Slave Life in Rio de Janeiro*, 203, and Stein, *Vassouras*, 188, 191. The key diseases of the middle passage were dysentery, fever, smallpox, ophthalmia, and diarrhea; African-trained doctors would probably do as well against these killers as the hapless European surgeons who also sometimes served aboard the slavers.

25. Charles C. Jones, *Negro Myths from the Georgia Coast* (Boston, 1888), 139–40; *Pennsylvania Gazette*, 11 Sept. 1740; Samuel Mordecai, *Richmond in By-gone Days: Being Reminiscences of an Old Citizen* (Richmond, 1856), 274–75; and Malvin E. Ring, *Dentistry: An Illustrated History* (New York, 1985), 212. For bleeding within a "hoodoo" context, see B. A. Botkin, *Lay My Burden Down* (Chicago, 1945), 33–34.

26. Pieter de Marees, *Description and Historical Account of the Gold Kingdom of Guinea*, trans. and ed. Albert van Dantzig and Adam Jones (1602; rpt. ed., Oxford, 1987), 38–39; similarly, see Richard F. Burton, *Wanderings in West Africa from Liverpool to Fernando Po*, 2 vols. (London, 1863), 2:16, 138. The practice has continued into the modern era; see Alexander Alland, Jr., *When the Spider Danced* (New York, 1975), 39, for an example from the Ivory Coast; and Ray Huffman, *Nuer Customs and Folk-Lore* (1931; rpt. ed., New York, 1970), 3.

27. M. L. E. Moreau de Saint-Méry, *Description . . . de la partie française de l'Ile Saint-Domingue*, 2 vols. (1797; rpt. ed., Paris, 1958), 1:63. Similarly, see Stedman, *Narrative of a Five Years' Expedition*, 2:374, 433. In Jamaica African Americans used *Paullinia jamaicensis* twigs called supplejacks to clean their teeth, and in Virginia they used dogwood; see H. Sloane, *The Natural History of Jamaica*, 2 vols. (London, 1707–25), 2:185, and C. F. Millspaugh, *American Medicinal Plants* (New York, 1887), 71, as quoted in Michel Laguerre, *Afro-Caribbean Folk Medicine* (South Hadley, MA, 1987), 31.

28. Robert Campbell, *A Pilgrimage to My Motherland: An Account of a Journey among the Egbas and Yorubas of Central Africa, in 1859–60*, in Howard H. Bell, ed., *A Search for a Place: Black Separatism and Africa, 1860* (Ann Arbor, 1969), 188.

29. See, for example, Ring, *Dentistry*, 141.

30. In addition to Africa, twig toothbrushes were known in this era in India, Japan, and the Middle East; see ibid., 55, 74, 93; but African-American practices would have likely had the greatest influence on changing American attitudes of the nineteenth century. On tooth decay among American slaves, see Theresa A. Singleton, "The Archaeology of Slave Life," in Edward D. C. Campbell, Jr., and Kym S. Rice, eds., *Before Freedom Came: African-American Life in the Antebellum South* (Charlottesville, VA, 1991), 173.

31. Stedman, *Narrative of a Five Years' Expedition,* 2:416.

32. Sally G. McMillen, *Motherhood in the Old South* (Baton Rouge, 1990), 79–80. Comparatively, Higman, *Slave Populations of the Caribbean,* 376, points out that conditions were similar in the West Indies, where those slaves most isolated from European medical attention survived longest. M. L. E. Moreau de Saint-Méry, *Description de l'Ile Saint-Domingue,* translated as *A Civilization that Perished* by Ivor D. Spencer (New York, 1985), 52, noted that black women of the period felt "the white man's medicines kill more" than did the medicines of black practitioners.

33. Quoted in Charles Joyner, *Down by the Riverside* (Urbana, IL, 1984), 212.

34. Drew Gilpin Faust, *James Henry Hammond and the Old South* (Baton Rouge, 1982), 77–82; the diary reference is from the Hammond Plantation Diary, 27 Oct. 1851.

35. Ulrich B. Phillips, *American Negro Slavery* (1918; rpt. ed., Baton Rouge, 1966), 323. In July of 1786 Carter sent one of his slaves who had been languishing eighteen months under Carter's own care to be doctored by William Berry's slave David, in King George County, Virginia; he also often used the services of "Old Man Doctor Lewis," a slave; see Savitt, *Medicine and Slavery,* 175; and Leslie Howard Owens, *This Species of Property* (New York, 1976), 35.

36. W. J. Titford, *Sketches towards a Hortus Botanicus Americanus* (1812), ix; and, similarly, J.K. [James Knight], "The Natural, Moral, and Political History of Jamaica . . . to the year 1742," 2:89–90, Add. MSS 12, 419, British Library, London, both quoted in Higman, *Slave Populations of the Caribbean,* 271.

37. Rebecca Hooks interview in George P. Rawick, ed., *The American Slave: A Composite Autobiography,* 31 vols. (Westport, CT, 1972–77), 25:175; similarly, see the testimony of Sally Brown, *Georgia Narratives,* in ibid., supp. ser. 1, 3, pt. 1:97–98, and Michael Craton, *Searching for the Invisible Man: Slaves and Plantation Life in Jamaica* (Cambridge, MA, 1978), 218, who notes that in Jamaica black midwifes and nurses were preferred by black patients.

38. Henry William Ravenel, "Recollections of Southern Plantation

Life," *Yale Review* 25, no. 4 (June 1936), 775–76. The distrust of white doctors seems to have been common in South Carolina; see Joyner, *Down by the Riverside*, 148.

39. Newbell Niles Puckett, *Folk Beliefs of the Southern Negro* (Chapel Hill, 1926), 385; and, similarly, see Jones, *Negro Myths*, 151.

40. T. Edward Bowdich, *Mission from Cape Coast Castle to Ashantee* (1819; rpt. ed., London, 1966), 264.

41. Rawick, *The American Slave*, 4, pt. 1:244–45.

42. Leonard E. Barrett, *Soul Force: African Heritage in Afro-American Religion* (Garden City, NY, 1974), 87–88. Comparatively, on the healing work of female doctors in colonial Colombia, see William Frederick Sharp, *Slavery on the Spanish Frontier* (Norman, OK, 1976), 137.

43. Savannah Unit, GWP, *Drums and Shadows*, 68–69.

44. Testimony of Patsy Moses, in Ronnie C. Tyler and Laurence R. Murphy, eds., *The Slave Narratives of Texas* (Austin, 1974), 88.

45. Savannah Unit, GWP, *Drums and Shadows*, 144–45, or similarly, 79.

46. Works Progress Administration, *Folklore File*, 2, no. 6 (MS, University of Virginia), as quoted in Savitt, *Medicine and Slavery*, 180. See also *Southern Agriculturalist* 1 (1829).

47. Robert Carter to Bennett Real, 15 Sept. 1781, as quoted in Owens, *This Species of Property*, 35. John Hamilton to William Hamilton, 4 Feb. 1860, as quoted in Eugene D. Genovese, *Roll, Jordan, Roll* (New York, 1976), 226; similarly, see the plantation instructions of Alexander Telfair of Savannah, Georgia, for Elsay, "doctress of the plantation," or the interview with Benjamin Fitzpatrick of Coosa River, Alabama, about his slave Mary, "physician and nurse," as noted in Phillips, *American Negro Slavery*, and Weymouth T. Jordan, *Herbs, Hoecakes, and Husbandry* (Tallahassee, 1960), 21. See the testimony of Bob Mobley, *Georgia Narratives*, in Rawick. *The American Slave*, supp. ser. 1, 4, pt. 2:337.

48. Ewbank, *Life in Brazil*, 247.

49. Thomas Bicknell, *A History of Barrington, Rhode Island* (Providence, 1898), 404; Delorain P. Corey, *The History of Malden, Massachusetts, 1633–1785* (Malden, 1899), 413, 778; William Bentley, *The Diary of William Bentley, D.D.*, 4 vols. (Gloucester, MA, 1962), 3:68; similarly, see Thomas F. De Voe, *The Market Book*, 2 vols. (New York, 1861), 1:370.

50. A. J. Oakes and M. P. Morris, "The West Indian Weedwoman of the United States Virgin Islands," *Bulletin of the History of Medicine* 32, no. 2 (March–April 1958), 164–69; and Laguerre, *Afro-Caribbean Folk Medicine*, 30. See also the interesting material in Barrett, *Soul Force*, 86–93.

51. Weymouth T. Jordan, *Ante-bellum Alabama* (Tallahassee, 1957), 77; Frances Anne Kemble, *Journal of a Residence on a Georgia Plantation in 1838–*

1839 (1863; rpt. ed., New York, 1961), 98; and Dr. Richard S. Cauthron, "A New Anti-periodic and a Substitute for Quinia," *Monthly Stethoscope* 2 (1857), 7–14, as quoted in Savitt, *Medicine and Slavery,* 174; Shick, "Healing and Race in South Carolina," 111; and, more generally, Laguerre, *Afro-Caribbean Folk Medicine,* 24, and Genovese, *Roll, Jordan, Roll,* 225.

52. Edward Long, *The History of Jamaica,* 2 vols. (London, 1774), 2:381.

53. Pascal James Imperato, *African Folk Medicine* (Baltimore, 1977), 56; Idris Andreski, *Old Wives Tales* (New York, 1971), 54; and George Schwab, *Tribes of the Liberian Hinterland,* in Papers of the Peabody Museum of American Archeology and Ethnology, Harvard University, 31 (Cambridge, MA, 1947), 385. For American examples, see Elizabeth Fox-Genovese, *Within the Plantation Household* (Chapel Hill, 1988), 169.

54. Dr. Warren Brickell of New Orleans contended in 1856 that it was almost universal for owners, overseers, and mistresses to tamper with the medical treatment of their slaves; see Walter Fisher, "Physicians and Slavery in Antebellum Southern Medical Journals," in August Meier and Elliot Rudwick, eds., *The Making of Black America* (New York, 1969), 159; and for a specific example, see Norman R. Yetman, ed., *Life under the "Peculiar Institution"* (New York, 1970), 202.

55. Edward Brathwaite, *The Development of Creole Society* (Oxford, 1971), 327; Isaac Dookhan, *A History of the Virgin Islands of the United States* (Epping, Essex, 1974), 152; Kemble, *Journal,* 71, 98; Phillips, *American Negro Slavery,* 322; Owens, *This Species of Property,* 35; Savitt, *Medicine and Slavery,* 180.

56. R. W. Gibbs, "Southern Slave Life," *De Bow's Review* 24 (April 1858), 321–24. Similarly, see other examples quoted in James O. Breeden, ed., *Advice among Masters: The Ideal in Slave Management in the Old South* (Westport, CT, 1980), 164, 169.

57. Craton, *Searching for the Invisible Man,* 130, 218; and Higman, *Slave Population in Jamaica,* 41.

58. Quoted in Karasch, *Slave Life in Rio de Janeiro,* 203.

59. Bowser, *African Slave in Colonial Peru,* 107. The first recognition of the medical properties of sarsaparilla in the English-speaking world would not be until a generation later in 1577 when knowledge of the Peruvian root was noted in Nicolas Monardes, *Joyfull News out of the New Founde Worlde* (London, 1577), 11:79, as noted in the *Oxford English Dictionary.* Later, sarsaparilla, as a diuretic, would be used to treat venereal diseases.

60. Savitt, *Medicine and Slavery,* 182; Dr. R. H. Whitfield of Gainsville, Alabama, in the *New Orleans Medical Surgical Journal* 12 (1855), 196–99, and 11 (1854), 20–21, as noted in Fisher, "Physicians and Slavery," 160; Mc-

Millen, *Motherhood in the Old South,* 70. Similarly, for the West Indies, see Craton, *Searching for the Invisible Man,* 219; Jerome S. Handler, Frederick Lange, and Robert V. Riordan, *Plantation Slavery in Barbados* (Cambridge, MA, 1978), 100.

61. W. D. Postell, *The Health of Slaves on Southern Plantations* (Baton Rouge, 1951), 112–14.

62. Kemble, *Journal,* 66, 364.

63. For criticism of black midwifes, see Long, *History of Jamaica,* 2:436; Mary Karasch, "From Porterage to Proprietorship: African Occupations in Rio de Janeiro, 1808–1850," in Stanley L. Engerman and Eugene D. Genovese, eds., *Race and Slavery in the Western Hemisphere: Quantitative Studies* (Princeton, 1975), 389; and Owens, *This Species of Property,* 35. For the statistical superiority of black midwifes, see Robert W. Fogel and Stanley L. Engerman, *Time on the Cross,* 2 vols. (Boston, 1974), 1:123; and Boorstin, *The Americans,* 1:216.

64. [Knight], "Natural, Moral, and Political History," 2:89–90; and Pinckard, *Notes on the West Indies,* 1:389.

65. Schwab, *Tribes of the Liberian Hinterland,* 184, 293.

66. Gilberto Freyre, *The Masters and the Slaves* (London, 1956), 310, 370; Richard Ligon, *A True and Exact History of the Island of Barbadoes, 1647–1650* (1653; rpt. ed., abridged, Jamaica, 1951), 43; Dunn, *Sugar and Slaves,* 72, 236; Frank W. Pitman, "Slavery in the British West India Plantations," *Journal of Negro History* 11 (Oct. 1926), 593–94; and Genovese, *Roll, Jordan, Roll,* 543.

67. Gwendolyn Midlo Hall, *Africans in Colonial Louisiana* (Baton Rouge, 1992), 126. See also, Karasch, *Slave Life in Rio de Janeiro,* 138–42.

68. Pieter de Marees is quoted in Samuel Purchas, *Purchas his Pilgrimes, in Five Books,* 6 vols. (1625; rpt. ed., Glasgow, 1905), 6:264–65; Bowdich, *Mission to Ashantee,* 318. Similarly, Burton noted that the Africans were "a cleanly race, and never passing a day—unless it be very cold—without bathing"; *Wanderings in West Africa,* 2:16, similarly, 2:291.

69. Moreau de Saint-Méry, *Description de l'Ile Saint-Domingue,* 1:63; see also Jean Baptiste Labat, *Voyages du Père Labat aux îles de l'Amérique* (1722; rpt. ed., Paris, 1956), 207.

70. Stedman, *Narrative of a Five Years' Expedition,* 1:81, 84, 90, 2:428.

71. On European and American medical knowledge of the skin and the usefulness of bathing, see Richard L. Bushman and Claudia L. Bushman, "The Early History of Cleanliness in America," *Journal of American History* 74, no. 4 (March 1988), 1222–24. Africans in the Gold Coast area also abhorred the European propensity for spitting on the ground; see Marees, *Description of Guinea,* 73.

72. Richard Price, *Alabi's World* (Baltimore, 1990), 157.

73. Quoted in Breeden, *Advice among Masters,* 156.

74. Crow, *Memoirs of the Late Captain,* 250; Alexander Falconbridge, *An Account of the Slave Trade on the Coast of Africa* (London, 1788), 51; Thomas Anburey, *Travels through the Interior Parts of America,* 2 vols. (London, 1789), 2:334; and J. P. Brissot de Warville, *New Travels in the United States of America Performed in 1788* (1791; rpt. ed., Cambridge, 1964), 281. Marees, *Description of Guinea,* 115, said natives of the Gold Coast made night fires "so that the heat of the fire may draw downwards all humidity and evil humours acquired through [exposure to rain]." However, his theory of "humours" seems more European than African.

75. Long, *History of Jamaica,* 2:510.

76. Absolom Jones and Richard Allen, *A Narrative of the Proceedings of the Black People during the Late Awful Calamity in Philadelphia in the Year 1793* (Philadelphia, 1794). Black nurses served in similar roles during the yellow fever epidemics of 1800 and 1855 in Norfolk, Virginia; in the latter case, nineteen black nurses from Charleston, South Carolina, were said to have done a superb job; see Savitt, *Medicine and Slavery,* 243.

77. Quoted in Savitt, *Medicine and Slavery,* 180–81. On "Aunt Jenny," Jane E. Wentworth, as nurse to Dartmouth students at the beginning of the nineteenth century, see William C. Nell, *The Colored Patriots of the American Revolution* (Boston, 1855), 121.

78. Roger Norman Buckley, ed., *The Haitian Journal of Lieutenant Howard, York Hussars, 1796–1798* (Knoxville, 1985), 105, 181.

79. Owens, *This Species of Property,* 35; Stein, *Vassouras,* 188 n.; Charles E. Wynes, "Dr. James Durham, Mysterious Black Physician: Man or Myth?" *Pennsylvania Magazine of History and Biography* 103, no. 3 (July 1979); Roi Ottley and William Weatherby, *The Negro in New York* (New York, 1967), 12; and Henry R. Stiles, *The History and Genealogies of Ancient Windsor, Connecticut, 1635–1891,* 2 vols. (Hartford, 1891), 1:458.

80. Adam Hodgson, *Letters from North America, Written during a Tour of the United States and Canada,* 2 vols. (London, 1824), 1:45; similarly, see Jones, *Negro Myths,* 138. Many white slave owners also sent their black servants to black doctors off the plantation; see Helen T. Catterall, ed., *Judicial Cases Concerning American Slavery and the Negro,* 5 vols. (Washington, DC, 1926), 2:520, 3:432, 460; and Kenneth M. Stampp, *The Peculiar Institution* (New York, 1963), 307. For a Jamaican example, see Craton, *Searching for the Invisible Man,* 218.

81. C. R. James, *The Black Jacobins* (New York, 1963), 94; similarly, see David Barry Gaspar, *Bondsmen & Rebels* (Baltimore, 1985), 246; Robert S. Starobin, *Denmark Vesey: Slave Conspiracy of 1822* (Englewood Cliffs, NJ,

1970), 4, 103; Frederick Douglass, *My Bondage and My Freedom* (1855; rpt. ed., New York, 1968), 236–40; and Stein, *Vassouras*, 190.

82. David J. McCord, ed., *The Statutes at Large of South Carolina*, 10 vols. (Columbia, 1837), 7:423. The same law was adopted by Georgia; see Allen D. Candler and Lucian L. Knight, eds., *The Colonial Records of the State of Georgia*, 26 vols. (Atlanta, 1904–16), 18:641–44.

83. Savitt, *Medicine and Slavery*, 175.

84. Wood, *Black Majority*, 290; Betty Wood, *Slavery in Colonial Georgia, 1730–1775* (Athens, 1984), 127; similarly, see Long, *History of Jamaica*, 2:463, or Thomas Roughley, *Jamaica Planter's Guide* (London, 1823).

85. *Charleston City Gazette and Daily Advertiser*, 22 June 1797. Welsh Neck Baptist Church Minutes, as quoted in Michael Mullin, ed., *American Negro Slavery* (Columbia, 1976), 281.

86. Rudolf Asveer Jacob van Lier, *Frontier Society* (The Hague, 1971), 83–84. In Cuba "the scarcity of formal medical services brought about a situation where the curanderos and the African healers and their pharmacopias were the only sources available to the majority of the people, black and white alike"; see Mercedes C. Sandoval, "Santeria as a Mental Health Care System: An Historical Overview," *Social Science and Medicine* 138, no. 2 (1979), 141.

87. See Caleb Perry Patterson, *The Negro in Tennessee* (Austin, 1922), 36, for a Tennessee statute of 1831 for discretionary probation; see also, comparatively, Stein, *Vassouras*, 190.

88. Roughley, *Jamaica Planter's Guide*, 45.

89. Deborah Gray White, *Ar'n't I a Woman?* (New York, 1985), 112.

90. On the practical usefulness of black folk medicine, see, for example, Bruce Jackson, "The Other Kind of Doctor: Conjure and Magic in Black American Folk Medicine," in Wayland D. Hand, ed., *American Folk Medicine* (Berkeley, 1976), 259–72.

91. Esteban Montejo, *The Autobiography of a Runaway Slave*, ed. Miguel Barnet (New York, 1973), 42.

92. Savannah Unit, GWP, *Drums and Shadows*, 65.

93. Henry Clay Bruce, *A New Man* (New York, 1855), 57–58.

94. [A. D. Galt], *Practical Medicine: Illustrated by Cases of the Most Important Diseases*, ed. John M. Galt (Philadelphia, 1843), 295–96, as quoted in Savitt, *Medicine and Slavery*, 177.

95. On herbal drugs, see Schwab, *Tribes of the Liberian Hinterland*, 383.

CHAPTER 6 *The Hidden Heritage of Mardi Gras*

1. See, for example, Gertrude Kurath, "Carnival," in Maria Leach et al., eds., *Funk & Wagnalls Standard Dictionary of Folklore, Mythology, and Legend*

(New York, 1972), 193; Lura Robinson, *It's an Old New Orleans Custom* (New York, 1948), 316 and passim; Robert Tallant, *Mardi Gras* (Garden City, 1948), passim; George Reinecke, "New Orleans Mardi Gras" (Paper presented at the annual meeting of the Association for the Anthropological Study of Play, Baton Rouge, 1983); and Samuel Kinser, *Carnival American Style* (Chicago, 1990), chap. 3.

2. The parade description is from the *Daily Crescent*, as quoted in Tallant, *Mardi Gras,* 111.

3. Quoted in Tallant, *Mardi Gras,* 113–14.

4. Frances Bever, "Mobile, Mother of Mystics," 2 (MS, Mobile Public Library, Local History Collection, Mobile); Bennett Wayne Dean, *Mardi Gras: Mobile's Illogical Whoop-De-Doo* (Mobile, 1971), 14–19; and Julian Lee Rayford, *Chasin' the Devil Round a Stump* (Mobile, 1962), passim.

5. Tallant, *Mardi Gras,* 113–14.

6. Kinser, *Carnival American Style,* 80–81, 88–89.

7. There are a number of varying traditions about the origin of the Cowbellions, but there is general agreement about much of the story; see Dean, *Mardi Gras,* 14–19; and Rayford, *Chasin' the Devil,* 1–64.

8. Dean, *Mardi Gras,* 17.

9. Kinser, *Carnival American Style,* 80–81, 86–87.

10. Susan Davis, *Parades and Power: Street Theater in Nineteenth-Century Philadelphia* (Philadelphia, 1986), 105, as quoted in Kinser, *Carnival American Style,* 81.

11. Krafft was supposed to have responded to a friend's question, "Hello, Mike, what society is this?" by replying, "This, this is the Cowbellion de Rakin Society." It is an unlikely question and probably legendary rather than historical. More likely would have been a question like "Hello, Mike, what are you doing?" and a reply something humorous like "This cowbellion doin' de rakin.'" Whatever the case of the original reply, it must have seemed funny enough that those who formed the secret society based upon it called themselves the "Cowbellion de Rakin."

12. Michael Scott, *Tom Cringle's Log* (1829–33; rpt. ed., London, 1969), 241–42.

13. Harriet Elizabeth Amos, "Social Life in an Antebellum Port: Mobile, Alabama, 1820–1860" (Ph.D. dissertation, Emory University, 1976), 186.

14. Hans Sloane, *A Voyage to the Islands of Madera, Barbados, Nieves, S. Christopher, and Jamaica,* 2 vols. (London, 1707), 1:xlviii–xlix.

15. Lafcadio Hearn, "The Scenes of Cable's Romances," *Century Magazine* 27 (1883–84), 45; and Herbert Asbury, *The French Quarter* (New York, 1936), 244.

16. Edward Warren, *A Doctor's Experiences on Three Continents* (Baltimore, 1885), 201.

17. Rayford, *Chasin' the Devil*, 65.

18. Matthew G. Lewis, *Journal of a West India Proprietor, 1815–1817* (London, 1834), 27; and Leon Beauvallet, *Rachel and the New World* (1856; rpt. ed., New York, 1967), 193; see also James Kelly, *Voyage to Jamaica* (Belfast, 1838), 20–21; Charles William Day, *Five Years' Residence in the West Indies*, 2 vols. (London, 1852), 1:289; and Richard F. Burton, *A Mission to Gelele, King of Dahome* (1864; rpt. ed., New York, 1966), 196, 215.

19. Tallant, *Mardi Gras*, 113. The Mistick Krewe may also have adopted a social nomenclature found in the African-American West Indies. On the island of Providencia black male social groupings are called "crews"; see Peter J. Wilson, *Crab Antics: The Social Anthropology of English-Speaking Negro Societies of the Caribbean* (New Haven, 1973), 169.

20. J. G. F. Wurdemann, *Notes on Cuba* (Boston, 1844), 83.

21. Day, *Five Years' Residence*, 1:47.

22. Ira de A. Reid, "The John Canoe Festival," *Phylon* 3 (1942), 349–70.

23. Lester B. Shippee, ed., *Bishop Whipple's Southern Diary, 1843–1844* (Minneapolis, 1937), 51.

24. See, for example, Henry Glassie, *All Silver and No Brass* (Bloomington, IN, 1975), 138–39.

25. Mrs. Lanigan, *Antigua and the Antiguans*, 2 vols. (London, 1844), 2:129–30.

26. James M. Phillippo, *Jamaica: Its Past and Present State* (Philadelphia, 1843), 80.

27. This model of Creole backcountry Mardi Gras is taken from Nicholas R. Spitzer, "Symbolic Interpretation of a Black Creole Mardi Gras in Rural French Louisiana" (Paper presented at the annual meeting of the Association for the Anthropological Study of Play, Baton Rouge, 1983). See also Harry Oster, "Country Mardi Gras," in Richard M. Dorson, ed., *Buying the Wind* (Chicago, 1964), 274–81.

28. Amos, "Social Life," 334.

29. James Creecy, *Scenes in the South and Other Miscellaneous Pieces* (Philadelphia, 1860), 21–23.

30. Timothy Flint, *Recollections of the Last Ten Years, Passed in Occasional Residences and Journeyings in the Valley of the Mississippi . . .* (Boston, 1826), 140.

31. Errol Hill, *The Trinidad Carnival* (Austin, 1972), 11; and Day, *Five Years' Residence*, 1:314–16.

32. Arthur Ramos, *The Negro in Brazil* (Washington, DC, 1939), 96; see also Donald Pierson, *Negroes in Brazil* (Chicago, 1942), 94; and Gilberto Freyre, *The Masters and the Slaves* (London, 1956), 374. Similar royal brother-

hoods date back to the late seventeenth century in Pernambuco; see Gerald Cardoso, *Negro Slavery in the Sugar Plantations of Veracruz and Pernambuco, 1550–1680* (Washington, DC, 1983), 134.

33. Henry Koster, *Travels in Brazil,* 2 vols. (London, 1817), 2:27.

34. Alice M. Earle, *Colonial Days in Old New York* (New York, 1896), 195–97; and Joel Munsell, ed., *Collections on the History of Albany from Its Discovery to the Present Time,* 4 vols. (Albany, 1865–71), 2:56, 323–26.

35. From an anonymous letter first published in the *Albany Centinel* and later reprinted in the *Daily Advertiser,* 29 June 1803, as quoted in Shane White, "Pinkster: Afro-Dutch Syncretization in New York City and the Hudson Valley," *Journal of American Folklore* 102, no. 403 (Jan.–March, 1989), 70. It is typical for African secret society maskers to go from house to house to receive small gifts in return for a blessing; see, for example, John Pemberton, III, "Egungun Masquerades of the Igbomina Yoruba," *African Arts* 11, no. 3 (April 1978), 42.

36. Henry Bull, "Memoir of Rhode-Island," *Rhode-Island Republican* (Newport), 19 April 1837, 1; comparatively, for New England see William Dillon Piersen, "Afro-American Culture in Eighteenth Century New England: A Comparative Examination" (Ph.D. dissertation, Indiana University, 1975), 211–31.

37. Phillippo, *Jamaica,* 93.

38. Ibid., 80; see also Chapter 2 herein. Kinser, *Carnival American Style,* 57, believes that black holiday celebrations in the Americas "were not carnivalesque" and "had no use for and probably no understanding of . . . socially grounded grotesqueness." Thus he tends to discount the influence of African-American cultural models on Mardi Gras until King Zulu and the Mardi Gras Indians of the late nineteenth or early twentieth century.

39. Flint, *Recollections of the Last Ten Years,* 140.

40. There is excellent coverage of the Zulu customs of New Orleans in Kinser, *Carnival American Style,* 232–49 and passim.

41. Day, *Five Years' Residence,* 1:49, 288, 315.

42. Henry Hegart Breen, *St. Lucia: Historical, Statistical, and Descriptive* (London, 1844), 190–200; and Lucien Peytraud, *L'Esclavage aux Antilles Françaises* (Paris, 1897), 182–83.

43. George Pinckard, *Notes on the West Indies,* 3 vols. (London, 1806), 3:208–9.

44. Fernando Ortiz, *Los Bailes y el teatro de los Negro en el folklore de Cuba* (Havana, 1951), 195.

45. Beauvallet, *Rachel and the New World,* 192–93. Such Indians were found in Haiti, Trinidad, and New Orleans as well as in Cuba and probably elsewhere. The whitening of the faces was certainly in imitation of Africa, not

of Indians. Michael P. Smith thinks Mardi Gras Indians may have "appeared, or perhaps reappeared," in New Orleans shortly after 1872 with the permission for night maskings. His photographs and text from the 1970s give a strong feeling for the continued African spirit of the Mardi Gras black Indians of New Orleans; see Michael P. Smith, *Spirit World*, catalog of an exhibition (New Orleans, 1984), 85 and passim.

46. *Daily Crescent*, 25 Feb. 1857, as quoted in Tallant, *Mardi Gras*, 111.

47. On the use of a whistle, see Kinser, *Carnival American Style*, 93, and Tallant, *Mardi Gras*, 255. The tradition of using a whistle may have come from Mobile; see Kinser, *Carnival American Style*, 347 n. 47. For the use of whistles as spirit-voiced commands in African secret societies, see Ruth M. Stone, "African Music Performed," in Phillis M. Martin and Patrick O'Meara, eds., *Africa* (2nd ed., Bloomington, IN, 1986), 245.

48. For the Albany quotation, see White, "Pinkster," 69.

49. Lewis, *Journal*, 53, 71.

50. Beauvallet, *Rachel and the New World*, 192–93.

51. Flint, *Recollections of the Last Ten Years*, 140. Black dancing during celebrations was common in New Orleans up to the 1820s; see Henry A. Kmen, *Music in New Orleans: The Formative Years, 1791–1841* (Baton Rouge, 1966), 221.

52. David Birmingham, "Carnival at Luanda," *Journal of African History* 29, no. 1 (1988), 96–97.

53. Phillippo, *Jamaica*, 243–44; W. J. Gardner, *A History of Jamaica from Its Discovery . . . to 1872* (London, 1873), 384; H. De la Beche, *Notes on the Present Condition of the Negroes of Jamaica* (London, 1825), 41–42; Edward Long, *The History of Jamaica*, 2 vols. (London, 1774), 2:425; Lewis, *Journal*, 53–55; and "Characteristic Traits of the Creolian and African Negroes in This Island . . . ," in *The Columbia Magazine; or, Monthly Miscellany* (Kingston, 1797), as quoted in Roger D. Abrahams and John F. Szwed, eds., *After Africa: Extracts from British Travel Accounts and Journals* (New Haven, 1983), 233. For similar sets in Saint Lucia, Dominica, and Trinidad, see Breen, *St. Lucia*, 190–200.

54. Orlando Patterson, *The Sociology of Slavery* (Rutherford, NJ, 1969), 239.

55. Roger Bastide, *African Civilizations in the New World* (New York, 1971), 185–86.

56. Piersen, "Afro-American Culture," 266–301, passim; Thurlow Weed, *Letters from Europe and the West Indies* (Albany, 1866), 365; Angelina Pollak-Eltz, "The Devil Dances in Venezuela," *Caribbean Studies* 8 (1968); Eduardo Galeano, *Memory of Fire*, 3 vols. (1982; English-language ed., New

York, 1985), 2:121–22; and Harold Courlander, *The Drum and the Hoe* (Berkeley, 1960), 105–9.

57. For an analysis of how this metamorphosis took place in Trinidad's carnival, for example, see Hill, *Trinidad Carnival*, passim. Similarly, see Freyre, *Masters and Slaves*, 472, on black contributions to Brazil's carnival festivities.

58. James E. Alexander, *Transatlantic Sketches*, 2 vols. (London, 1833), 2:128–30.

59. On the important role of black balls in New Orleans from 1800 to 1820, see Kmen, *Music in New Orleans*, 8–45, passim, and Kinser, *Carnival American Style*, 25. African royal balls in Louisiana go back to the late eighteenth century; see Gwendolyn Midlo Hall, *Africans in Colonial Louisiana* (Baton Rouge, 1992), 320.

60. See George E. Brooks, Jr., "The Signares of Saint-Louis and Goree: Women Entrepreneurs in Eighteenth-Century Senegal," in Nancy J. Hafkin and Edna G. Bay, eds., *Women in Africa* (Stanford, 1976), 40.

CHAPTER 7 *The Mixed Bloodlines of the Early Ku Klux Klan*

1. An early version of my research of this topic was presented as a paper at the Citadel Conference on the South, Charleston, in April 1987 and was included in a published collection of selected essays from the conference; see William D. Piersen, "Family Secrets: How African-American Culture Helped Shape the Early Ku Klux Klan," in Winfred B. Moore, Jr., and Joseph F. Tripp, eds., *Looking South*, Contributions in American History, no. 136 (Westport, CT, 1989), 41–50.

2. On the general practice of African secret societies, see Georges Balandier and Jacques Maquet, *Dictionary of Black African Civilization* (New York, 1974), 226–27, 303–4. On whistles as the spirit voices, see Ruth M. Stone, "African Music Performed," in Phyllis M. Martin and Patrick O'Meara, eds., *Africa* (2nd ed., Bloomington, IN, 1986), 245; and Geoffrey Gorer, *Africa Dances* (1935; rpt. ed., New York, 1962), 216.

3. Mr. and Mrs. W. B. Romine, *A Story of the Original Ku Klux Klan* (Pulaski, TN, 1934), 8.

4. Ibid., 9.

5. Stanley F. Horn, *Invisible Empire: The Story of the Ku Klux Klan, 1866–1871* (Cos Cob, CT, 1939), 10; Allen W. Trelease, *White Terror: The Ku Klux Klan Conspiracy and Southern Reconstruction* (Westport, CT, 1971), 4.

6. Trelease, *White Terror*, 5. On the use of whistles, see U.S. Congress, *Report of the Joint Select Committee to Inquire into the Conditions of Affairs in the Late Insurrectionary States*, 42nd Cong., 2nd sess., H. Report no. 22, 13 vols.,

1872 (hereafter cited as *KKK Report*), Mississippi, 1160 (Report 41, pt. 12, 2:1159). One Klansman was said to have used a mouth flap to create an weird vibrating effect; *KKK Report*, Mississippi, 1160.

7. Romine and Romine, *Story of the Original Klan*, 9–10.

8. Ibid., 10.

9. Trelease, *White Terror*, 9.

10. Romine and Romine, *Story of the Original Klan*, 10–11. Elsewhere the Romines suggest that the Klan consciously intended to make use of the Negroes' fears of "ghosts" from the beginning; ibid., 13. William Pierce Randel, *The Ku Klux Klan* (Philadelphia, 1965), 8–9, believes that at their second meeting the six originals sheeted their horses and went out to frighten blacks. The return of the Shiloh ghosts remained a standard part of the Klan repertoire; see, for example, *KKK Report*, Alabama, 432, and Mississippi, 1151.

11. Romine and Romine, *Story of the Original Klan*, 13.

12. Trelease, *White Terror*, 4–5; and Gladys-Marie Fry, *Night Riders in Black Folk History* (Knoxville, 1975), 122–32.

13. John C. Lester and Daniel L. Wilson, *Ku-Klux Klan: Its Origin, Its Growth and Disbandment* (Nashville, 1884), 58.

14. H. Grady McWhiney and Francis B. Simkins argue in "The Ghostly Legend of the Ku Klux Klan," *Negro History Bulletin* 14 (Feb. 1951), 109–12, that the whole concept of black fear of Klansmen as ghosts was a legend based on mistaken white stereotypes; blacks feared the violence, not the masks.

15. Testimony of Lorenzo Ezell, quoted in Norman R. Yetman, ed., *Life under the "Peculiar Institution"* (New York, 1970), 114–15. Ezell says this happened in 1868 when he was eighteen. Within the year messengers had been sent from Pulaski to South Carolina to establish new dens, and presumably they told the South Carolina initiates about the strategy of appearing as the spirits of Confederate war dead.

16. Horn, *Invisible Empire*, 19. For a North Carolina example, see the testimony of Wil Bost in Belinda Hurmence, ed., *My Folks Don't Want Me to Talk about Slavery: Twenty-one Oral Histories of Former North Carolina Slaves* (Winston-Salem, 1984), 98.

17. Fry, *Night Riders*, 69–73, 113; and on the continuity with the earlier patrol system, see Gladys-Marie Fry, "Fake Ghosts and 'Pretend' Hell," *The World & I*, Oct. 1987, 476.

18. See, for example, Romine and Romine, *Story of the Original Klan*, 10.

19. A picture of the original robe of J. R. Brunson of Klan Den Number 1 is found in ibid., 27.

20. The Brunson robe is in possession of the Giles County Historical Society, Pulaski, TN.

21. Note photo illustration section in Horn, *Invisible Empire.*

22. *KKK Report,* Alabama, 9:813–14.

23. On white as a ghostly color for blacks, see Newbell Niles Puckett, *Folk Beliefs of the Southern Negro* (Chapel Hill, 1926), 119; and Savannah Unit, Georgia Writers' Project, Work Projects Administration, *Drums and Shadows* (1940; rpt. ed., Athens, 1986), passim.

24. On the Confederate (and doubtless after-the-fact) symbolism, see Romine and Romine, *Story of the Original Klan,* 15: "As the Klan stood primarily for the purity and preservation of the home and for the protection of the women and children, especially the widows and orphans of Confederate soldiers, white, the emblem of purity was chosen for the robes. And to render them startling and conspicuous red, emblem of the blood which Klansmen were ready to shed in defense of the helpless was chosen for the trimmings. Also a sentimental thought probably was present in adopting the color scheme, as white and red were the Confederate colors." Fry, *Night Riders,* 123, accepts this theory in order to explain the otherwise anomalous choice of red robes as a disguise for the would-be ghosts.

25. Romine and Romine, *Story of the Original Klan,* 28, says that the sister of John B. Kennedy, one of the original organizers, "designed and made" the original robe. Testimony before the congressional committee investigating the Klan maintained that the robes were "made in the families"; *KKK Report,* Mississippi, 1159.

26. *KKK Report,* South Carolina, 1142.

27. The adjectives come from a description of Klan regalia in Lester and Wilson, *Ku Klux Klan,* passim, and will be familiar to anyone who has read Anglo-American descriptions of African-American dress. On the African-American aesthetic in regard to textiles, see Maude Southwell Wahlman and John Scully, "Aesthetic Principles in Afro-American Quilts," in William Ferris, ed., *Afro-American Folk Art and Crafts* (Jackson, 1983), 79–97.

28. *KKK Report,* Mississippi, 1152.

29. Ibid., 1159–60.

30. On the power of the color red in African and African-American culture (and especially costuming), see Puckett, *Folk Beliefs of the Southern Negro,* 220–21, who calls red "the fetish color." Thomas Ewbank notes that in Brazil an African conjurer possessed "the scarlet cap and gown of the enchanter"; *Life in Brazil* (New York, 1856), 406. Martha Warren Beckwith, *Black Roadways* (Chapel Hill, 1929), 108, similarly observes that in Jamaica men who dealt in spirits wore red flannel shirts or a crosspiece of red under

their ordinary clothes. For other comparative evidence, see Victor Tuner, *The Forest of Symbols* (Ithaca, 1967), 74; Robert Ferris Thompson, *Flash of the Spirit* (New York, 1984), 131, 184, and passim; and Robert Brain, *Art and Society in Africa* (Hong Kong, 1980), passim.

31. See, for example, Brain, *Art and Society,* 243, 245; Robert Ferris Thompson, *African Art in Motion* (Berkeley, 1974), 167, 181–82; Thompson, *Flash of the Spirit,* 258–66; and Fernando Ortiz, "La Antigua Fiesta Afrocubana del 'Dia de Reyes,'" *Archivos del Folklore Cubana* 1, no. 2, 145, and no. 3, 238; and John W. Nunley and Judith Bettelheim, *Caribbean Festival Arts* (Seattle, 1988), figs. 117–20. The *ireme* are individually named nanigos with the Cuban Abakuá who wear tall pointed headdresses and fringed and appliquéd jumpsuit-like costumes. For an English-language description of the Abakuá Society's rites in Cuba, see Harold Courlander, "Abakwa Meeting in Guanabacoa," *Journal of Negro History* 29 (1944). If a precise and slavish imitation was intended, the Klansmen missed the *sombrereta* (or little hat) on the back of the hood, which is vital to the leopard-maskers but would probably not be important to onlooking white observers.

32. See figs. 102–7 and the accompanying discussion in Fernando Ortiz, *Los Bailes y el teatro de los Negro en el folklore de Cuba* (Havana, 1951), 360–65.

33. On the Red Sect, see Alfred Metraux, *Voodoo in Haiti* (1959; English-language ed., New York, 1972), 292–98; and Zora Neale Hurston, *Tell My Horse* (1938; rpt. ed., Berkeley, 1981), 213, 220, 221, 225. In Africa, too, horned masks were not uncommon; see R. S. Wassing, *African Art* (1968; English-language ed., New York, 1988), 139, 140, 143.

34. Rachel Beauvoir, from an unpublished manuscript at Tufts University, as quoted in Nunley and Bettelheim, *Caribbean Festival Arts,* 144.

35. James C. Fletcher and Daniel P. Kidder, *Brazil and the Brazilians* (Boston, 1866), 137, 126. Today the term *capoeira* denotes an African-Brazilian martial arts dance. For the Ogboni and Oro secret societies in Brazil, see Roger Bastide, *The African Religions of Brazil* (1960; English-language ed., Baltimore, 1978), 103, 198; for similar African terrorist activities by leopard societies found from Sierra Leone to the Congo, see Wassing, *African Art,* 118.

36. Hugh Crow, *Memoirs of the Late Captain H. Crow of Liverpool . . .* (London, 1830), 313–15.

37. See, for example, Paul E. Lovejoy, *Transformations in Slavery: A History of Slavery in Africa* (Cambridge, 1983), 100.

38. Great Britain, *Parliamentary Papers,* 11 (531), pt. 1, Q. 5899 (1842), "Report of Select Committee on British Possessions on the West Coast of Africa," as quoted in K. Onwuka Dike, *Trade and Politics in the Niger Delta, 1830–1885* (Oxford, 1956), 161–62, and for an 1856 example, 121. Likewise,

see the similar report in 1875 of Bishop Samuel Crowther: "Some months ago an intelligent, well-educated Englishman degraded himself so far as to conform to the idolatrous practices of the heathens at Bonny; to join their secret club, he performs all the idolatrous rites required"; *Church Missionary Intelligencer,* 1876, 475.

39. Compare the Romine photograph with the charms pictured in Thompson, *Flash of the Spirit,* 126–27. A. B. Ellis, *The Yoruba-Speaking Peoples of the Slave Coast of West Africa* (1894; rpt. ed., Oosterhout, 1970), 118, points out that it was common for such Yoruba charms to be worn "tied around the waist"; examples are pictured in *African Arts* 11, no. 3 (April 1978), 45, 53, 55. John W. Nunley, *Moving with the Face of the Devil* (Urbana, IL, 1987), 72–73, reports that maskers from the Yoruba-derived Ode-lay Society of Sierra Leone commonly carry protective charms to protect themselves from witches. Examples of Central African *minkisi* are displayed in Wyatt MacGaffey, *Art and Healing of the Bakongo Commented by Themselves: Minkisi from the Laman Collection* (Stockholm, 1991), passim. On red and white as mojo "hand" colors, see Puckett, *Folk Beliefs of the Southern Negro,* 234–35. In the Sea Islands, off the U.S. coast, such protective bags are traditionally worn around the waist; Janie Gillard Moore, "A James Island Childhood: Africanisms among Families of the Sea Islands of Charleston, South Carolina," in Mary A. Twining and Keith E. Baird, eds., *Sea Island Roots* (Trenton, 1991), 112.

40. Frances Anne Kemble, *Further Records, 1848–1883* (New York, 1891), 214.

41. There is no doubt that the decorated liberty poles did look something like obeah staffs—long sticks from which usually hung parrot feathers, animal teeth, and other magical talismans. What is especially interesting is that white southerners knew it and consciously intended to exploit this similarity. For the use of obeah sticks elsewhere in the Americas, see Richard Price, *Alabi's World* (Baltimore, 1990), 120, 330.

42. For the Shakespearean theory, see Romine and Romine, *Story of the Original Klan,* 8; and for a less theatrical version, see Horn, *Invisible Empire,* 14–15.

43. Quoted in Roger D. Abrahams and John F. Szwed, eds., *After Africa: Extracts from British Travel Accounts and Journals* (New Haven, 1983), 236–37, 270, and passim; see also Douglas MacMillan, "John Kuners," *Journal of American Folklore* 39 (Jan.–March 1926), 53–54; Judith Bettelheim, "Jamaican Jonkonnu and Related Caribbean Festivals," in Margaret E. Crahan and Franklin W. Knight, eds., *Africa and the Caribbean* (Baltimore, 1979), 84, 92; and Hurston, *Tell My Horse,* 40. Such masks are extremely similar to Yoruba Egungun hunting devils; see Nunley, *Moving with the Devil,* 124, fig. 44, and 127, fig. 46. The horsehead and cowhead masks were found

primarily in the rural areas of Jamaica and seem to Judith Bettelheim "more directly African," especially in their fierceness, than other masks. She points out that the horsehead was an old form in Britain, too, but finds the roots of the Caribbean heads to be primarily African, probably from the Mende areas such as the Kore society of the Bambara; Nunley and Bettelheim, *Caribbean Festival Arts,* 55.

44. Work Projects Administration files, "Slave Narratives," North Carolina, as quoted in Fry, *Night Riders,* 143. In Africa hunting devils were among the fiercest of secret society maskers; see Nunley, *Moving with the Devil,* 121.

45. Masks with such false heads on top of the masker's head were common in West Africa. See, for example, the plates in Brain, *Art and Society,* 105–6, 146–47.

46. McWhiney and Simkins have argued persuasively that most blacks knew there were men behind the masks, so the authors conclude that Klansmen wore the masks for their own enjoyment and sense of racial superiority; "Ghostly Legend of the Klan," 109–12.

47. Gorer, *Africa Dances,* 216.

48. Ellis, *Yoruba-Speaking Peoples,* 107; see also Oludare Olajubu, "Iwi Egungun Chants: An Introduction," in Bernth Lindfors, ed., *Forms of Folklore in Africa* (Austin, 1977), 155.

49. Robert Campbell, *A Pilgrimage to My Motherland: An Account of a Journey among the Egbas and Yorubas of Central Africa, in 1859–60,* in Howard H. Bell, ed., *Search for a Place: Black Separatism and Africa, 1860* (Ann Arbor, 1969), 203.

50. Anne Moody, *Coming of Age in Mississippi* (New York, 1968), 121.

51. *KKK Report,* Mississippi, 1151.

52. Lester and Wilson, *Ku Klux Klan,* 98.

53. See, for example, Nunley, *Moving with the Devil,* 57, 249, n. 15. The conical crown of the warrior chief of the Yoruba is fronted by a veil to hide the face; see John Pemberton, III, "The Dreadful God and the Divine King," in Sandra T. Barnes, ed., *Africa's Ogun* (Bloomington, IN, 1989), 117. On executioners, see Captain J. F. Landolphe, *Mémoires du Capitaine Landolphe . . . rédigés sur son manuscrit, par J. S. Quesné,* 2 vols. (Paris, 1823), 2:70, as quoted in H. Ling Roth, *Great Benin* (1903; rpt. ed., Northbrook, IL, 1972), 57.

54. Thompson, *Flash of the Spirit,* 227, 236–37; Puckett, *Folk Beliefs of the Southern Negro,* 283–84 and passim; and Hurston, *Tell My Horse,* 227.

55. Bertram Wyatt-Brown, *Honor and Violence in the Old South* (New York, 1986), 207: "The headgear varied as well, but the customary symbols of the charivari were certainly unmistakable. Caps were tall and conical or crowned with horns, a phallic representation as old as the charivari itself. The cowbird's or cuckold's horns, the horns of the Devil, were chosen for the

Klansman's headpiece with no self-consciousness or contrived intent: such was simply a tradition."

56. There is a good picture of the rowdy charivari (or shivaree, as it was known in Tennessee) behavior in the John Stokes painting *Wedding in the Big Smokies, Tennessee* (1872). See the reproduction in James C. Kelly, "Landscape and Genre Painting in Tennessee, 1810–1985," *Tennessee Historical Quarterly* 44, no. 2 (summer 1985), 73.

57. Cajun Mardi Gras in Louisiana did feature a masking tradition with some similarities: "tacky, motley one-piece uniforms, topped with a high conical cap, resembling a dunce hat, and masks of coarse screen with holes cut out for eyes, nose, and mouth"; see Harry Oster, "Country Mardi Gras," in Richard M. Dorson, ed., *Buying the Wind* (Chicago, 1964), 274. However, the dates are uncertain, and as I argued in the previous chapter regarding *Courir de Mardi Gras* there is a good chance aspects of Cajun Mardi Gras were syncretized with African-American elements.

58. Consider, for example, the horned headdress. Similar headdresses were described in Africa by François Froger, *Relation d'un voyage fait en 1695–97 au Côtes d'Afrique* (Paris, 1698); Jean Labat, *Nouvelle relation de l'Afrique occidental*, 4 vols. (Paris, 1728), 4:288; and Louis Gustave Binger, *Du Niger au Golfe du Guinée*, 2 vols. (Paris, 1892), 1:378.

CHAPTER 8 *Mammy, Indeed!*

1. Edward Kimber, *London Magazine* 1746, as quoted in Mechal Sobel, *The World They Made Together* (Princeton, 1987), 137. *Southern Evangelical Messenger* 2 (29 April 1820), 32; and on this subject in general, see John Edward Philips, "The African Heritage of White America: Some Neglected Aspects of New World Africanisms" Paper presented at the Twenty-Seventh Annual Meeting of the African Studies Association, Los Angeles, 1984; Sidney M. Mintz and Richard Price, *An Anthropological Approach to the Afro-American Past: A Caribbean Perspective*, ISHI Occasional Papers in Social Change, no. 2 (Philadelphia, 1976), 16; J. L. Dillard, *Black English* (New York, 1973), chap. 5; and Melville J. Herskovits, *The New World Negro* (Bloomington, IN, 1969), 171.

2. Mary Chaplin is quoted by her husband in his journal entry of 15 May 1851; see Theodore Rosengarten, ed., "The Journal of Thomas B. Chaplin (1822–1890)," in *Tombee Portrait of a Cotton Planter* (New York, 1986), 532.

3. Thomas L. Nichols, *Forty Years of American Life* (1864), as quoted in Dillard, *Black English*, 191.

4. *Southern Presbyterian Review* 1 (June 1847), 90. Le Page du Pratz, *The*

History of Louisiana (1758; rpt. ed., New Orleans, 1949), 362. Sir Charles Lyell, *A Second Visit to the United States of North America*, 2 vols. (New York, 1849), 2:20. Some scholars had understood this quite early. From Alabama L. W. Payne noted, "For my part, after a somewhat careful study of East Alabama dialect, I am convinced that the speech of the white people, the dialect I have spoken all my life and the one I have tried to record here, is more largely colored by the language of the Negroes than by any other single influence"; "A Word List from East Alabama," *Dialect Notes* 3 (1903), 279.

5. Sidney Andrews, *The South since the War* (Boston, 1866), 227–29. Anne Royall, as quoted in Dillard, *Black English*, 190.

6. Louis H. Blair, *The Prosperity of the South Dependent upon the Elevation of the Negro* (Richmond, 1889), 105. Gwendolyn Midlo Hall, *Africans in Colonial Louisiana* (Baton Rouge, 1992), 194; Charles Joyner, *Down by the Riverside* (Urbana, IL, 1984), 208. Similarly, see the observation of Caroline Gilman: "although, at the time of which I speak, I preferred to talk to the Negroes in their dialect I never used it to the whites"; *Recollections of a Southern Matron* (New York, 1838), 41.

7. Frances Anne Kemble, *Journal of a Residence on a Georgia Plantation in 1838–1839* (1863; rpt. ed., New York, 1961), 252. Similarly, see the 1842 observation of Charles Dickens: "All the women who have been bred in slave states speak more or less like Negroes, from having been constantly in their childhood with black nurses," as quoted in Dillard, *Black English*, 192.

8. Kemble, *Journal*, 280–81.

9. Maria Taylor Byrd to William Byrd, III, Feb. 1760(?), as quoted in Sobel, *The World They Made Together*, 138.

10. As Robert Dirks notes in his discussion of the British West Indies, "Englishmen in general looked down on Creoles no matter how wealthy. Their speech and food habits—their Creole drawl, their habit of eating with their hands, and their favoring such foods as okra pepper pot—were taken as too nearly Negro for comfort"; *The Black Saturnalia* (Gainesville, FL, 1987), 46.

11. Edward Long, *The History of Jamaica*, 2 vols. (London, 1774), 2:276–77, 328, 427; and, comparatively, see William Beckford, *A Descriptive Account of the Island of Jamaica*, 2 vols. (London, 1790), 1:390–92, and James Houstoun, *Works of James Houstoun, M.D.* (London, 1817), 241–42. Sylvia Wynter, "Lady Nugent's Journal," *Jamaica Journal* 1, no. 1 (1967), 28. "Journal of Josiah Quincy, Junior, 1773," Massachusetts Historical Society, *Proceedings* 49 (1916), 456–57.

12. J. G. Stedman, *Narrative of a Five Years' Expedition against the Revolted Negroes of Surinam in Guinana on the Wild Coast of South America from the Years 1772 to 1777*, 2 vols. (1796; rpt. ed., Barre, MA, 1971), 2:361. Kemble, *Journal*, 282.

13. See, for example, Clement Eaton, *A History of the Old South* (New York, 1966), 2–3; and Juanita V. Williamson and Virginia M. Burke, eds., *A Various Language: Perspectives on American Dialects* (New York, 1971).

14. On the question of vocabulary, see David Dalby, "Black through White: Patterns of Communication" (Hans Wolff Memorial Lecture, Indiana University, 1970); Roger D. Abrahams and John F. Szwed, eds., *After Africa: Extracts from British Travel Accounts and Journals* (New Haven, 1983), 2; and Robert Ferris Thompson, *Flash of the Spirit* (New York, 1984), 104. On the use of "Huddy," see Charlotte Forten's observations in "Life on the Sea Islands," pt. 1, *Atlantic Monthly* 13 (May 1864), 592; the diary of William Francis Allen, 3 July 1864, as quoted in Dena J. Epstein, *Sinful Tunes and Spirituals* (Urbana, IL, 1977), 356; and Andrews, *The South since the War*, as quoted in Abrahams and Szwed, *After Africa*, 359. On uses of "Hodi Massra" as a greeting in Surinam, see the journal of Johann Riemer for 1779, as quoted in Richard Price, *Alabi's World* (Baltimore, 1990), 190, 193, 203. For the use of "How de massa?" see James E. Alexander, *Transatlantic Sketches* (London, 1833), as quoted in Abrahams and Szwed, *After Africa*, 303.

15. W. J. Cash, *The Mind of the South* (1941; rpt. ed., New York, 1961), 53. In the same way, Eugene D. Genovese, *Roll, Jordan, Roll* (New York, 1976), 267, credits black preachers for having the primary influence on southern white oratory.

16. Bryan Edwards, *The History, Civil and Commercial, of the British Colonies in the West Indies*, 2 vols. (Dublin, 1793), 2:77; James Stewart, *A View of the Past and Present State of the Island of Jamaica* (1808; rpt. ed., Edinburgh, 1823), 264; and, comparatively, Jean Baptiste Labat, *Voyages du Père Labat aux îles de l'Amérique* (1722; rpt. ed., Paris, 1956), 193; and M. L. E. Moreau de Saint-Méry, *A Civilization that Perished: The Last Years of White Colonial Rule in Haiti*, ed. and trans. Ivor D. Spencer (1797; English-language ed., New York, 1985), 58. See also Abrahams and Szwed, *After Africa*, 78–79. For comparative comments on African oratory, see John Beecham's comment that on the Gold Coast "the natives of this part of Africa are remarkable for oratory, and will discourse fluently on a given subject for hours"; quoted in John Beecham, *Ashantee and the Gold Coast* (1841; rpt. ed., New York, 1970), 167.

17. Newbell Niles Puckett, *Folk Beliefs of the Southern Negro* (1926; rpt. ed., New York, 1969), 28. Richard Austin Freeman, *Travels and Life in Ashanti and Jamaica* (New York, 1898), 61. Alexander Alland, Jr., *When the Spider Danced* (New York, 1975), 5.

18. Joseph Holt Ingraham, *The Southwest by a Yankee*, 2 vols. (New York, 1835), 2:56. On the topic of fancy talk and the white reaction to it, see the important chapter "Who Speaks Black English?" in Dillard, *Black English*.

19. Willard B. Gatewood, *Aristocrats of Color* (Bloomington, IN, 1990),

19. On the role of the black mammy, see Jessie W. Parkhurst, "The Black Mammy in the Plantation Household," *Journal of Negro History* 23 (July 1938).

20. Elizabeth W. Allston Pringle, *Chronicles of Chicora Wood* (New York, 1922), 54. Susan Dabney Smedes, *Memorials of a Southern Planter* (1887; rpt. ed., New York, 1965), 125.

21. Thomas Wentworth Higginson, *Army Life in a Black Regiment* (1869; rpt. ed., New York, 1984), 48, 50, 135, 239–40.

22. Frederick Douglass, *The Life and Times of Frederick Douglass, Written by Himself* (Hartford, 1881), 100; similarly, see *Narrative of the Life of Frederick Douglass, an American Slave* (1845; rpt. ed., New York, 1982), 97.

23. Ingraham is quoted in Genovese, *Roll, Jordan, Roll*, 23. Frances Butler Leigh, *Ten Years on a Georgia Plantation since the War* (London, 1883), 226.

24. "A Journey from Philadelphia to Charleston, 1783," Virginia State Library, quoted in Thad W. Tate, *The Negro in Eighteenth-Century Williamsburg* (1965; rpt. ed., Williamsburg, 1987), 37.

25. Kemble, *Journal*, 175.

26. See, for example, Margaret Washington Creel, *"A Peculiar People": Slave Religion and Community-Culture among the Gullahs* (New York, 1988), 281–82, who observes how much such politeness depended upon the African heritage of the slaves. See also Melville J. Herskovits, *Myth of the Negro Past* (Boston, 1941), 150–53; and John A. Davis, "The Influence of Africans on American Culture," *Annals of the American Academy of Political and Social Sciences* (1964), 354, 79.

27. An early translation of the Pieter de Marees account is found in Samuel Purchas, *Purchas his Pilgrimes, in Five Books*, 6 vols. (1625; rpt. ed., Glasgow, 1905), 6:265. European etiquette of the period suggested that indoors one should cover a fart with a cough, but this was, of course, a mark of rare refinement; see John F. Kasson, *Rudeness & Civility* (New York, 1990), 25. The Blair letter describing the contest between Betsy Blair and Sally Sweeny is quoted in Edmund Morgan, *Virginians at Home* (Williamsburg, 1952), 37.

28. John Pendleton Kennedy, *Swallow Barn; or, A Sojourn in the Old Dominion* (1832; rpt. ed., Baton Rouge, 1986), 454; and Lady Emmeline Stuart-Wortley, *Travels in the United States . . . during 1849 and 1850* (New York, 1855), 118–19.

29. Leigh, *Ten Years on a Georgia Plantation*, 95. William Alexander Percy, *Lanterns on the Levee* (1941; rpt. ed., Baton Rouge, 1973), 286.

30. Mrs. A. C. Carmichael, *Domestic Manners and Social Conditions of the . . . West Indies*, 2 vols. (London, 1833), 1:284; and Richard Ligon, *A True and Exact History of the Island of Barbadoes* (1657; rpt. ed., London, 1976), 47. Allen is quoted in Epstein, *Sinful Tunes and Spirituals*, 350.

31. Hunter Dickinson Farish, ed., *Journal and Letters of Philip Vickers*

Fithian, 1773–1774: A Plantation Tutor of the Old Dominion (Williamsburg, 1957), 129. Africans commonly prostrated themselves on the ground before chiefs, kings, and other great men.

32. James S. Buckingham, *The Slave States of America*, 2 vols. (London, 1842), 2:427. Forten, "Life on the Sea Islands," 592. Edward Channing Gannett came to the same general conclusion about Port Royal: "The old are treated with great reverence, and often exercise a kind of patriarchal authority. Children are carefully taught 'manners,' and the common address to each other, as well as to the 'buckra people,' is marked by extreme courtesy"; see his article "The Freedmen at Port Royal," *North American Review* 101 (1865), 10.

33. Frederick Douglass, *My Bondage and My Freedom* (New York, 1855), 60. Similarly, Hagar Brown taught her children, "Anybody older than you, you must honor them"; quoted in Joyner, *Down by the Riverside*, 64. Comparatively, see the observation of a resident of Dominica: "The Africans are extremely attentive to, and careful of, their old people: to be old, secures the kind offices and care of their friends, and of all who know them; and negroes vie with each other, in displaying kindness to their father and mother, aunty or sissy, for by all these affectionate appellations, do they designate them, though not at all related"; see "A Resident," *Sketches and Recollections of the West Indies* (London, 1828), 65; and Labat, *Voyages du Père Labat*, 192. According to Edward Long, respect for elders was among the highest moral precepts among the African slaves: "Murder is with most of them esteemed the highest impiety—Filial disobedience, and insulting the ashes of the dead, are placed next"; see Long, *History of Jamaica*, 2:416.

34. "Sketches of South Carolina, Number Four: 'Slaves and Slavery,'" *Knickerbocker Magazine* 21 (May 1843), 348. Ann Abadie, ed., *William Faulkner: A Life on Paper* (Jackson, MS, 1980), 86. Pringle, *Chronicles of Chicora Wood*, 168.

35. See, for example, the discussion of this topic in Creel, *"A Peculiar People,"* 281–82.

36. Robert Campbell, *A Pilgrimage to My Motherland: An Account of a Journey among the Egbas and Yorubas of Central Africa, in 1859–60*, in Howard H. Bell, ed., *Search for a Place: Black Separatism and Africa, 1860* (Ann Arbor, 1969), 189.

37. Cash, *Mind of the South*, 51.

38. Bertram Wyatt-Brown, "The Mask of Obedience: Male Slave Psychology in the Old South," *American Historical Review* 93, no. 5 (Dec. 1988), 1232, sees the two shame/honor cultures as a parallel development. Genovese, *Roll, Jordan, Roll*, 116, 120–21, also noted the similarities between white and black in their aristocratic ethos of southern courtesy but believed that the South was a guilt culture unlike the shame culture of Africa.

39. Clinkscales and Faulkner are quoted in Bertram Wyatt-Brown, *Honor and Violence in the Old South* (New York, 1986), 71.

40. Annie Laurie Broidrick, "Recollections of Thirty Years Ago," MS, 6–7, as quoted in Genovese, *Roll, Jordan, Roll,* 354. Similarly, see Mary Boykin Chesnut's observations in 1861 about her servant Polly's judgments on proper behavior; C. Vann Woodward, ed. *Mary Chesnut's Civil War* (New Haven, 1981), 69.

41. M. Cain to Minerva R. Cain, 14 April 1833, as quoted in Genovese, *Roll, Jordan, Roll,* 357.

42. John Egarton, *Southern Food* (West Hanover, MA, 1987), 13. William F. Neal, *Bill Neal's Southern Cooking* (Chapel Hill, 1985), 9.

43. Kemble, *Journal,* 236–37.

44. Ibid., 60. Northern whites agreed; see William C. Fowler, *The Historical Status of the Negro in Connecticut* (Albany, 1872), 131, and Anne Grant, *Memoirs of an American Lady* (1808; rpt. ed., New York, 1903), 265.

45. Robert Q. Mallard, *Plantation Life before Emancipation* (Richmond, 1892), 18; similarly, see Mary Howard Schoolcraft, *Plantation Life: The Narrative of Mrs. Henry Rowe Schoolcraft* (1852; rpt. ed., New York, 1969), 234. Evan Jones, *American Food: The Gastronomic Story* (New York, 1981), 34; and Fawn M. Brodie, *Thomas Jefferson: An Intimate History* (New York, 1975), 303.

46. On the African-American contribution to southern cooking, see Mary Tolford Wilson, "Peaceful Integration: The Owner's Adoption of His Slave's Food," *Journal of Negro History* 49, no. 2 (April 1964); Egarton, *Southern Food;* Neal, *Southern Cooking;* Genovese, *Roll, Jordan, Roll,* 540–49; Joyner, *Down by the Riverside,* 78; Helen Mendes, *The African Heritage Cookbook* (New York, 1974), 35–36, 74, 79, 83–84; and note the suggestive comments in Howard Peacock, "The Making of a Cajun Chef," *The World & I* (Oct. 1987), 329–30. John Thorne, *Rice and Beans,* suggests that hoppin John derived its name from the Caribbean *pois à pigeon* (pigeon peas), which had been carried to the West Indies from Africa; the Thorne reference is found in Jane Stern and Michael Stern, *Real American Food* (New York, 1986), 115.

47. American Indians in Virginia roasted green ears of corn, according to Robert Beverley, *The History and Present State of Virginia* (1705; rpt. ed., 1947), 144, but European Americans more commonly cut the kernels from the cob. West Africans, on the other hand, when first introduced to the New World crop in Africa developed their own taste for roasted ears; see T. Aubrey, M.D., *The Sea-Surgeon: or, Guinea Man's Vade Mecum . . . for the Use of Young Sea-Surgeons* (London, 1729), 126–28; and T. Edward Bowdich, *Mission from Cape Coast Castle to Ashantee* (1819; rpt. ed., London, 1966), 319, who reports that this style of eating corn was practiced in Ashanti but not found among the

Fantees (who being on the coast were more influenced by Atlantic ways). For a continuation of the blacks' preference for roasting ears in the West Indies and Brazil, see Richard S. Dunn, *Sugar and Slaves* (New York, 1973), 278–79, and J. K. Tuckey, *Tuckey's Voyage . . .* (London, 1805), 10–12.

48. Neal, *Southern Cooking*, 13, 175, 58; and Jones, *American Food*, 38 n., who ties the common southern good luck tradition of eating hoppin John on New Year's Day to the custom of hiding a shiny new dime among the peas before serving them, the luck going to the one who gets the dime. This is likely an American variant of the old European King's Day traditions (which center on finding a prize in a cake) adapted to the African/African-American taste for collard greens and black-eyed peas; however, there may also have been a syncretism with African good luck customs of the New Year as well.

49. On black influences on the Great Awakening in New England; see William D. Piersen, *Black Yankees: The Development of an Afro-American Subculture in Eighteenth-Century New England* (Amherst, 1988), chap. 6; for the South, see the conclusions of the Reverend Samuel McCorkle, as quoted in Guion G. Johnson, *Ante-bellum North Carolina* (Chapel Hill, 1937), 404; Alfloyd Butler, "The Blacks' Contribution of Elements of African Religion to Christianity in America: A Case Study of the Great Awakening in South Carolina" (Ph.D. dissertation, Northwestern University, 1975); Sobel, *The World They Made Together*, 3, 189, 206; and Alan Gallay, "Planters and Slaves in the Great Awakening," in John B. Boles, ed., *Masters & Slaves in the House of the Lord* (Lexington, KY, 1988), 29.

50. George Wilson Bridges, *Annals of Jamaica*, 2 vols. (London, 1827), 2:442–43; on the West African value of musicality and fluidity of speech, see Alland, *When the Spider Danced*, 4. William P. Harrison, ed., *The Gospel among the Slaves* (Nashville, 1893), 151–52.

51. Simon Peter Richardson, *The Lights and Shadows of Itinerant Life: An Autobiography* (Nashville, 1900), 70–71, 88–89.

52. See, for example, Albert J. Raboteau, *Slave Religion* (Oxford, 1978), 68–73; and Sterling Stuckey, *Slave Culture* (New York, 1987), passim, who finds the ring shout at the center of African-American culture.

53. Richardson, *Lights and Shadows*, 91, 99–100.

54. Daniel Alexander Payne, *Recollections of Seventy Years* (1886; rpt. ed., New York, 1969), 256.

55. Harrison, *Gospel among the Slaves*, 202; see also Mary Boykin Chesnut, *A Diary from Dixie*, ed. Ben Ames Williams (Boston, 1949), 148–49; and the report of Simon Peter Richardson that whites came to his Florida services just to hear the Negroes sing, *Lights and Shadows*, 90. John F. Watson, "Methodist Error . . ." (Trenton, 1819), as quoted in Eileen Southern, *The Music of Black Americans: A History* (New York, 1971), 91, 95–96.

56. Frederick Law Olmstead, *The Cotton Kingdom*, 2 vols. (New York, 1861), 1:311.

57. *Farmer's Gazette* (Sparta, GA), 8 Aug. 1807, as quoted in Ulrich B. Phillips, *American Negro Slavery* (1918; rpt. ed., Baton Rouge, 1966), 316–17. These black all-night songfests were a common feature of camp meetings; see Southern, *Music of Black Americans*, 95.

58. Quoted in Phillips, *American Negro Slavery*, 420. On the interaction of blacks and whites within the white churches of the South, see Boles, "Introduction," *Masters & Slaves*, 10–11.

59. Sobel, *The World They Made Together*, 218–19.

60. W. E. B. Du Bois, *The Souls of Black Folk* (1903; rpt. ed., New York, 1970), 157; Herskovits, *Myth of the Negro Past*, 230–32; and Butler, "The Blacks' Contribution," 163–66.

61. Ezra Adams is quoted in George P. Rawick, ed., *The American Slave: A Composite Autobiography* 31 vols. (Westport, CT, 1972–77), 2:8. Edward A. Pollard, *Black Diamonds Gathered in the Darkey Homes of the South* (1859; rpt. ed., New York, 1968), 76; similarly, see Virginia Clay-Clopton, *A Belle of the Fifties: Memoirs of Mrs. Clay of Alabama*, ed. Ada Sterling (New York, 1905), 4.

62. Thomas R. Cobb, *An Historical Sketch of Slavery from the Earliest Periods* (Philadelphia, 1858), 220; Tattler, "Management of Negroes," *Southern Cultivator* 8 (Nov. 1850), 162–64; and, more generally, see Elizabeth Fox-Genovese, *Within the Plantation Household* (Chapel Hill, 1988), 112. Long, *History of Jamaica*, 2:278. George Washington Cable, "Creole Slave Songs," in Bernard Katz, ed., *The Social Implications of Early Negro Music in the United States* (New York, 1969), 60; likewise, see Richard M. Dorson, "Conjure, Hoodoo, and Gris-Gris," in his *Buying the Wind* (Chicago, 1964), 268–69, and, comparatively, see Gerald Cardoso, *Negro Slavery in the Sugar Plantations of Veracruz and Pernambuco, 1550–1680* (Washington, DC, 1983), 136; and Michael Craton, *Testing the Chains: Resistance to Slavery in the British West Indies* (Ithaca, 1982), 46.

63. For an introduction to this topic, see James Harvey Young, "Self-dosage," in Charles Reagan Wilson and William Ferris, eds., *Encyclopedia of Southern Culture* (Chapel Hill, 1989), 1361–62.

64. David Hackett Fisher, *Albion's Seed: Four British Folkways in America* (New York, 1989), 282, contends without reference to his source that the custom was common among southern whites, who had brought it with them from Britain (particularly from Wessex and Mercia). On broomstick weddings in the American South, see Raboteau, *Slave Religion*, 228–29, and Genovese, *Roll, Jordan, Roll*, 475–81. On poor whites jumping the broom, see the testimony of Willis Cozart of Person County, North Carolina, as quoted in Belinda

Hurmence, ed., *My Folks Don't Want Me to Talk about Slavery: Twenty-one Oral Histories of Former North Carolina Slaves* (Winston-Salem, 1984), 90.

65. On the cult of Nana in Africa and Brazil, see Thompson, *Flash of the Spirit*, 68–72. For the use in 1860 of ornamental brooms to wash the stones in front of a church in Bahia, Brazil, to insure fertility, see Maximilian I, *Recollections of My Life*, 3 vols. (London, 1868), 3:170–76; Roger Bastide, *The African Religions of Brazil* (1960; English-language ed., Baltimore, 1978), 276, 478, thinks the key to this Brazilian ceremony is in the washing and is therefore related to Obatala, the god of sky and procreation.

66. Moreau de Saint-Méry, *Civilization that Perished*, 43. Work Projects Administration, *The Negro in Virginia* (New York, 1940), 81–82. Elmo Steele, whose great-grandfather was an African, remembered his grandfather telling him that the broomstick wedding was an African tradition: "Dey used branches from bushes for brooms, an' one ob dese brooms wuz laid across de floor, an' de boy an' gal run an' jumped over it an' dey wuz married." But on the whole Mr. Steele's recitation of his grandfather's remembrance of Africa appears extremely unreliable, so this reference must be taken with proper caution; see the testimony of Elmo Steele in James Mellon, ed., *Bullwhip Days: The Slaves Remember* (New York, 1988), 283.

67. Piersen, *Black Yankees*, 97. Kemble, *Journal*, 192.

68. Beauchamp Plantagenet, "A Perfect Description of Virginia," in Peter Force, ed., *Tracts and Other Papers . . .* (Washington, DC, 1836), 1 (8): 14, as quoted in Daniel C. Littlefield, *Rice and Slaves* (Baton Rouge, 1981), 100. Littlefield, *Rice and Slaves*, 103–6. Peter H. Wood, "'It Was a Negro Taught Them': A New Look at African Labor in Early South Carolina," *Journal of Asian and African Studies* 9, nos. 3–4 (1974), 168–70; and John Solomon Otto, "Traditional Cattle-Herding Practices in Southern Florida," *Journal of American Folklore* 97, no. 385 (July–Sept. 1984), 300. Peter H. Wood, *Black Majority* (New York, 1974), 122–24; John Michael Vlach, *The Afro-American Tradition in Decorative Arts* (Cleveland, 1978), 97–107; and Hall, *Africans in Colonial Louisiana*, 236.

69. Vlach, *Afro-American Tradition*, 122–38; and Sobel, *The World They Made Together*, 100–26.

70. George Washington to William Pearce, 25 Jan. 1795, *The Writings of George Washington*, 34:103, as quoted in Sobel, *The World They Made Together*, 47. Carmichael, *Domestic Manners and Social Conditions*, 2:268. An interesting modern example of the same conflict in work patterns is seen in Anne Moody, *Coming of Age in Mississippi* (New York, 1968), 117. Fox-Genovese, *Within the Plantation Household*, 174.

71. Rev. I. E. Lowery, *Life on the Old Plantation in Ante-bellum Days* (Columbia, SC, 1911), 34–35.

72. Matthew G. Lewis, *Journal of a West India Proprietor, 1815–1817* (London, 1834), as quoted in Abrahams and Szwed, *After Africa*, 111.

73. On the use of "Mister" and "Miz" with first names as the required racial etiquette for blacks to use with whites of all ages, see William H. Wiggins, *O Freedom* (Knoxville, 1987), 77.

74. Roger D. Abrahams argues this case for the corn-shucking competitions of the South, but the point has broader implications; see his *Singing the Master* (New York, 1992), 30.

75. See, for example, Bruce Jackson, *Wake Up Deadman: Afro-American Worksongs from Texas Prisons* (Cambridge, MA, 1974). In later years blacks would come to prefer the greater personal freedoms of task work, probably because gang labor was becoming more of an economic strategy than, as in Africa, a social one. See, for example, Drew Gilpin Faust, *James Henry Hammond and the Old South* (Baton Rouge, 1982), 74–75, 92.

76. Douglass, *Life and Times*, 43. James C. Fletcher and Daniel P. Kidder, *Brazil and the Brazilians* (Boston, 1866), 30. Miles Mark Fisher, *Negro Slave Songs in the United States* (1953; rpt. ed., New York, 1990), 21.

77. Genovese, *Roll, Jordan, Roll*, 554–56.

78. John Lambert, *Travels through Canada, and the U.S.*, 3 vols. (London, 1810), 2:138.

79. Quoted in Southern, *Music of Black Americans*, 103. Similarly, see the comments of John U. Petit, an American residing in nineteenth-century Brazil, who noted, "The melodies of the North American plantations (by which he meant minstrelsy tunes] . . . are, like the smallpox, contagious through all ranks of [Brazilian] society"; Fletcher and Kidder, *Brazil and the Brazilians*, 535.

80. Robert C. Toll, *Blacking Up: The Minstrel Show in Nineteenth Century America* (New York, 1974), 28, 45–46.

81. For Whitlock and Cotton, see *New York Clipper*, 13 April 1878, and *New York Mirror*, 1897, as quoted in Toll, *Blacking Up*, 45–46. Stratton is quoted in Tony Russell, *Blacks, Whites, and Blues* (New York, 1970), 11–12.

82. Epstein, *Sinful Tunes and Spirituals*, 3–17. Robert B. Winans, "The Folk, the Stage, and the Five-String Banjo in the Nineteenth Century," *Journal of American Folklore* 89, no. 354 (Oct. 1976), 407–37.

83. See, for example, Bill C. Malone, *Country Music U.S.A.: A Fifty Year History* (Austin, 1968), 90–91, 102; Charles W. Wolfe, *Tennessee Strings* (Knoxville, 1977), 47, 70, 72; Mike Paris and Chris Comber, *Jimmie the Kid* (New York, 1977), 29; and Robert Cantwell, *Bluegrass Breakdown: The Making of an Old Southern Sound* (Urbana, IL, 1984), 255.

84. Wolfe, *Tennessee Strings*, 50, 60, 69; Malone, *Country Music*, 65, 311; Paris and Comber, *Jimmie the Kid*, 15; Russell, *Blacks, Whites, and Blues*,

passim; Jay Caress, *Hank Williams: Country Music's Tragic King* (New York, 1981), 19–22; and Cantwell, *Bluegrass Breakdown*, 258.

85. Carlisle is quoted in Paris and Comber, *Jimmie the Kid*, 29; Malone, *Country Music*, 112, 115; Arnold Shaw, "Country Music and the Negro," *Billboard's World of Country Music* 79, no. 43 (28 Oct. 1971), 82. On Olmstead and yodeling, see Harold Courlander, *Negro Folk Music, U.S.A.* (New York, 1963), 81–82; and for the Kongo reference, see Robert Ferris Thompson, "The Song that Named the Land: The Visionary Presence of African-American Art," in Robert V. Rozelle, Alvia Wardlaw, and Maureen A. McKenna, eds., *Black Art, Ancestral Legacy: The African Impulse in African-American Art* (Dallas, 1989), 97–98.

86. Caress, *Hank Williams*, 23. Shaw, "Country Music and the Negro," 83. Wolfe, *Tennessee Strings*, 60. Douglas B. Green, *Country Roots* (New York, 1976), 50. Shaw, "Country Music and the Negro," 83, credits black performers with molding Dock Boggs, Roscoe Holcomb, and Hobart Smith as well.

87. Foley is quoted in Shaw, "Country Music and the Negro," 83.

88. Billy Charles Malone, "A History of Commercial Country Music in the United States, 1920–1964" (Ph.D. dissertation, University of Texas, Austin, 1965), 19. See also Malone, *Country Music*, 311; and Green, *Country Roots*, 51. Dock Boggs, "I Always Loved the Lonesome Songs," *Sing Out!* 14, no. 3 (July 1964), 32–39, as quoted in Russell, *Blacks, Whites, and Blues*, 51. Schultz also taught both Ike Everly and Mose Roger to play the two-finger guitar style often called "nigger pickin'."

89. Robert J. Sye, "Blacks in Country-Western Music" (MS, Library of the Country Music Foundation, Nashville), 4; Shaw, "Country Music and the Negro," 83; and Steven D. Price, *Old as the Hills: The Story of Bluegrass Music* (New York, 1975), 27.

90. Malone, "History of Country Music," 91. Green, *Country Roots*, 57.

91. D. Epstein, *Sinful Tunes and Spirituals*, 120–22; Winans, "Folk, Stage, and Banjo," 407–37; Green, *Country Roots*, 51, 57; Sye, "Blacks in Country-Western Music," 4; Shaw, "Country Music and the Negro," 33–34. Russell, *Blacks, Whites, and Blues*, 53; on the blues connections, see ibid., passim. And for Deford Bailey, see George D. Hay, *A Story of the Grand Ole Opry* (Nashville, 1945), 18.

92. Thomas D. Clark, *The Rampaging Frontier* (1939; rpt. ed., Bloomington, IN, 1964), 260–61. On the ubiquity of black fiddlers, see Southern, *Music of Black Americans*, 64–68. For black influence on white fiddling, see Epstein, *Sinful Tunes and Spirituals*, 114; Alan Jabbour's liner notes for *The Hammon Family* record album (Washington, DC, 1973), 25. And for the wider implications of black fiddle and dance calling, see Piersen, *Black Yankees*, 104–5.

93. Andrew Burnaby, *Travels through the Middle Settlements in North America* (1775; rpt. ed., 1960), 57; Nicholas Cresswell, *The Journal of Nicholas Cresswell* (New York, 1924), as quoted in Southern, *Music of Black Americans,* 64; John Davis, *Travels of Four Years and a Half in the United States of America during 1798, 1799, 1800, 1801, and 1802* (1803; rpt. ed., New York, 1909), 414; and *Concise Historical Account of All the British Colonies in North America* (Dublin, 1776), 213, as quoted in Sobel, *The World They Made Together,* 167. Cantwell, *Bluegrass Breakdown,* 71–72, 124.

94. Chesnut, *Diary from Dixie,* 275. Labat, *Voyages du Père Labat,* 196. Similarly, the Portuguese took over the *lundu,* an African dance from Brazil, making it popular in Europe; see Mary C. Karasch, *Slave Life in Rio de Janeiro, 1808–1850* (Princeton, 1987), 243.

95. On the black roots of white rock, see Michael Bane, *White Boy Singin' the Blues* (New York, 1982).

96. Robert Ferris Thompson, "Kongo Influences on African-American Artistic Culture," in Joseph E. Holloway, ed., *Africanisms in American Culture* (Bloomington, IN, 1990), 162–63.

97. It seems likely that the rousing yell that made southern soldiers distinctive was influenced by the African-American tradition of black dancers bellowing a bloodcurdling yell before leaping to the center of a dance ring; see Piersen, *Black Yankees,* 105.

98. Dillard, *Black English,* 221–22.

INDEX

Acuff, Roy (country musician), copies African-American style, 183

Adam (West African), stolen by slavers, 38

Adams, Edward C. L. (South Carolina writer): "Color Red" tale, 38–39; "God's Gifts" tale, 22

Adams, Ezra (ex-slave), says whites learn superstitions from blacks, 175

African-American music
—as gift from God, 32; influence on white music, 127, 181–88; loudness of, 127, 131
—instruments: banjo, 128, 131, 182, 185, 186; bells, 126, 129, 133; bones, 126, 128, 182; drum, 128, 130, 131; fiddle, 128, 131, 185–87; flute, 125; guitar, 184–86; harmonica, 184–85; horns, 128; jar, 126; rattles, 63, 124–29, 132; tambourine, 131, 132, 182; tin pan, 132
—processions, 121, 125–34
—songs: blues, 185; about enslavement, 45–46; extort gifts, 68–70, 126–28, 130, 180; form of resistance, 53–54, 72–73; improvisational, 57–60, 72; praise songs, 68–71; religious songs, 174–75; satiric content, 54, 57–73, 127; spirituals, 185; street cries, 61, 180, 192; work songs, 62, 63, 68–69, 179–80, 184; yodel, 184

African elite: children as hostages in slave trade, 90; children educated in Europe, 89–90, 96–97; freed from slavery, 88, 91–92; heroic captives in literature, 86–88, 91–92; large population of, 75; vulnerability to enslavement, 75; way of life, 77
—in Americas: class status of, 76–77, 80–81; indirect rule by, 77, 93, 94; make poor slaves, 77–78, 92; positions as slaves, 77, 94; recognized as superior by whites, 79; recognized during festivals, 82, 129–30
—as leaders of maroon settlements: Barbados, 123, 127; Brazil, 84–85; Colombia, 84; Jamaica, 85; Mexico, 84; Panama, 84; Virginia, 85

African songs: extort gifts, 56–57; foster social harmony, 54, 56–58; improvisational nature, 54, 56–60; praise songs, 58; rhythms, 187; satiric content, 54–60, 179; work songs, 57–58, 179; yodel, 184

Akan (West African people): use variolation, 102; mentioned, 26

Akropong (West African people), on "God's Gifts," 26

Akus (West African people): dental hygiene, 106; fine manners, 168

Alabama: Klan in, 147; mentioned, 184. *See also* Mardi Gras in Mobile

Albany, N.Y.: African-American festival, 130, 132; African royal in, 82; devil maskers, 132

Aldridge, Ira, claims royal African ancestry, 95

Alland, Alexander (visitor to West Africa), on oratory, 162

Allen, Richard (Philadelphia religious leader), organizes public nursing, 113

Allen, William Francis (visitor to South Carolina), on African-American manners, 166